Journey into Truth

Instructions in the

Catholic Faith

To Dave and Ellen,

   With best wishes and prayers
for a long, loving, happy and
fruitful marriage. God bless
you both!

        John

        Sydney, May 9, 2015

JOURNEY INTO
TRUTH

Instructions in the Catholic Faith

FR JOHN FLADER

connorcourt
PUBLISHING

Connor Court Publishing Pty Ltd

PO Box 224W

Ballarat VIC 3350

sales@connorcourt.com

www.connorcourt.com

ISBN: 9781925138306 (pbk.)

Cover design by John Chiaravalle

Nihil obstat: Rev. Peter Joseph, STD

Imprimatur: ✠Most Reverend Peter A. Comensoli, Apostolic Administrator

The *Nihil obstat* and *Imprimatur* are a declaration that a book or pamphlet is considered to be free from doctrinal or moral error. It is not necessarily implied that those who have granted them agree with the contents, opinions or statements expressed.

The Scripture quotations are from the Revised Standard Version, Second Catholic Edition, Ignatius Edition, of the Bible, copyrighted 2006, by the Division of Christian Education of the National Council of Churches in the United States of America, and are used by permission. All rights reserved.

Printed in Australia

CONTENTS

DEDICATION

In memory of Bishop Alvaro del Portillo, successor of St Josemaría Escrivá and first Prelate of Opus Dei, who was for me an inspiring example of love for the Church, prayerfulness, humility and fidelity.

PREFACE

"This is eternal life: that they may know you, the only true God, and Jesus Christ, whom you sent" (*Jn* 17:3). Quoting this text from St John the greatest theologian in history, St Thomas Aquinas, explained in his *Compendium of Theology* that *who* and *what* we believe is crucial to our happiness in this life and our eternal salvation in the next. Without knowledge of saving truth we will be easily confused, pursue the wrong goals, end up mired in vice and ultimately be unhappy.

But God, St Thomas explains, doesn't make this too hard for us. What he taught us at great length in the Scriptures and Tradition is clear enough, but many lack the leisure to study it all and in depth. If God wants us to be happy, it can't require that we all get doctorates in theology! Following St Paul, Thomas teaches that the important thing is that we have faith, hope and love: an abiding, informed faith "that feeds our minds with knowledge of the truth"; a prayerful, confident hope "that fixes our wills on the right ends"; and a compassionate, God-seeking love "that puts our affections in the right order".

St Augustine concluded that God had made us restless: our souls are never at peace until they rest in Him. St Thomas thought God had made us curious: we always want to learn more; the more we know, the more we realise we don't know. Faith aids our search for the truth about God, the universe, ourselves; it is "a taste of that knowledge which will make us happy in the life to come" and once you've got a taste for it you will want more!

Fr John Flader's book, *Journey into Truth*, is a very good place to start. Anyone wanting to obtain "the full measure of knowledge of God" needs to study the Catholic Faith, not just to assent to it. This book will help those thinking of joining the Catholic Church, those already in the Church who want to know more, and those who are just plain curious. It will help them come to know the person of Jesus Christ and what he has entrusted to the Catholic Church to guard, expound and transmit to us. Such knowledge is essential for restless souls, curious minds, wayfarers on pilgrimage toward God.

Journey into Truth follows the structure of the *Catechism of the Catholic Church*, providing an overview of whom and what we believe (the Creed), how we celebrate what we believe (the Sacraments), how we live what we believe (the Moral Life) and how we pray what we believe. It is a *trustworthy* presentation of the Catholic Faith, containing a vast array of references to Sacred Scripture, the Catholic Tradition, and modern thinking. Yet for all the breadth and depth of its learning, this book is very accessible, using everyday language to introduce us to the riches of the Catholic Faith.

Fr Flader does not shy away from raising very contemporary questions. As a very experienced spiritual director and teacher through a weekly newspaper column he has an acute awareness of *what's on people's minds*. He is as comfortable in the worlds of evolutionary biology and information technology as in the tomes of St Thomas Aquinas! He offers summary boxes and discussion questions to focus our attention on the basics and to keep us wondering.

I highly recommend Fr Flader's book for study and discussion. It is an important contribution to that new evangelisation which the popes have called us to since the Second Vatican Council – a fresh presentation of the Gospel to formerly or formally Christian cultures, institutions and individuals. I pray that it will be disseminated and used widely. And I thank the author for his great fidelity to God and service to his people.

+Anthony Fisher op
Bishop of Parramatta
Holy Week 2014

INTRODUCTION

This book was not my idea. The idea came from Roman Vedat, director of Arts Media, a Sydney company dedicated to promoting understanding and appreciation of the Catholic faith through DVDs and CDs. Roman came to me in 2011 with an ambitious proposal: to film a series of talks on the Catholic faith for the benefit of groups of people coming into the Church through the Rite of Christian Initiation of Adults (RCIA) as well as for adult faith formation groups, schools, families and anyone else interested in studying the Catholic faith in depth.

I told Roman I would consider the idea and get back to him. On one hand, the idea was very attractive. I have always enjoyed teaching the faith and the idea of producing a resource to this end was appealing. But the implementation of the proposal would involve considerable time, both to prepare the talks and then to film them. After considering the matter at length I finally decided to accept the proposal. The result, after hundreds of hours of work, is this book and the DVD series of the same name, for which this is the text.

From the beginning we worked closely with Cathy Dennis of the Catechumenate Office of the Archdiocese of Sydney to determine how many talks to give, their length and their content. Mgr Peter Williams, of the Diocese of Parramatta, also offered helpful suggestions. The title *Journey into Truth* came when we were well along with the project. Why this particular title?

First, because the process of coming to know the faith and grow in the practice of it is very much like a journey. Really the journey lasts a lifetime, whether someone comes into the Church as an adult or has grown up in it from childhood. It is a journey with a clearly marked goal, a goal which is never fully reached but toward which one constantly moves. The goal is the knowledge and practice of the Catholic faith.

Since one can always grow in this knowledge and practice the journey is ongoing. Pope Benedict XVI spoke of it at the beginning of his Apostolic Letter *Porta Fidei* calling for a Year of Faith in 2012 to commemorate the fiftieth anniversary of the opening of the Second Vatican Council and the twentieth of the publication of the *Catechism of the Catholic Church*: "Ever since the start of my ministry as Successor of Peter, I have spoken of the need to rediscover the journey of faith so as to shed ever clearer light on the joy and renewed enthusiasm of the encounter with Christ" (*PF* 2).

Growth in the faith, then, is a journey, but it is also a journey into truth. It goes without saying that the Catholic faith is a matter of truth, of objective truth. What Jesus Christ teaches and the Church passes on to us is not mere opinion or sentiments. It is truth. Coming into the Church or growing in the faith is not only a matter of having pleasant feelings or of belonging to a supportive community. It is first a matter of learning the truth about God, about man, about the Church and the sacraments, about morality, about the meaning of life, about life after death... The whole of our faith is based on these truths. They form the foundation on which we build our relationship with Jesus Christ and with the faith community.

As Pope Francis wrote in his encyclical *Lumen Fidei* (2013), "Faith without truth does not save, it does not provide a sure footing. It remains a beautiful story, the projection of our deep yearning for happiness, something capable of satisfying us to the extent that we are willing to deceive ourselves. Either that, or it is reduced to a lofty sentiment which brings consolation and cheer, yet remains prey to the vagaries of our spirit and the changing seasons, incapable of sustaining a steady journey through life" (n. 24).

So our faith must rest on the solid foundation of truth, of the truths of faith. But truth is not only propositions to be believed. It is also, and especially, a person to be known and loved: Jesus Christ, "the way, the truth and the life" (*Jn* 14:6). Throughout *Journey into Truth* we emphasise the importance of coming to a personal relationship with Jesus Christ, who leads us to the Father. Pope Francis invited the whole Church to do this in his Apostolic Exhortation *The Joy of the Gospel* (2013): "I invite all Christians, everywhere, at this very moment, to a renewed personal encounter with Jesus Christ, or at least an openness to letting him encounter them; I ask all of you to do this unfailingly each day. No one should think that this invitation is not meant for him or her, since no one is excluded from the joy brought by the Lord" (n. 3).

From the outset it was clear that *Journey into Truth* should be based on the *Catechism of the Catholic Church,* that marvelous compendium of the principal teachings of the Church which was first published in 1992. Pope Benedict XVI, in *Porta Fidei,* urged all in the Church to study the Catechism. He wrote that the Year of Faith "will have to see a concerted effort to rediscover and study the fundamental content of the faith that receives its systematic and organic synthesis in the *Catechism of the Catholic Church*" (n. 11). *Journey into Truth* follows the Catechism closely and attempts to draw out its most important teachings. It also incorporates other material from the Fathers of the Church, Popes, saints and other sources to illustrate the material in the Catechism.

Moreover, it was clear that this program should follow what Pope St John Paul II indicated in his Apostolic Exhortation *Catechesi tradendae* (1979) about the handing on of the faith, or catechesis. There the Pope defined catechesis as "an education in the faith of children, young people, and adults which includes especially the teaching of Christian doctrine imparted, generally speaking, in an organic and systematic way, with a view to initiating the hearers into the fullness of Christian life" (*CT* 18).

Journey into Truth sets out to teach the main elements of Catholic doctrine, based on the premise that every Catholic should know these truths well. As we have said, it is on the foundation of these objective truths that we build our life, our relationship with God and with others. And Jesus himself said, "The truth shall set you free" (*Jn* 8:32). Nothing is so enslaving as ignorance, and nothing so liberating as truth. It is the difference between trying to make our way forward in pitch darkness and doing so in the light of day.

Then too, *Journey into Truth* imparts the faith in an organic, systematic way, following the Catechism. In this way it is easy to see how all the elements of Catholic teaching are related to one another, forming a coherent whole. Moreover, the program is comprehensive, covering all the principal teachings of the faith, not only the Creed, but the sacraments, our moral life and our life of prayer.

Finally, the program sets out to initiate those who use it into the fullness of Christian life, into a deep and personal relationship with Jesus Christ. It is not merely a matter of knowing the truths about God, but of using those truths to come to a love for God. As Pope St John Paul II puts it, "Catechesis aims ... at developing understanding of the mystery of Christ in the light of God's Word, so that the whole of a person's humanity is impregnated by that Word. Changed by the working of grace into a new creature, the Christian thus sets himself to follow Christ and learns more and more within the Church to think like him, to judge like him, to act in conformity with his commandments, and to hope as he invites us to" (*CT* 20).

In the third century, Origen described this journey in a homily given to people seeking to enter the Church: "When you were numbered among the catechumens and first undertook to obey the laws of the Church, you crossed the Red Sea. As you halt each day on your journey through the desert, you devote some time to listening to God's law and looking on the face of Moses, unveiled for you by the glory of the Lord. And if you come to the spiritual waters of baptism and in the presence of the priests and levites are initiated into those great and awe-inspiring mysteries (which are familiar to those who have the right to know about them), then you too will cross the Jordan through the ministry of the priests. You will enter the promised land, where Jesus, following Moses, takes you in his charge and becomes your leader on this new journey" (*Homily 4, 1* on the book of Joshua).

Using Journey into Truth for a group

When this program is used with the DVDs in the context of a group, for example an RCIA group, an adult faith formation group, a school a family, etc., the following suggestions may prove helpful.

At the beginning of each chapter of the book there is a brief summary of the main points to be studied in that lesson. It will be helpful for the moderator of the group to read these points to the group before watching the DVD so that all are aware from the outset of what they will be learning.

It may be helpful to stop the DVD from time to time, especially at the end of a topic, to emphasise or discuss the main points of what has just been seen. In this way those in the group will find it easier to grasp the principal teachings.

At the end of each chapter is a series of questions for discussion. They are intended only as suggestions to facilitate the learning process and they may be used in any way the group desires, or not used at all. If the people want to ask questions of the moderator this may be the most beneficial for them. If they have questions other than those listed here they should feel free to raise them so that they can be discussed. It is up to the moderator to decide how best to help the group understand the material that has been presented.

In order that the members of the group derive the maximum benefit from the program, it will be advisable for them to read the material of each lesson *before* they watch the DVD, and to think about the answers to the questions. In this way they will be better prepared to understand the content of the DVDs. To this end it will be helpful if they each have a copy of the book.

At the end of each chapter there are some "Points to remember". This is perhaps one of the most important tools of the program, since it helps the members of the group to identify and retain the principal points of what they have just studied. It may be useful at the beginning of each session to remind those present of the "Points to remember" from the previous session and even to ask them questions about them by way of revision.

It is my hope that *Journey into Truth*, with the book and DVDs, will help many people come to appreciate the richness and beauty of the Catholic faith, so that they in turn can be God's instruments in helping others find and love God. In this way they will be more effective in carrying out the new evangelisation to which all the recent Popes have been calling the Church.

Fr John Flader

ABBREVIATIONS USED

AA	Second Vatican Council, Decree on the Apostolate of the Laity *Apostolicam actuositatem* (1965)
CA	Pope John Paul II, Encyclical *Centesimus Annus* (1991)
CCC	*Catechism of the Catholic Church*, Second Edition (1997)
CCL	*Code of Canon Law* (1983)
CDF	Congregation for the Doctrine of the Faith
CT	Pope John Paul II, Apostolic Exhortation *Catechesi tradendae* (1979)
CV	Pope Benedict XVI, Encyclical *Caritas in veritate* (2009)
DS	Denzinger-Schönmetzer, *Enchiridion Symbolorum et Definitionum* (1963)
DV	Second Vatican Council, Dogmatic Constitution on Divine Revelation *Dei verbum* (1965)
FC	Pope John Paul II, Apostolic Exhortation *Familiaris consortio* (1981)
GCD	Congregation for the Clergy, *General Catechetical Directory* (1997)
GE	Second Vatican Council, Declaration on Christian Education *Gravissimum educationis* (1965)
GS	Second Vatican Council, Pastoral Constitution on the Church in the Modern World *Gaudium et spes* (1965)
HV	Pope Paul VI, Encyclical *Humanae vitae* (1968)
LE	Pope John Paul II, Encyclical *Laborem exercens* (1981)
LG	Second Vatican Council, Dogmatic Constitution on the Church *Lumen gentium* (1964)
MF	Pope Paul VI, Encyclical *Mysterium fidei* (1965)
PF	Pope Benedict XVI, Apostolic Letter *Porta Fidei* (2012)
PO	Second Vatican Council, Decree on the Ministry and Life of Priests *Presbyterorum ordinis* (1965)
SC	Second Vatican Council, Constitution on the Liturgy *Sacrosanctum Concilium* (1963)
SS	Pope Benedict XVI, Encyclical *Spe Salvi* (2007)
STh	St Thomas Aquinas (1225-1274), *Summa Theologiae*
UR	Second Vatican Council, Decree on Ecumenism *Unitatis redintegratio* (1964)

Abbreviations Used

1. MAN'S SEARCH FOR GOD

The heavens are telling the glory of God; and the firmament
proclaims his handiwork (Ps 19:1)

SUMMARY

Following the order used by the *Catechism of the Catholic Church*, we begin our study of the Catholic faith not with God but with man, with man in his search for truth and happiness. This search leads us to God, who is the ultimate answer to our deepest human longings.

We then study how we can come to know that this God for whom we long really exists. First we consider reasons based on the physical world, especially the order or purpose we find in nature, and then reasons based on the human person, including the existence of our spiritual soul and the testimony of our conscience.

Finally, we consider how we find meaning in life precisely through our personal relationship with this God, who loves us very much and who has a place in heaven for each of us.

Welcome to "Journey into Truth", our excursion into the marvellous truths of the Catholic faith. It will be like a tour of the faith and I will be your tour guide.

But before we set off, let us say a prayer. Heavenly Father, moved by love you created this vast universe out of nothing, showing forth

1

your wisdom and power. You created human beings in your image and likeness, giving us an intellect and a free will. Help us through these classes to know you ever better so that we can love you with our whole heart and be with you forever in heaven. We make our prayer through Christ our Lord. Amen.

Over the next 24 lessons, I will take you on a journey through the essentials of what it means to be Catholic. We will study both what we believe and how we practise what we believe. I think you will find it a fascinating trip. Our faith is very rich and it contains many hidden treasures. After all, it comes from God himself, through his Son Jesus Christ.

I will use the *Catechism of the Catholic Church* as our roadmap. It is a magnificent document, first published by the Church in 1992 and then revised in 1997. We will use the Second Edition of the Catechism, which incorporates the 1997 revisions. If you would like to study the faith in greater depth, I suggest you obtain a copy of the Catechism. Or you might like to use the *Compendium of the Catechism of the Catholic Church*, a shorter question-and-answer version of the Catechism, which came out in 2005.

You may also find helpful my books *A Tour of the Catechism*, which are a commentary on the key ideas of the Catechism. Volume One, *The Creed*, was published by Connor Court in 2011. And of course you will want a Bible, a Catholic one.

We will follow the four parts of the Catechism in the order in which they appear there. This means we will start with the Creed, or Profession of Faith, which is a statement of the basic beliefs of Catholics. From there we will go on to the Sacraments, the means Jesus Christ gives us to live out our faith to the full in the search for holiness or love for God. Then we will study our Moral Life in Christ, starting with some basic ideas of morality in general – like the law of God, the different types of sin, the role of conscience, the virtues, the emotions, etc. – and going on to consider particular moral issues, following the Ten Commandments.

And finally we will study Christian Prayer, and in particular the Our Father. At the end, you should be well acquainted with the basics of the faith taught to us by Jesus Christ.

But throughout the journey we will also talk about our personal relationship with the God who loves us so much that he became man and died on the cross for us. After all, we want to learn the truth about God so that we can know him personally and love him. It is this personal relationship that gives life its true meaning – and that prepares us here on earth for the intimate, loving relationship we will have with God in heaven.

And we come to God through his son Jesus Christ. Pope John Paul II wrote that "at the heart of catechesis", the teaching of the faith, "we find, in essence, a person, the person of Jesus of Nazareth." He went on to say that "The primary and essential object of catechesis is ... the mystery of Christ" (CT 5).

Naturally these talks do not pretend to be an in-depth treatment of the faith. Much more time would be needed for that. But they will present all the essentials we ought to know in order to enter the Church or, for that matter, to be a good Catholic.

Really, what we are trying to do reminds me of a cartoon I saw many years ago. It showed a tour bus with a big sign reading "Europe in 7 Days", with a stream of people running out the front door of the bus into Notre Dame Cathedral in Paris, and another line running out of the Cathedral into the back door of the bus. Our tour won't be quite that fast, but it will be a challenge to cover the Catholic faith in the limited time available.

So now fasten your seatbelt and let us begin. Our topic today is "Man's search for God" or, as the Catechism puts it: "Man's capacity for God." A more simple and personal way to describe it would be "Man's search for meaning".

In this lesson we will look at three main topics: the desire for God, how we come to know God, and the meaning of life.

1. The desire for God

The Catechism tells us that man has a natural desire for God, written in his heart (cf. *CCC* 27). If we took a poll and asked people whether they were looking for God, many would answer flatly no. But deep down everyone is looking for God. How can we say this? We see it in the natural tendencies of the intellect and will, which all human beings have.

The intellect, or mind, has a natural desire for truth and it does not stop searching until it finds the answer to the most fundamental questions, questions like: What is the origin of the universe, with all its harmony and complexity? What is the meaning of life? Is there life after death? The answer to these deeper questions is ultimately God himself.

The will, sometimes referred to as the heart, – the faculty by which we choose, desire, love, etc., – has a natural desire for the good, and with it for happiness. It finds happiness when it finds a good. But finite, limited goods like money, possessions, fame, etc., cannot fully satisfy the longings of the heart. The will is spiritual, in some way unlimited, and ultimately only the infinite good, God himself, can fully satisfy it.

For this reason, St Augustine wrote, speaking to God: "For you have made us for yourself, and our heart is restless until it rests in you" (*Conf.* 1, 1, 1; *CCC* 30). A little later in that same work, his *Confessions*, which is a classic of spiritual writing, he says: "When I am completely united to you, there will be no more sorrow or trials; entirely full of you, my life will be complete" (*Conf.* 10, 28, 39; *CCC* 45). Summing up, everyone wants to be happy. But only God can fully satisfy the longing for happiness. Therefore, everyone, whether they know it or not, is looking for God. This can often be the starting point in our effort to help others, especially non-believers, to find God.

Another way we can see the truth of the proposition that all people have a desire for God is the fact that all civilisations have had some form of religion. Some may have believed in a multiplicity of gods, or in a god identified with nature, or in a god who didn't care about man, but all have had some form of religion, some belief in a being beyond themselves, often with a priesthood, prayers, sacrifices, rituals, etc. In short, man is by nature a religious being (cf. *CCC* 28).

2. How we can come to know God

If all people are looking for God, how can we come to know him? We start with our intellect, our mind, which looks for what the Catechism calls "converging and convincing arguments", which give certainty about the truth of God's existence (cf. *CCC* 31). The Catechism considers two different types of arguments, some based on the physical world and others based on the human person.

Arguments based on the physical world

St Thomas Aquinas (1225-1274) is well known for his five arguments for the existence of God, all of which are based on aspects of the physical world, aspects such as cause and effect, movement, contingency or dependence, order and beauty (cf. *CCC* 32).

Perhaps the easiest argument to understand without a philosophical mind is that from order or purpose in nature. In simple terms, we observe in the world of nature great order or purpose; for example, the parts of the human body, which all function according to an admirable plan. Consider for example the exquisite design of the digestive system, the reproductive system, the respiratory system, or the immune system. Now order, or purpose, comes about by design or intention, not by chance. Therefore, if all of nature has order and purpose, it must have a designer, one who is supremely intelligent and powerful, and this being we call God.

Archbishop Michael Sheehan, in his classic and still popular *Apologetics and Catholic Doctrine*, uses the analogy of the camera, which has various parts which all work together to produce a photograph. No one would say that the camera put itself together by chance. Yet the human eye is far more complex than a camera. It too must have been put together by an intelligent designer, who can only be God.

Sir Isaac Newton reflects this thinking in his *Opticks*, written in 1721: "How are the bodies of animals to be contrived with so much art, and for what ends were their natural parts? Was the eye contrived without skill in optics, and the ear without knowledge of sounds? ... Does it not appear from phenomena that there is a Being incorporeal, living, intelligent ...?"

Even a non-believer like Sir Frederick Hoyle, British astronomer who died in 2001, wrote in the "Annual Review of Astronomy and Astrophysics" in 1982: "A common sense interpretation of the facts suggests that a superintellect has monkeyed with physics, as well as with chemistry and biology, and that there are no blind forces worth speaking about in nature."

Hoyle and Chandra Wickramasinghe, a mathematician and also a non-believer, in the early 1980s pondered the question of how life began in the universe. They set out to calculate the probability of the first living thing, the simplest living organism, putting itself together by chance through the random shuffling of amino acids in the "prehistoric soup", or atmosphere, surrounding the earth. They came up with the infinitesimal probability of one in $10^{40,000}$! That is one in ten with 40,000 zeros after it. They naturally concluded that life could not possibly have arisen by chance and that there had to be a creator. But rather than admit the existence of God, they considered this creator to be a superintellect somewhere in outer space which sent the first living thing to earth! Hoyle once said that the probability that life just occurred by chance on earth is about as great as a tornado blowing through a junkyard and constructing a 747 aircraft.

An argument for design in the universe which is much under discussion at the present time is what has come to be known as the "anthropic principle". The word anthropic, by the way, comes from the Greek word for man. Expressed in simple terms, the principle says that a whole series of constants in physics, including the force of gravity, the electromagnetic force, etc., have to be almost exactly what they are in fact for the universe to support life, human life in particular. If any one of them were changed even slightly, life would be impossible. Scientists are in awe at the fact that the probability of these forces being what they are is mathematically exceedingly, exceedingly small. The only two explanations are either that there is an intelligence behind the creation and structure of the universe, or that there must be billions or even trillions of other universes in order for there to be even a small probability of a universe in which life is possible. Of course there is no evidence for other universes.

In short, wherever we observe order and purpose we know there had to be an intelligent cause of that order. In nature we observe such order, and therefore there must be an intelligent being who brought it about, and this is precisely our understanding of God.

Already in the Old Testament, long before Christ, we see how man could know God through creation. The book of Wisdom says: "For from the greatness and beauty of created things comes a corresponding perception of their Creator" (*Wis* 13:5). Likewise, we read in Psalm 19: "The heavens are telling the glory of God; and the firmament proclaims his handiwork" (*Ps* 19:1). St Paul sums it up: "Ever since the creation of the world [God's] invisible nature, namely, his eternal power and deity, has been clearly perceived in the things that have been made" (*Rom* 1:20).

And a few centuries later St Augustine wrote: "Question the beauty of the earth, question the beauty of the sea, question the beauty of the air distending and diffusing itself, question the beauty of the sky ... question all these realities. All respond: 'See, we are beautiful.' Their beauty is a profession [*confessio*]. These beauties are subject to change. Who made them if not the Beautiful One [*Pulcher*] who is not subject to change?" (*Sermo* 241, 2; *CCC* 32)

Arguments based on the human person

Passing to arguments based on the human person, we realise that there is more to man than just a material body. In our openness to truth and beauty, our freedom, our conscience reminding us of what is right and wrong, we see the existence of a spiritual element which transcends the world of matter. This spiritual element we call the soul and, in the words of the Catechism, it "can have its origin only in God" (*CCC* 33). This is easy to understand. Where does spirit come from? It cannot possibly come from matter. It can only come from another spirit, and the source of everything spiritual is the infinite pure spirit, God.

Likewise, the testimony of conscience, which reveals the existence of a moral law which man himself did not make, raises the question: where did this moral law come from? All are aware that good is to be done and evil avoided. But why are they aware? Clearly this moral law is prior to and above the human person, who only comes to discover the law and to know that it applies to him. This law can only come from the supreme lawgiver whom we call God.

The universal belief in God mentioned earlier is another argument – not necessarily a proof – for the existence of God. If the whole world believes something, there must be some basis for that belief. If all civilisations have had a religion and believed in some form of God, and among them some of the most intelligent people that have ever lived, there is at least a high probability that God exists.

Thus, in different ways, we can come to know that there exists a reality which is the first cause and final end of all things, a reality that everyone calls God. Naturally it is not necessary to understand all these arguments fully in order to be a Catholic, but it is helpful to know that the arguments exist and that they have helped many to come to believe in God.

The Catechism goes on to say that while we can come to know the existence of a personal God, that is, one with intellect and will, we cannot come into real intimacy with God by reason alone. For this, God chose to give us his revelation and the grace to share in his divine life. Thus, while the rational proofs for God's existence cannot give us faith – faith is always a gift from God – they can predispose us to faith and help us to see that faith in God is not opposed to reason.

Has the Church ever declared that we can know the existence of God starting from reason alone? The First Vatican Council, a gathering of the world's bishops held in 1869-70, declared that indeed we can. The Council teaches: "Our holy mother, the Church, holds and teaches that God, the first principle and last end of all things, can be known with certainty from the created world by the natural light of human reason" (*Dei Filius* 2; *CCC* 36).

But while man can theoretically know God by reason alone, in fact many people find it very difficult to come to know God in this way. The Catechism explains this with a quotation from Pope Pius XII's Encyclical *Humani generis* (1950):

> For the truths that concern the relations between God and man wholly transcend the visible order of things, and, if they are translated into human action and influence it, they call for self-surrender and abnegation. The human mind, in its turn, is hampered in the attaining of such truths, not only by the impact of the senses and the imagination, but also by disordered appetites which are the consequences of original sin. So it happens that men in such matters easily persuade themselves that what they would not like to be true is false or at least doubtful (*Humani generis*, 2; *CCC* 37).

This point makes reference to a very important difficulty that many people have in coming to believe in God: the fact that they are living sinful lives and they don't want to believe in a God who may judge them and possibly punish them. This often goes together with pride: people want to be their own god, to be in charge of their life, to decide for themselves what to do or not to do. They don't want to worship anyone above themselves. Therefore, they convince themselves that there is no God. As the popular saying goes, "When you don't live as you believe, you end up believing as you live".

It is because of these difficulties in coming to know God by reason alone that God chose to reveal himself to man. In the words of the First Vatican Council, he did it so that these truths could be known "by all men with ease, with firm certainty and with no admixture of error" (*Dei Filius* 2; *CCC* 38). We will study revelation in the next lesson.

3. THE MEANING OF LIFE

This desire for God written in our nature, together with the knowledge we have of God, both from his creation and from revelation, points to the ultimate meaning and purpose of life. Although we will study this topic again later when we consider creation, we know that we, like the whole universe, were made by God and we exist for him. This is why St Augustine says, "You made us for yourself and our heart is restless until it rests in you" (*Conf* 1, 1, 1).

In order to discover the meaning of our life, and to enter into a personal relationship with this God who loves us so much that he became man for us, it is good to set aside some time each day to stop and be still in God's presence. There we can talk with him, entrust to him our concerns, our hopes and joys, our sufferings, and simply listen to him. He is always there waiting for us and he wants us to come to him. Jesus invites us to do this: "Come to me, all who labour and are heavy laden, and I will give you rest" (*Mt* 11:28). If we do this, we will come little by little to have a personal relationship, a personal friendship with the best friend anyone can have, the God-man Jesus Christ.

Pope Benedict XVI said to a million young people in Madrid for World Youth Day 2011:

> Yes, dear friends, God loves us. This is the great truth of our life; it is what makes everything else meaningful. We are not the product

of blind chance or absurdity; instead our life originates as part of a loving plan of God. To abide in his love, then, means living a life rooted in faith, since faith is more than the mere acceptance of certain abstract truths: it is an intimate relationship with Christ, who enables us to open our hearts to this mystery of love and to live as men and women conscious of being loved by God (Vigil ceremony, 20 August 2011).

Summing up, we all have a natural desire for God, whether we know it or not. Our intellect seeks truth – not just circumstantial truths but ultimate truths, like where did the world come from and is there life after death? And our will seeks the good, and with it happiness. Nothing finite can completely satisfy this desire. Only God, the infinite good, can.

We can come to know that there is a God by two approaches: arguments based on the physical world, including its beauty, order and harmony, and arguments based on the human person, including the existence of our spiritual soul, our conscience, and the universal belief in God.

And finally, the meaning, the purpose of our life, is God. He is the answer to our deepest longings. We exist because he made us and we exist for him. And he wants us to spend eternity with him in heaven. That concludes our first lesson on man's search for God. May God bless you and guide you gently through the week.

QUESTIONS FOR DISCUSSION

1. This series of instructions in the Catholic faith is called
   Journey into Truth. Do you think it is important to learn
   truths about God, the Church and man, or is it enough
   just to feel the warmth of belonging to a supportive faith
   community? Why?

2. Do you agree that man has a natural desire for God written
   in his heart? How would you defend this statement and
   explain it to a friend?

3. What reason for the existence of God do you find most
   convincing?

4. Why is it that a person who is not living a good moral life
   will find it difficult to believe in God?

5. Why is having a personal relationship with God so
   important?

POINTS TO REMEMBER

- All human beings are looking for God, whether they know
  it or not, because their intellect seeks truth and their will
  seeks happiness, and God is the answer to their deepest
  longings.

- We can know from the obvious order and purpose in
  nature that there has to be an intelligent, all powerful being
  who put it there, and this being is God.

- If we have a spiritual soul, there must be a spiritual being
  who gave it to us and this being is God.

- Knowing that we are not just the result of blind chance
  but that we have been created by an all-powerful and all-
  loving Father God gives life its deepest meaning

2. REVELATION AND OUR RESPONSE OF FAITH

In many and various ways God spoke of old to our fathers by the prophets; but in these last days he has spoken to us by a Son, whom he appointed the heir of all things, through whom he created the ages (Heb 1:1)

SUMMARY

Having begun our journey into the truths of the Catholic faith by considering man's search for God, we now study God's approach to man, which is revelation.

We study first the nature of revelation and how God reveals himself in two ways: first, through his work of creation, which tells us much about him, as we have already seen. We call this *natural revelation*. Second, God reveals himself through his word, both the spoken word, especially the Word of God, Jesus Christ, and the written word contained in the Bible. This we call *supernatural revelation*.

We go on to consider how supernatural revelation is passed on to us in two ways: through the Church's living Tradition, which is the whole life of the Church, and through Sacred Scripture, the Bible. In order to safeguard, interpret authentically and pass on this revelation down the ages, we have the Church, founded by Jesus Christ. We also study the very interesting topic of how the Church came to know which of the many writings circulating in the early Church were divinely inspired and therefore part of the New Testament of the Bible.

Finally, we study how we respond to God's revelation through faith and what characteristics faith has.

Welcome back to our journey into truth, our excursion into the truths of the Catholic faith. In the last lesson we studied man's desire and search for God and how we can come to know God through reason alone. In this lesson we will consider God's approach to man: his revelation. We will consider three topics: the nature of revelation, the transmission of revelation, and our response to revelation through faith.

Let us begin with a prayer. Heavenly Father, having shown us something of yourself through your wondrous work of creation, you went even further and revealed yourself to us in words. Finally you sent your divine Word, your one and only Word, the Son of God, who took flesh in the womb of the Blessed Virgin Mary, to bring us the fullness of revelation. Help us to respond to your truth with faith, with complete trust in you, like Mary. We make our prayer through Christ our Lord. Amen.

1. THE NATURE OF REVELATION

We begin with the nature of revelation. There are two ways of coming to know another person. One is by observing the person and his works. The other is by listening to what the person may choose to tell us about himself or herself.

Similarly there are two ways of knowing God. We have seen how man can know God with certainty by natural reason alone, by reflecting on various aspects of his creation. But we can also know God through what he tells us about himself. We could never arrive at this second order of knowledge by ourselves, and it is only because of God's mercy that he chooses to reveal himself to us. This way of knowledge we call revelation. Revelation is God's communication of himself, making known his divine plan through words and deeds, most fully by sending us his divine Son, Jesus Christ. As the Catechism puts it, through revelation God has given "the definitive, superabundant answer to the questions that man asks himself about the meaning and purpose of his life" (CCC 68).

How does God reveal himself? God began, as we saw in the last lesson, by providing evidence of himself through creation itself. Just as we can know something about an artist through his work of art, so we can know much about God through his work of creation. For this reason the book of Wisdom says: "For from the greatness and beauty of created things comes a corresponding perception of their Creator" (*Wis* 13:5). This revelation of God through creation is called *natural revelation*.

But God went beyond this. He invited our first parents, Adam and Eve, to an intimate relationship with him, revealing himself to them in words. Then, throughout the centuries up to the coming of Christ, God revealed himself again and again, through such figures as Noah, the patriarchs Abraham, Isaac and Jacob, Moses, King David and the numerous prophets, among them Isaiah, Jeremiah and Ezekiel. His revealed word throughout the period before the coming of Christ was recorded in numerous writings. They are what we call the Old Testament, and they make up the first part of the Bible.

Finally, some two thousand years ago, God went even further. He sent his eternal Son to earth in the person of Jesus Christ. Jesus is the very Word of God who took flesh in the womb of the Blessed Virgin Mary. The Catechism says of Jesus: "Christ, the Son of God made man, is the Father's one, perfect and unsurpassable Word. In him he has said everything; there will be no other word than this one" (*CCC* 65). This revelation of God in words and deeds is what we call *supernatural revelation*.

In view of God's constant and ongoing revelation of himself, and especially of his sending his Son to earth in Jesus, it has rightly been said that whereas other religions are man in search of God, Christianity is God in search of man.

2. The Transmission of Divine Revelation

We come now to our second topic, the transmission of divine revelation. God wanted his revelation to reach all people of all times so that all might be saved and go to heaven. How was he going to achieve this? In two ways: through the Church's living Tradition and through the written word inspired by God, known as Sacred Scripture, or the Bible. Tradition and Scripture are what we call the sources of revelation.

The Apostolic Tradition

Let us look first at Tradition, which is the first and fullest source of divine revelation. We are speaking here of the tradition of the Church, and therefore of the time from Christ on. It includes the spoken word, the example Christ's apostles gave and the institutions they established. The apostles, for those who do not know, were twelve men specially chosen by Christ to assist him in the care of the Church. We see this Tradition, for example, in the way the apostles celebrated Mass, the way they prayed for the dead and conducted funerals for them, and the way they structured the Christian communities. In a word, Tradition is the whole life of the Church: its beliefs, worship, structures of government, art, customs, etc. For this reason it is often called the "living Tradition of the Church".

An example of a belief of the Church that is found in Tradition is the belief in Purgatory with its practice of praying for the dead so that they may go to heaven. There is no text in the New Testament which expressly teaches this doctrine, yet St Isidore of Seville in the seventh century says that the custom of praying for the dead and offering sacrifices for them was so widespread in his time that it was believed to have been taught by the apostles themselves (cf. *On ecclesiastical offices*, 1).

The Second Vatican Council (1962-1965) gives a description of Tradition and its role in the Church: "This living transmission, accomplished in the Holy Spirit, is called Tradition, since it is distinct from Sacred Scripture, though closely connected to it. Through Tradition, 'the Church, in her doctrine, life, and worship perpetuates and transmits to every generation all that she herself is, all that she believes'" (*DV* 8 §1; *CCC* 78).

Where do we find this Tradition? We find it on one hand in the numerous writings of the early Church. There are many hundreds of such writings, and they reveal what the early Christians believed and how they lived their faith. In addition, we find it on tombstones, burial vaults, church buildings, frescoes, mosaics, etc., many of which have been preserved from the early centuries. In a real sense, even the Sacred Scriptures, especially the Gospels, can be understood as the written form of some of this oral Tradition. The Scriptures take the oral preaching of the apostles, including the words and deeds of Jesus, and transmit it to writing.

How are Scripture and Tradition related? First of all, both Tradition and Scripture come from one common source (cf. *CCC* 80). The source is Jesus Christ and his teaching, which both Tradition and Scripture pass on to us. The Catechism says that "flowing out from the same divine well-spring, [they] come together in some fashion to form one thing and move towards the same goal... 'Sacred Tradition and Sacred Scripture make up a single sacred deposit of the Word of God,' in which, as in a mirror, the pilgrim Church contemplates God, the source of all her riches" (*DV* 10; *CCC* 97). In simple terms, Scripture and Tradition are two distinct modes of transmission of the same divine message.

What is more, Tradition "transmits in its entirety the Word of God which has been entrusted to the apostles by Christ the Lord and the Holy Spirit" (*DV* 9: *CCC* 81). It is clear from this, as indeed common sense tells us, that Tradition is a much broader, more complete, source of Divine Revelation than Scripture. And it is prior, having begun from the very preaching of Christ. Indeed, the first of the Scriptures were not written until some twenty years after the death of Christ. As the Catechism says, "the first generation of Christians did not yet have a written New Testament" and yet they were perfectly able to function as an established Church (cf. *CCC* 83).

The role of the Church

Where does the Church fit into our reception of the truths of Revelation, or is it not necessary? It is absolutely necessary. The Catechism says that "the apostles entrusted the 'Sacred deposit' of faith, contained in Sacred Scripture and Tradition, to the whole of the Church" (*CCC* 84).

It is the Church that has the task of discerning whether a particular idea, custom, etc., is faithful to the original Tradition. Obviously there must be some authority with this role or otherwise many different, even contradictory, customs and teachings could arise, with no one to decide which were faithful to Christ's teaching. Christ provided for this by entrusting this task "to the living, teaching office of the Church alone. Its authority in this matter is exercised in the name of Jesus Christ" (*CCC* 85). Today this task is exercised by the bishops in communion with the Pope, or, as we shall see, by the Pope on his own.

To assist the Church in remaining faithful to his teaching, Christ promised to send the apostles the Holy Spirit, the third person of the Blessed Trinity, whom he called the "Spirit of truth." He told the apostles: "When the Spirit of truth comes, he will guide you into all the truth" (*Jn* 16:12). Also, when he sent his disciples, or followers, out to teach, he told them: "He who hears you, hears me" (*Lk* 10:16). It is clear from these words that whoever hears the apostles and their successors, the bishops, hears Christ himself. Christ trusts the Church to teach faithfully the truth he has passed on to it.

Always, Christ's teaching must be preserved intact. Not even the Church can change it. In the words of the Catechism, the teaching authority of the Church, known as the Magisterium, "is not superior to the Word of God, but is its servant. It teaches only what has been handed on to it ... All that it proposes for belief as being divinely revealed is drawn from this single deposit of faith" (*CCC* 86).

These teachings of the Church, the more solemn of which are known as dogmas, should be seen as helps, as sure guideposts on our spiritual journey. As the Catechism explains, "Dogmas are lights along the path of faith; they illuminate it and make it secure" (*CCC* 89). Indeed, they are like lighthouses, fixed points, sending out their beacons of truth to guide us to the safe harbour of heaven.

Sacred Scripture

That brings us to Sacred Scripture. As we have said, apart from Tradition, the other source of divine Revelation is Sacred Scripture, the written word of God. The Catechism gives us the classical definition of Scripture: "the speech of God as it is put down in writing under the breath of the Holy Spirit" (*DV* 9). That is, Sacred Scripture is God's own word, written down by men under the inspiration of the Holy Spirit.

When we say "Sacred Scripture" we are referring of course to the Bible. The Bible, as we know, is divided into two main parts: the Old Testament, comprising the Jewish writings up to the time of Christ, and the New Testament, made up of the inspired writings of the Christian era, in the first century. The Church has always held the Scriptures in the highest regard, finding in them not a human word, but the very word of God. The Second Vatican Council puts it like this: "In the sacred books, the Father who is in heaven comes lovingly to meet his children, and talks with them" (*DV* 21; *CCC* 104).

What distinguishes Sacred Scripture from other writings? The Second Vatican Council answers: "All the books of the Bible, both Old and New Testaments, and all their parts have God as their author, because they were written down under the inspiration of the Holy Spirit" (*CCC* 105). In other words, the author of Sacred Scripture is not Matthew or John or Paul but God himself, who makes use of human writers.

What does it mean to say that these writings were inspired by the Holy Spirit? The Council answers: "To compose the sacred books, God chose certain men who, all the while he employed them in this task, made full use of their own faculties and powers so that, though he acted in them and by them, it was as true authors that they consigned to writing whatever he wanted written, and no more" (*DV* 11; *CCC* 106). That is, through inspiration, God respects the writers' own personality and freedom, so that, for example, each has a different style. But they write what God wants written and no more. Because they are inspired by God, all the Scriptures are free from error. In the words of the Council, "we must acknowledge that the books of Scripture firmly, faithfully, and without error teach that truth which God, for the sake of our salvation, wished to see confided to the Sacred Scriptures" (*DV* 11; *CCC* 107).

Naturally, in interpreting them we must take into account the different forms of expression, the different literary types, such as history, allegory, poetry, prayer, etc. We must also take into account such factors as the conditions of the time and culture in which they were written, and the modes of feeling, speaking, and writing of those times (cf. *CCC* 110).

A very important matter to take into account when interpreting Scripture is the unity of the whole of Scripture. Even though the books and writers are very different one from another, there is an overall unity by reason of the unity of God's plan and the central focus on Christ in the whole of Scripture. Thus, while any one text may be difficult to understand when taken out of context, – think, for example, of Christ's words "Do not think that I have come to bring peace on earth; I have not come to bring peace, but a sword" (*Mt* 10:34). – the text can be understood in the light of the whole message of Christ, who obviously did come to bring peace, a peace such as the world cannot give (cf. *Jn* 14:27).

The Canon of Scripture

In addition to the writings we now know as the New Testament, many others abounded, among them the *Didache,* or *Doctrine of the Twelve Apostles,* the letters of Pope St Clement I and of St Ignatius of Antioch, the Epistle of Barnabas, *The Shepherd* of Hermas, and the apocryphal *Proto-Gospel of James* and the *Gospel of St Thomas.* Who decided which of these writings circulating among the communities in the first 100 years after Christ were to be considered as the inspired word of God, or Sacred Scripture, and which were not?

The Catechism answers: "It was by the Apostolic Tradition that the Church discerned which writings are to be included in the list of the sacred books" (*CCC* 120). In other words, it was the Church, guided by the Holy Spirit, which accepted some writings as inspired and rejected others, while still holding some of the rejected ones in high regard. The list of inspired works is called the *canon*, or list, of Scripture. It comprises the 46 books of the Old Testament and the 27 of the New Testament found in any Catholic Bible.

How do Christians look on the Old Testament? As with the New Testament, we regard the Old Testament as being divinely inspired and having a permanent value (cf. *CCC* 121). In the words of the Catechism, they are "a storehouse of sublime teaching on God and of sound wisdom on human life, as well as a wonderful treasury of prayers; in them, too, the mystery of our salvation is present in a hidden way" (*CCC* 122).

The New Testament hands on the ultimate truth of God's Revelation. Its central object is Jesus Christ: his deeds, teachings, his death and resurrection, and the Church's beginnings under the guidance of the Holy Spirit (cf. *CCC* 124). At the heart of the New Testament are the four Gospels, written by Matthew, Mark, Luke and John. They are the principal sources for the life and teaching of Christ (cf. *CCC* 125). The Church shows her great veneration for the Gospels in the more solemn Masses, where the deacon carries the book of the Gospels in procession, accompanied by two candle bearers. He incenses the book before reading from it and kisses it at the end. We too should have a great veneration for the Gospels.

From the very times of the apostles, the Church has emphasised the unity of the two testaments, seeing in the Old Testament numerous types or figures of New Testament realities (cf. *CCC* 128). We therefore read the Old Testament in the light of the New, and the New in the light of the Old. St Augustine gives us the well-known statement: "The New Testament lies hidden in the Old and the Old Testament is unveiled in the New" (*Quaest. in Hept.* 2, 73; *CCC* 129). And Hugh of St Victor sums it up: "All Sacred Scripture is but one book, and this one book is Christ" (*CCC* 134).

Does the Church encourage us to read the Bible? Most definitely! The Second Vatican Council declared that the Church "forcefully and specifically exhorts all the Christian faithful ... to learn 'the surpassing knowledge of Jesus Christ' by frequent reading of the divine Scriptures" (*DV* 25; cf. *Phil* 3:8; *CCC* 133). As St Jerome puts it: "Ignorance of the Scriptures is ignorance of Christ" (*Commentariorum in Isaiam libri xviii* prol; *CCC* 133).

What can we do in practical terms to become familiar with the Bible? Daily reading, for at least a few minutes, of the New Testament is an excellent way to come to know the message of Christ and to nourish one's life of piety. Indeed, by reading just one chapter a day, which takes only a few minutes, one can read the whole New Testament in much less than a year.

Also very helpful is spending a little time each day meditating on the Scriptures, reading them slowly and considering what they have to say to us. They will be a true lamp lighting up our way and a source of many inspirations.

3. MAN'S RESPONSE TO GOD: FAITH

Having considered God's revelation to man, communicated down the ages through Scripture and Tradition, we now look at what our response to this Revelation should be. The answer is of course faith – to believe everything God has said. Since God is Truth and knows all truth, and since he can neither deceive nor be deceived, the only reasonable response is for us to believe, to have faith in everything God reveals.

The act of faith includes not only the assent of the intellect to the truths revealed by God, but also a surrender of one's whole being and life to God. As the Catechism says, "By faith, man completely submits his intellect and his will to God. With his whole being man gives his assent to God the revealer. Sacred Scripture calls this human response to God ... 'the obedience of faith'" (cf. *Rom* 1:5; 16:26; *CCC* 143). The

Catechism gives two great examples of this obedience of faith: Abraham in the Old Testament and the Blessed Virgin Mary in the New.

Most people realise that faith is really a commitment of one's whole life, a surrender to God. And it is precisely for this reason that people who are not living in keeping with God's law find it difficult to convert to the faith, or to return to the practice of the faith. They are not prepared to submit their entire life to God and do his will. For this reason St John Chrysostom says: "Unclean living makes it difficult for a person to know the truth. Just as a man who is blinded by error cannot for long keep to the right road, so too it is very difficult for someone who is leading a bad life to accept the demands our sublime mysteries make on us. To embrace truth one needs to be detached from all one's passions... This freedom of soul must be total, if one is to attain truth" (*Hom. on 1 Cor. 8, ad loc.*).

Coming into the Church involves being willing to accept whatever God has revealed. And this is freedom. "The truth shall set you free" (*Jn* 8:32), Jesus said. Accepting God and submitting our whole being to him is like falling into the strong arms of a loving Father.

What are the characteristics of faith?

First of all, faith is a *grace,* a gift from God. It is not something one acquires through reason alone. Reason can prepare for faith, it can offer well-founded reasons for believing, but in the end faith is always a gift from God. If we find it hard to believe some truth, we should ask God for the gift of faith.

Secondly, the knowledge that faith gives is *certain.* The reason is simple: faith is founded on the very word of God, who is truth. Thus we can be more certain of what God has told us than of what we have come to know by ourselves. We, after all, are sometimes mistaken. As St Thomas Aquinas says, "The certainty that the divine light gives is greater than that which the light of natural reason gives" (*STh* II-II, 171, 5, obj. 3; *CCC* 157).

Thirdly, despite its certainty, faith always has an element of *obscurity*. This is so because we do not see the first-hand evidence of what we believe. We believe it on the authority of God who reveals it.

Fourthly, in the words of St Anselm, "Faith *seeks understanding*" (*Prosl. Prooem.; CCC* 158). It seeks to understand better both the God who has revealed himself and the contents of the revelation, and this understanding in turn strengthens faith. St Augustine expresses it in similar terms: "I believe, in order to understand; and I understand, the better to believe" (*Sermo* 43, 7, 9; *CCC* 158). This desire for understanding will lead us to read more and study our faith, to grow more deeply in it. This is a life-long process, a wonderful journey into the fullness of truth.

And finally, we should never forget that the faith we have as Catholics is not only our own personal faith, but first and foremost *the faith of the Church*. The Church is our mother, who has believed and taught the faith for two thousand years. We have received it from her and we profess it in the Church in the words she has given us. It is expressed in the Profession of Faith we recite in Mass each Sunday, which comes from the Councils of Nicaea and Constantinople in the fourth century and which Catholics and other Christians have professed ever since.

That concludes our study of divine revelation. In the next lesson we will begin our consideration of the contents of the Profession of Faith, to see in more detail what Catholics believe. Until then, may God bless you and keep you in his love.

Questions for discussion

1. How would you explain in simple terms what Tradition is and why the Church gives it so much importance?

2. What distinguishes Sacred Scripture from other spiritual writings?

3. What roles does the Church have with respect to Tradition and Scripture and why is the Church so important?

4. What are some ways in which we can become more familiar with the Bible?

5. Why should we always respond to God's word and the teachings of the Church with faith?

Points to remember

• The truth revealed by God through his Son Jesus Christ has been passed on to us through Sacred Scripture and the living Tradition of the Church.

• Tradition is the first and fullest source of divine revelation and it transmits in its entirety the Word of God entrusted by Christ to the Church.

• Sacred Scripture is the word of God put down in writing under the inspiration of the Holy Spirit.

• Because all the books of Sacred Scripture have been inspired by the Holy Spirit they have a unity among themselves and they are free from error.

• The Church has the role of safeguarding, interpreting authentically and passing on the Word of God contained in Sacred Scripture and Tradition.

3. The Unity and Trinity of God

Hear, O Israel: the Lord our God is one Lord (Deut 6:4)

Summary

Having considered man's search for God and God's revelation of himself to man, we now begin our study of the content of this revelation, following the ancient profession of faith known as the Apostles' Creed.

We study first the origin of Creeds and why from the very beginning the Church has formulated these professions of faith.

We go on to consider the unity of God and our firm belief that there is only one God. We study the name of God revealed to Moses and why we should always approach and speak of God with great reverence.

Then we consider the Trinity of God: that in the one God there are three divine persons, Father, Son and Holy Spirit and how this truth is central to our faith. We study how we know that each of the divine persons is God and how the persons are related to each other.

Finally, we study God's almighty power, which is compatible with his love and mercy.

Welcome once again to our journey into truth. In the last lesson we looked at God's revelation, his seeking us out and announcing his truth to us. We recall that we find that truth, the fullness of revelation, in Jesus Christ, the very Word of God. It is preserved for us in the two forms of

Scripture and Tradition, which spring from the one source, Jesus Christ, and are handed on to us through the Church. And we considered our response to God's revelation: faith.

In this lesson we will begin our study of the core beliefs of Catholics contained in the profession of faith known as the Apostles' Creed. We will consider four topics: the origin of creeds, the unity of God, the trinity of God and God's almighty power.

But, as usual, let us begin with a prayer. Heavenly Father, you reveal yourself to us as one God in a trinity of persons, Father, Son and Holy Spirit, a mystery we can never fully comprehend. Grant us the gift of awe and reverence before this great truth, and faith to believe whatever you have revealed. We make our prayer through Christ our Lord. Amen.

1. THE ORIGIN OF CREEDS

What is a creed and where do creeds come from? The word *creed* comes from the Latin word *credo*, meaning "I believe". The first words of most creeds are precisely "I believe". From the beginning the Church expressed and handed on the faith in brief formulas which would be easy for all to learn and memorise. They were known by various names: "professions of faith"; "creeds", or "symbols of faith" from the Greek word *symbolon*, a summary (cf. *CCC* 187).

As the first profession of faith is made at Baptism, which is done in the name of the Father and of the Son and of the Holy Spirit, the Creed is traditionally divided into three parts, each making reference to one of the three divine persons (cf. *CCC* 189-190).

The two Creeds that have a special place in the Church are the Apostles' Creed, which is the ancient baptismal Creed of the Church of Rome, and the Nicene-Constantinopolitan or simply Nicene Creed, which was formulated in the first two ecumenical Councils, at Nicaea in 325 and Constantinople in 381 (cf. *CCC* 193-195). As we recall, an ecumenical council is a gathering of the world's bishops.

The Apostles' Creed is often said at the beginning of the Rosary and it is a prayer that all Catholics ought to know by heart. The Nicene Creed is the one we say in Mass each Sunday. It is also used by the Orthodox and many Protestant communities. It thus unites us with the Church since the fourth century and with other Christians. The Catechism's presentation of the faith follows especially the Apostles' Creed, which it calls "the oldest Roman catechism", but it also makes frequent use of the Nicene Creed (CCC 196).

At the end of its introduction to the Creeds, the Catechism says: "To say the Credo with faith is to enter into communion with God, Father, Son, and Holy Spirit, and also with the whole Church which transmits the faith to us and in whose midst we believe." It adds an expressive statement of St Ambrose, from the fourth century: "This Creed is the spiritual seal, our heart's meditation and an ever-present guardian; it is, unquestionably, the treasure of our soul" (*Expl. Symb.* 1; CCC 197). So when we say the Creed we should do so with a deep sense of faith, in union with our brothers and sisters in the Church from the earliest times and with those around the world today.

We will now begin our journey through the Apostles' Creed phrase by phrase, word by word, to see the deep meaning of each part.

2. THE UNITY OF GOD

The first phrase is "I believe in God". As the Catechism explains, "The whole Creed speaks of God and when it also speaks of man and of the world it does so in relation to God" (CCC 199).

In the Nicene Creed we profess our belief in "one God". This is fundamental. There is only one God. In the Old Testament God reveals himself as One: "Hear, O Israel: the Lord our God is one Lord" (*Deut* 6:4-5). Jesus too says that God is "the one Lord" whom you must love "with all your heart, and with all your soul, and with all your mind, and with all your strength" (*Mk* 12:29-30).

Naturally, as we shall see, our belief that Jesus Christ is Lord, or God, and that the Holy Spirit too is God is not contrary to our belief in the one God. Although God is a Trinity, three persons in one God, there is still only one God. In the words of the Fourth Lateran Council (1215), "We firmly believe and confess without reservation that there is only one true God, eternal, infinite (*immensus*), and unchangeable, incomprehensible, almighty, and ineffable, the Father and the Son and the Holy Spirit; three persons indeed, but one essence, substance or nature entirely simple" (*CCC* 202).

Does God have a name? Yes, he does. He is not some anonymous force, and he revealed his name to Moses from the burning bush. Those familiar with the Old Testament will recall that Moses' asked God to reveal his name. After identifying himself as the God of Abraham, Isaac and Jacob, God told Moses that his name is Yahweh, a Hebrew word meaning "I am who I am" (*Ex* 3:13-15). This can also be translated "I am he who is", or "I am who am".

What are we to make of this name? In simple terms it means that God alone *is*. He is the fullness of being and of every perfection, without beginning or end. All creatures receive all that they are and have from him. But he alone is his very being. He exists necessarily; he is necessary being. In other words, whereas all creatures have received their existence or being from another – they do not exist necessarily; they *have* being or *participate in* being – God *is* his very being and he is the cause of the being of everything else. Thus God is radically different from everything else.

Jesus too applies the name Yahweh to himself when he says, for example, "When you have lifted up the Son of man, then you will realise that 'I Am'" (*Jn* 8:28). The name "I am" naturally remains in some way mysterious, just as God is mystery. As the Catechism explains, it helps us see God as "infinitely above everything that we can understand or say: he is the 'hidden God,' his name is ineffable, and he is the God who makes himself close to men" (*CCC* 206).

In the presence of this mysterious and holy God, Moses takes off his sandals and covers his face with a veil (cf. *Ex* 3:5-6). We too should have a sense of great awe and reverence in the presence of God. Out of great respect for God's name, the people of Israel never pronounced the name Yahweh. When they read the Sacred Scriptures, they replaced the revealed name by the divine title 'Lord' (in Hebrew *Adonai*, in Greek *Kyrios*). Thus when we say that Jesus is Lord we mean it in this same sense, that he too is God; he is divine.

How does God relate to human beings? This mysterious and holy God is not removed from the life of men, nor is he a harsh God. Rather he is merciful and gracious. After the Israelites had offended God by making and worshipping a golden calf, God still walked among them and proclaimed, "Yahweh, Yahweh, a God merciful and gracious, slow to anger, and abounding in steadfast love and faithfulness." And Moses said that "the Lord is a forgiving God" (*Ex* 34:5-6, 9; *CCC* 210).

It is important to remember this because some people try to oppose the God of the Old Testament – supposedly a God of wrath, ever ready to punish – to the God of the New Testament, who would be a God of love and mercy. But there is only one God and he is always a God of mercy.

What is more, this God is truth. We read in the *Second Book of Samuel:* "And now, O Lord God, you are God, and your words are true" (*2 Sam* 7:28). That is, God is Truth itself and he cannot deceive. He knows everything because he created everything, and he is always true to his word. As a consequence, we can abandon ourselves in complete confidence to the truth and faithfulness of his word in all things. This abandonment is the "obedience of faith" we spoke about in the last lesson.

At the same time, God is love. Throughout the Old Testament, and of course in the New, God pours out his love on his people. In phrases taken from the Old Testament, "His love for his people is stronger than a mother's for her children. God loves his people more than a bridegroom his beloved; his love will be victorious over even the worst infidelities ..." (cf. *Hos* 11:1; *Is* 49:14-15, 62:4-5; *Ezek* 16; *CCC* 219).

What is more, God's love is everlasting. We read in the prophet Isaiah: "For the mountains may depart and the hills be removed, but my steadfast love shall not depart from you" (*Is* 54: 10). St John goes even further to say that "God *is* love" (*1 Jn* 4:8). The Catechism explains: "God's very being is love. By sending his only Son and the Spirit of Love in the fullness of time, God has revealed his innermost secret: God himself is an eternal exchange of love, Father, Son and Holy Spirit, and he has destined us to share in that exchange" (*CCC* 221).

This should move us to respond to God's infinite love for each one of us, no matter who we are or how sinful we have been, by making an effort to grow in love for him, especially through prayer and the sacraments, and by seeking always to do his will. And it should move us to trust God absolutely. St Teresa of Avila gives us the well-known advice: "Let nothing trouble you. Let nothing frighten you. Everything passes. God never changes. Patience obtains all. Whoever has God wants for nothing. God alone is enough" (*Poesias* 30; *CCC* 227).

3. THE TRINITY OF GOD

So it is clear that there is only one God. But this one God reveals himself as a trinity of persons. Christians are baptised "in the name of the Father and of the Son and of the Holy Spirit." And before being baptised they, or their godparents, are asked to answer "I do" to questions about the three divine persons in the three parts of the Apostles' Creed. Belief in God as a trinity of persons is fundamental to our faith. As St Caesarius of Arles says, "The faith of all Christians rests on the Trinity" (*Sermo* 9, *Exp. symb.*; *CCC* 232).

We are baptised in the *name* of the three divine persons, not in the *names*, because the three persons are only one God. The Catechism expresses the importance of this truth in the following words: "The mystery of the Most Holy Trinity is the central mystery of Christian faith and life. It is the mystery of God in himself. It is therefore the source of all the other mysteries of faith, the light that enlightens them. It is the most fundamental and essential teaching in the 'hierarchy of the truths of faith'" (*GCD* 43; *CCC* 234). For our consolation, it is impossible for a human being to understand fully how there can be three persons in one God. It will always remain a mystery for us. Only God knows himself in his innermost being.

The Father is God

The first person of the Trinity is clearly revealed as Father. Many religions invoke God as "Father." The Israelites, the ancient Jews, called God "Father" because he is the Creator of the world, but also because God entered into a covenant, an agreement, with Israel, "his firstborn son" (*Ex* 4:22; *CCC* 238).

What do we understand by the name "Father" when we apply it to God? The Catechism answers: "By calling God 'Father' the language of faith indicates *two main things*: that God is the *first origin* of everything and transcendent authority; and that he is at the same time *goodness and loving care* for all his children" (*CCC* 239). The Catechism explains that God's loving care can also be expressed by the image of motherhood, which emphasises the intimacy between Creator and creature. For example, God says: "As a mother comforts her child, so I will comfort you" (*Is* 66:13).

We can understand something of God's fatherhood through our experience of human fatherhood. But, in so doing we must be careful. As the Catechism explains, while earthly parents are "in a way the first representatives of God for man ... human parents are fallible and can disfigure the face of fatherhood and motherhood." God, on the other hand, "transcends human fatherhood and motherhood, although he is their origin and standard: no one is father as God is Father" (*CCC* 239). Thus those who have had an unpleasant experience of their father or mother should not think that God is like their parents. Rather, he transcends human fatherhood and motherhood and is their origin and standard. We measure human parents by the standard of God and not vice versa.

Naturally too, we must always remember that God transcends the human distinction between the sexes. He is neither man nor woman: he is God (cf. *CCC* 239). Nonetheless, it is common to refer to God as "he", because he reveals himself as Father.

The Son is God

Looking now at the second person of the Trinity, the Son, we see that within the Trinity God is "eternally Father in relation to his only Son, who is eternally Son only in relation to his Father" (*CCC* 240). St John calls the eternal Son of God the "Word" in the first chapter of his Gospel. There he writes: "In the beginning was the Word, and the Word was with God, and the Word was God" (*Jn* 1:1). This Word is the second person of the Trinity.

St John goes on to say: "The Word became flesh and dwelt among us" (*Jn* 1:14). The Word made flesh is of course Jesus Christ. So Jesus is not just a human being. He is the very eternal Son of God who took human flesh and dwelt among us. In the Nicene Creed we say of the Son: "I believe in one Lord Jesus Christ, the Only Begotten Son of God, born of the Father before all ages, God from God, Light from Light, true God from true God, begotten, not made, consubstantial [that is, of one being or substance] with the Father; through him all things were made."

Speaking of the Son becoming man, we go on to say, "For us men and for our salvation he came down from heaven, and by the Holy Spirit was incarnate of the Virgin Mary, and became man." Jesus himself affirms that he is truly God, truly one with the Father, when he says: "I and the Father are one" (*Jn* 10:30).

The Holy Spirit is God

Thus the Father and the Son are clearly God, divine persons. But what about the Holy Spirit? Is he too a divine person or perhaps just the spirit of God, as we might speak of the spirit of the Pope?

In the Last Supper Jesus promised to send "another Paraclete", "the Spirit of Truth" (*Jn* 14:16-17), and the Holy Spirit came down on the apostles in a dramatic way on the feast of Pentecost (cf. *Acts* 2:1 ff). We know that the Holy Spirit is truly a divine person when Jesus sends the apostles out to baptise "in the name of the Father and of the Son and of the Holy Spirit" (cf. *Mt* 28:19). All three are given equal status, so that if the Father and the Son are divine persons, so must be the Holy Spirit.

The Eleventh Council of Toledo, in the year 675, said of the relationship between the Holy Spirit and the other two divine persons: "The Holy Spirit, the third person of the Trinity, is God, one and equal with the Father and the Son, of the same substance and also of the same nature ... Yet he is not called the Spirit of the Father alone, ... but the Spirit of both the Father and the Son" (*CCC* 245).

In the Nicene Creed we profess the divinity of the Holy Spirit in these words: "I believe in the Holy Spirit, the Lord, the giver of life, who proceeds from the Father and the Son, who with the Father and the Son is adored and glorified, who has spoken through the prophets."

Within the Blessed Trinity, the Holy Spirit proceeds eternally from both the Father and the Son. In the words of the Council of Florence (1438), "The Holy Spirit ... proceeds eternally from both as from one principle and through one spiration..." (*CCC* 246). The word "spiration" refers to breathing – the Holy Spirit is "breathed forth" by the Father and the Son.

St Paul sums up his faith in the Trinity at the end of his second letter to the Corinthians, in words now used as one of the greetings at the beginning of Mass: "The grace of the Lord Jesus Christ and the love of God and the communion of the Holy Spirit be with you all" (*2 Cor* 13:13).

The Church's belief in the Trinity

We can summarise the Church's belief in the Trinity in four statements.

1. *The Trinity is One.* We do not believe in three Gods, but in one God.

2. *The divine persons are really distinct from one another.* The Fourth Lateran Council (1215) teaches: "They are distinct from one another in their relations of origin: 'It is the Father who generates, the Son who is begotten, and the Holy Spirit who proceeds'" (*CCC* 254).

3. *The divine persons are related to one another.* The Father is related to the Son as the one begetting to the one begotten, the Son is related to the Father as the one begotten to the one begetting, and the Holy Spirit is related to the Father and the Son as the one proceeding from both. Apart from these relations, the divine persons have everything in common: the divine being, nature, eternity, power, wisdom, etc.

4. *All the works that God does outside of himself – e.g. creation, revelation, providence, etc. – are common to all three divine persons acting as one.* For example, while we sometimes attribute creation to the Father, in reality all three divine persons create the world acting together. According to the Council of Florence, "The Father, the Son, and the Holy Spirit are not three principles of creation but one principle" (*CCC* 258). And the Second Council of Constantinople (553) professes "one God and Father *from whom* all things are, and one Lord Jesus Christ, *through whom* all things are, and one Holy Spirit *in whom* all things are" (*CCC* 258).

4. GOD IS ALMIGHTY

Of all the divine attributes, the only one we name in the Creed is his almighty power, his omnipotence: "I believe in God the Father Almighty." The Catechism mentions three characteristics of God's omnipotence.

1. God's omnipotence is *universal.* "Nothing is impossible with God" (*Lk* 1:37). He can do all things. He created the universe out of nothing and it remains completely subject to him and at his disposal (*CCC* 269).

2. God's omnipotence is *loving or merciful.* God is the Father Almighty and he shows his fatherly omnipotence by the way he takes care of all our needs, by making us his adopted children, and above all by his infinite mercy, ever ready to forgive our sins (*CCC* 270).

3. God's omnipotence is *mysterious.* We see this in God's apparent powerlessness in the face of the evil and suffering in the world. Many people wonder why, if God is almighty, he doesn't prevent suffering. The Catechism answers that "in the most mysterious way God the Father has revealed his almighty power in the voluntary humiliation and Resurrection of his Son, by which he conquered evil" (*CCC* 272).

What does this teaching on God mean for us personally?

Our belief in the unity and trinity of God is the foundation of our spiritual life. It fills us with faith in a mystery we will never fully understand. We accept on faith that God is at the same time one God in three persons.

Also, as we will see later, this God who exists from all eternity and who created the universe out of nothing dwells in our soul from the moment of Baptism. This is our great dignity as Christians. We are truly temples of God. The indwelling of the Trinity is a great mystery of the love of God, who comes to dwell in the souls of his children, in an anticipation of heaven. As a consequence, our life should be directed towards God throughout the day in praise, thanksgiving, petition and sorrow. If we live focussed on God, we will have great peace and we will live in the hope of being with the Blessed Trinity forever in heaven. The consideration that God is love, full of mercy and compassion, moves us to love him in return and to know that he will always forgive us if we are sorry for our offences.

And finally, the consideration of God's almighty power fills us with confidence that God can do all things, that he can answer all our prayers. We ask for the gift of faith to believe, like Mary, that nothing is impossible for God (cf. *Lk* 1:37).

In the next class we will study God's work of creation: his creation of heaven and earth, of angels and man, his divine providence, and the original sin of our first parents with its effects in us. Until then may God bless you and fill you with his love.

Journey Into Truth

QUESTIONS FOR DISCUSSION

1. What is a Creed, or Profession of Faith, and why does the Church have Creeds?
2. How would you explain to a friend that Catholics believe in only one God, even though we believe that God is a trinity of persons?
3. Why should we always speak of God and relate to him with great reverence?
4. Why do we call God Father and what does this mean for you personally?
5. What do we mean when we say that God is almighty and what consequences does this have for how we relate to him?

POINTS TO REMEMBER

- There is only one God, and he reveals his name to Moses as Yahweh: I am who am.
- The one God reveals himself as a trinity of persons: Father, Son and Holy Spirit.
- The trinity of God is the central mystery, or truth, of our faith.
- The three divine persons have everything in common – the divine nature, wisdom, power, etc. – except the distinction between Father, Son and Holy Spirit.
- God is Almighty: he can do all things.

4. CREATION AND ORIGINAL SIN

In the beginning God created the heavens and the earth (Gen 1:1)

SUMMARY

Having considered the unity and trinity of God, we now study the first great work of God outside himself, the creation of the universe.

We begin by looking at creation in general, where we see how God created the universe out of nothing, giving it order, harmony and purpose. The universe did not result from chance, in which case there would be no order and purpose. And God created it out of love to show forth his glory and majesty and to share his being and goodness with creatures.

We go on to study the creation of heaven and earth. By heaven we mean the spiritual realm of angels, and by earth the visible universe, with the various creatures forming a hierarchy with man at the summit.

Then we consider the creation of man in the image and likeness of God, and how man is radically different from every other creature.

Finally we study original sin, the sin of our first parents, which affected them and all their descendants after them. We consider too the important topic of how the account of creation in the Bible relates to the theory of evolution.

Welcome back to our journey into the wonders of the Catholic faith.

In the last lesson we studied God in himself, his unity as one God and the Trinity of persons in the one God. In this lesson we look at the first great work of God: the creation of the universe.

Let us begin with a prayer. Heavenly Father, you reveal your almighty power, your wisdom and your love in the great work of creation. As we consider this mystery, help us to grow in faith, in gratitude for the gift of creation and in trust in your fatherly providence, knowing that you guide the whole of creation, including each one of us, gently to our end. We make our prayer through Christ our Lord. Amen.

In this lesson we will consider four main topics: creation in general, the creation of heaven and earth, the creation of man, and original sin. So sit back, relax and get ready for a fascinating journey into where we came from, why we are as we are and where we are going.

1. CREATION IN GENERAL

In the Apostles' Creed we profess our belief in God the Father almighty, "Creator of heaven and earth." We find this truth in the very first words of the Bible in the book of *Genesis*: "In the beginning God created the heavens and the earth" (*Gen* 1:1). What do we mean by the "heavens and the earth"? We mean everything that exists, both spiritual and material.

As you can imagine, belief in creation is important, very important. It answers those basic questions that people of all times have asked: Where did the world come from? Why are we here? Or simply, what is the meaning of life? There are two possible answers to these questions. Either the universe was created by an eternally existing, intelligent, all-powerful being whom we call God, and it is he who gave it its marvellous order, laws, harmony and purpose; or the world came about by chance, in which case it is subject to the blind forces of matter and it has no meaning. There are no other possibilities.

The Bible is clear on the fact that God created the world and that he had a definite plan in mind. But in recent decades scientists too are seeing more and more evidence that the world had a beginning in time, and they are baffled by the fact that it has just the right conditions to support life. Among all the Bible passages about creation, the first three chapters of *Genesis* are especially important. They tell us about the origin of the world, its order and goodness, the vocation of man, and finally the whole drama of sin and the hope of salvation. In order to understand what we are going to say about creation and original sin, it is important to read those chapters.

The purpose of creation: the glory of God

Why did God create the world? If God is responsible for the beginning of the world, God is also its end or purpose. The First Vatican Council teaches: "The world was made *for the glory of God*" (*Dei Filius*, Can. 5). What do we mean by this? We are not saying that God made the world in order to increase his glory and happiness. After all, he is all perfect and happy in himself. Rather, as St Bonaventure explains, God created all things "not to increase his glory, but to show it forth and to communicate it" (*In II Sent.* I, 2, 2, 1). When we look at creation, for example the stars on a clear night, a bird, a flower, or a beautiful sunset, we see clearly the hand of God. In the words of the psalm, "The heavens are telling the glory of God; and the firmament proclaims his handiwork" (*Ps* 19:1).

But what moved God to create? His love and goodness. St Thomas Aquinas says, using a very graphic expression, "Creatures came into existence when the key of love opened his hand" (*Sent.* 2, Prol.; *CCC* 293). In short, God did not need to create the world. He did it freely, moved by love, to share his being and happiness with creatures.

And he created the world out of nothing. He did not start from matter which already existed. There was no matter until he created it. He started from nothing and made this vast universe, with its billions of galaxies. The Scriptures say: "Look at the heaven and the earth and see everything that is in them, and recognise that God did not make them out of things that existed" (2 *Mac* 7:28; cf. *CCC* 296-298).

What is more, God created an ordered world, with beauty and harmony and laws of nature which are constant everywhere. This in itself tells us that the world did not result from chance, in which case it would be chaotic and unintelligible. Rather it came from the mind of God, who is the supreme intelligence. And God created a good world. We read in the book of *Genesis*, after the various days of creation: "And God saw that it was good ... very good" (*Gen* 1:4, 31; *CCC* 299).

It is clear too that God created the world for man. The Catechism says: "The universe, created in and by the eternal Word, the 'image of the invisible God', is destined for and addressed to man, himself created in the 'image of God' and called to a personal relationship with God" (*Col 1:15; Gen* 1:26; *CCC* 299). As we mentioned earlier with respect to the "anthropic principle", modern day scientists and philosophers find abundant evidence that the universe seems to have been "fine-tuned" to support human life.

What relationship does God have with the world? Although he transcends creation, that is he is outside and above the world, not part of it, God is always present to the world. He holds it in being, he knows everything that happens in it, and he watches over it through what we call his providence, guiding each creature gently to its end. Nothing happens that he does not will or at least permit. This leads us to an attitude of great trust and serenity in God's fatherly providence, even when things seem to be going wrong. If we don't understand what is happening, God does.

In his providence God makes use even of evil, including human sin, to bring about good. He created a world in which there was no evil, but sin and suffering entered through the original sin of our first parents. God is in no way the cause of sin, but he permits it because he respects the freedom of his creatures and, mysteriously, he knows how to derive good from it. As St Augustine says, "For almighty God..., because he is supremely good, would never allow any evil whatsoever to exist in his works if he were not so all-powerful and good as to cause good to emerge from evil itself" (*Enchiridion* 3, 11; *CCC* 311).

2. THE CREATION OF HEAVEN AND EARTH

What do we mean when we say "God created the heavens and the earth"? We mean simply that he created absolutely everything, both the spiritual (the heavens) and the material (the earth). Let us begin with the spiritual, the angels. Who or what are angels? They are spiritual beings without a body who act as servants and messengers of God. They have intelligence and free will and they are more perfect than all visible creatures (cf. *CCC* 328, 330).

The angels are always in the presence of God in heaven, and at the same time some of them act as God's messengers to men and as protectors of human beings. These latter are called guardian angels. St Basil says of them: "Beside each believer stands an angel as protector and shepherd leading him to life" (*Adversus Eunomium* III, 1; *CCC* 336). This is a consoling reality. We all have an angel looking after us personally. It is very good to have devotion to our guardian angel.

That angels exist is a truth of faith, that is to say a dogma, which all Catholics are to believe. There are numerous references to angels in the Bible, from the book of *Genesis* at the beginning to the book of *Revelation* at the end, and the Tradition of the Church has always accepted their existence (cf. *CCC* 328). For example, the angel Gabriel announced to Mary that she was to be the mother of Jesus (cf. *Lk* 1:26-38). In fact, the word angel comes from a Greek word meaning messenger. The Church celebrates the feast of the Archangels Michael, Gabriel and Raphael on September 29 each year, and of the Guardian Angels on October 2.

In addition to angels, who are spiritual, God also created the visible universe. The work of creation is described in the first chapter of the book of *Genesis*. There it is presented as a succession of six days on which God "worked", followed by the seventh day on which he "rested". Are we meant to take this literally, as six days of 24 hours? In 1909 the Vatican's Pontifical Biblical Commission declared that we need not, and that the word "day" can be understood in the sense of a longer space of time.

In the account of creation we see how each creature possesses its own particular goodness and perfection. After each of the six days of creation we read: "And God saw that it was good." That is, each creature reflects in its own way something of God's infinite wisdom, beauty and goodness. Therefore we should respect every creature, avoiding any disordered use of things, which would show contempt for God the Creator (cf. *CCC* 33˙9).

We also see how there is a hierarchy of creatures, from the less perfect to the more perfect, with man at the summit of visible creation. As the Catechism says, God "destined all material creatures for the good of the human race. Man, and through him all creation, is destined for the glory of God" (*CCC* 353; cf. 342, 343).

3. THE CREATION OF MAN

Turning now to man, the book of *Genesis* tells us that "God created man in his own image, in the image of God he created him, male and female he created them" (*Gen* 1:27). What does this tell us? In general, we say that man is created in the image of God in that he has a spiritual soul, with an intellect and a free will like God. The Catechism says: "Of all visible creatures, only man is 'able to know and love his creator.' He is 'the only creature on earth that God has willed for its own sake', and he alone is called to share, by knowledge and love, in God's own life ... This is the fundamental reason for his dignity" (*GS* 12, 24; *CCC* 356).

The Catechism goes on to say: "Being the image of God the human individual possesses the dignity of a person, who is not just something, but someone. He is capable of self-knowledge, of self-possession and of freely giving himself and entering into communion with other persons.

And he is called by grace to a covenant with his Creator, to offer him a response of faith and love that no other creature can give in his stead" (*CCC* 357). Truly, this is what gives man his dignity. He has an intellect and a free will, to know and love God, and he is called to be with God forever in heaven.

What do we mean by the word "soul"? In simple terms we mean the spiritual principle in man. We know that we have a soul or spiritual principle because we are able to think, to know immaterial realities like honesty or angels, to plan for the future, to choose freely among various courses of action, to love others, etc. By our spiritual soul we are radically different from any other creature on earth. We have rational intelligence and free will, which no other creature on earth has. We are not just a little more intelligent than apes; we are radically different from apes. One manifestation of man's rational intelligence is the fact that with it he continually makes progress: in communication, transportation, medicine, etc. Other creatures cannot do this. They cannot think. They simply live according to their nature, following their instincts.

Although it is by our soul that we are most especially made in God's image, our body also shares in this dignity since it is animated by the soul. In this we see the duty to take care of our body, since God has created it and it is an essential part of our nature. How are body and soul related to each other? In the traditional terminology, the soul is the "form" of the body. As the Catechism says, "It is because of its spiritual soul that the body made of matter becomes a living, human body; spirit and matter, in man, are not two natures united, but rather their union forms a single nature" (*CCC* 365). This goes against the idea of the Greek philosopher Plato, for example, who considered that the soul was in the body like the pilot in a ship. In man, body and soul form a unity, a single person.

Where does the soul come from: from our parents? No, the Church teaches that every spiritual soul is created immediately by God when the person is conceived (cf. CCC 366). Will the soul die with the body? No, the soul, being spiritual, is immortal. It does not cease to exist when it separates from the body at death, and it will be reunited with the body at the end of the world.

In the Book of *Genesis* we read that God created man "male and female" (*Gen* 1:27). Man and woman are complementary as masculine and feminine and each is a companion, a helpmate, for the other in what is the first communion of persons. In marriage they come together "in one flesh" to express their love and to transmit human life to children. They thus cooperate in the creative work of God through what we call "pro-creation". It is truly an awesome gift and responsibility. While men and women are different from each other, they are equal in dignity as children of God, made in his image and likeness.

And as *Genesis* says, they are called to "subdue" the earth as stewards of God. This "subduing" of the earth is not meant to be an arbitrary destructive domination, but rather a responsible stewardship of the creation given to man by God (cf. *Gen* 1:28; *CCC* 373).

4. ORIGINAL SIN

This brings us to a very important topic: original sin. It answers the question: where does evil come from? We have all asked ourselves that question, and the answer lies ultimately in the sin of our first parents, whom the book of *Genesis* calls Adam and Eve. We call their sin original sin.

But let us begin by looking at Adam and Eve in their original state. Our first parents were not only created good but they were given a special friendship with God, along with harmony within themselves, with each other and with creation. This state of happiness is sometimes called the state of "original justice." It included four gifts. First, a "supernatural gift", which was a sharing in the very life of God, known as *sanctifying grace* (cf. *CCC* 375).

In addition, they had three so-called "praeternatual gifts", meaning gifts which were beyond nature, but not above it, as is the supernatural gift of sanctifying grace. There were three praeternatural gifts:

1. *Freedom from suffering and death* (cf. *CCC* 376). Although Adam and Eve were meant to work, this work would not involve toil and suffering, and they would not have to die.

2. *Freedom from concupiscence,* or mastery of self. That is, their passions or emotions were under the control of their intellect and will, and they did not experience a disordered desire for pleasure, for earthly goods or for self-assertion (cf. *CCC* 377).

3. *Freedom from ignorance.* Adam and Eve knew everything they needed to know and their intellect did not find difficulty in grasping truth.

This whole state of harmony was destined to be lost when Adam and Eve committed what we call the original sin. You can read about it in the third chapter of the book of *Genesis.* According to the Bible, Adam and Eve were tempted by a serpent, which Scripture and Tradition see as a fallen angel called "Satan" or the "devil." The Church teaches that Satan was at first a good angel, but he and the other devils rejected God and were banished forever from his sight. Now they go about tempting human beings to turn away from God. Even though the devils can tempt us and cause great harm, their power is limited. They are only creatures, after all, and God's power is always greater, so they can only do what God allows them to do. And, in any case, we have a guardian angel to protect us.

How did the original sin come about? God had forbidden Adam and Eve to eat the fruit of one tree in the garden, the "tree of the knowledge of good and evil" (*Gen* 2:17). In tempting them, the devil told them that if they ate the fruit of the tree, they would be "like God, knowing God and evil" (*Gen* 3:5). As we know, Adam and Eve did eat the fruit of the tree. Their sin was one of pride, of preferring themselves to God, of wanting to be like God, not wanting to obey God even in this small matter.

We know the consequences of their sin. Adam and Eve lost, both for themselves and for all mankind after them, the gifts they had been given:

first, their intimate friendship with God or sanctifying grace, so that they now feared the God whom they had loved. They lost too their inner harmony or freedom from concupiscence, seen in their shame at their nakedness. They lost their freedom from suffering and death, so that now Adam would earn his bread with the sweat of his brow, Eve would bear children in pain and they would eventually die. And having lost their freedom from ignorance, their minds would find it more difficult to grasp the truth (cf. *Gen* 3:1-24).

The original sin of our first parents has been passed on from parents to children ever since. We are all born deprived of sanctifying grace and we experience such effects as disordered passions, pride, selfishness and laziness, and a certain tendency to sin, to do what is wrong. But the story does not end with the fall of Adam and Eve. God promised that from the offspring of Eve would come one who would crush the head of the serpent (cf. *Gen* 3:15). This is the first promise of a Redeemer, one who would be the offspring of the second Eve, Mary. This is of course Jesus Christ, who defeated Satan by his death on the Cross and redeemed us, restoring us to friendship with God. We receive the grace of redemption for the first time in Baptism. But Baptism, while erasing the guilt of original sin and restoring the soul to grace, does not take away some of the effects of that sin, such as suffering, death and the inclination to sin.

While the biblical account of creation and original sin in *Genesis* uses figurative language, it does express a real event that took place at the beginning of human history. According to the Catechism, "Revelation gives us the certainty of faith that the whole of human history is marked by the original fault freely committed by our first parents" (*CCC* 390).

The account of Genesis and the theory of evolution

Many people ask whether the account of creation in *Genesis* is compatible with the theory of evolution, one version of which says that man descended from some other living thing. The most comprehensive and authoritative answer to date comes from Pope Pius XII in his Encyclical *Humani generis* (1950). There the Pope makes three main points:

1. "The teaching of the Church leaves the doctrine of evolution an *open question,* as long as it confines its speculations to the development, from other living matter already in existence, of the human body." That is, man in his body may have evolved from some other living thing.

2. "That souls are immediately created by God is a view which the Catholic faith imposes on us." Therefore God would have implanted a human soul in the first living thing to become human.

3. As regards the theory of *polygenism,* or many first pairs of humans, the Pope says: "Christians cannot lend their support to a theory which involves the existence, after Adam's time, of some earthly race of men, truly so called, who were not descended ultimately from him, or else supposes that Adam was the name given to some group of our primordial ancestors. It does not appear how such views can be reconciled with the doctrine of original sin, as this is guaranteed to us by Scripture and tradition, and proposed to us by the Church. Original sin is the result of a sin committed, in actual historical fact, by an individual man named Adam, and it is a quality native to all of us, only because it has been handed down by descent from him" (cf. *Rom* 5:12-19).

Interestingly enough, the science of genetics seems to arrive at the same conclusion, although there is still some disagreement about the exact interpretation of the data. Scientists are now saying that a study of the Y-chromosome, which is passed from fathers to sons, shows that all males alive today have a single common ancestor, sometimes dubbed "Y-chromosome Adam". Similarly, studies of mitochondrial DNA, which is passed from mothers to daughters, have shown that all living females have descended from one woman, dubbed "Mitochondrial Eve".

In short, all human beings have descended from the same first parents and therefore all form one family. This should lead us to an attitude of solidarity and fraternity towards all peoples on earth, avoiding any hint of racism, nationalism or discrimination on any basis whatsoever. We are all one in Christ Jesus. As St Josemaría Escrivá used to say: "There is only one race in the world: the race of the children of God" (*Christ is Passing By*, 13).

In the next lesson we will look at our personal relationship with this loving God, a relationship known as prayer. Until then, may God bless you and guide you gently through the week.

QUESTIONS FOR DISCUSSION

1. Does it make any difference to you whether the universe was created by God or it resulted from chance?

2. Why do you think God created angels, and what importance do they have in our life?

3. Many people believe that man is not radically different from apes, but just a little more intelligent and with no more dignity than that of apes. How would you answer them?

4. What are the principal effects of original sin which affect all of us today?

5. Can a Christian believe in both God and evolution?

POINTS TO REMEMBER

- God created the universe out of nothing to show forth his glory.

- The universe has order and purpose because it was created by God.

- Angels are pure spirits with intelligence and free will who act as servants and messengers of God, some as guardian angels of human beings.

- Human beings were created in the image and likeness of God, with intelligence and free will, capable of knowing and loving God.

- Our first parents, Adam and Eve, were given special gifts from God but they lost those gifts for themselves and their descendants through the original sin.

5. PRAYER AND DEVOTIONS

Watch and pray that you may not enter into temptation; the spirit indeed is willing, but the flesh is weak (Mt 26:41)

SUMMARY

We now make a pause in the study of the Creed in order to consider how we relate to the God who created us out of love and who wants us to be with him forever in heaven. This relationship we call prayer and it takes different forms.

We begin by studying the nature of prayer: what it is and how it is always a gift from God to which we respond. What is important is not to know how to define prayer but to practise it.

We go on to consider the different forms of prayer, in particular vocal prayer, meditation or mental prayer, contemplation and aspirations. It is important to be growing constantly in our prayer life, which unites us with God.

We then consider some general aspects of prayer such as suitable places for prayer, times for prayer, and how to overcome difficulties in prayer such as lack of time, lack of feelings and distractions.

Welcome back to *Journey into Truth*. Although we are still very much at the beginning of our journey of discovery into the wonders of the Catholic faith, we have already seen that God is truly a loving father, who made the universe out of nothing, who watches over it and over each one of us in his fatherly providence, and who shares his divine life with his children, first with Adam and Eve and then with all of us.

This makes us want to enter into a personal relationship with this Father and his Son Jesus Christ. We cannot wait until we have finished studying about God to begin our relationship with him. The relationship can take different forms, but the most accessible one for everyone is prayer.

Let us begin, as usual, with a prayer. Heavenly Father, you are truly Our Father, who art in heaven. We want to come to a personal relationship with you, and with your Son Jesus Christ. We want to love you as we love our earthly parents, and to live in your presence, aware that you are always with us. Help us to respond to your initiative of love by developing a deep life of prayer, of communion with you, through Christ our Lord. Amen.

In this lesson we will consider three main topics: the nature of prayer, the different ways of praying, and some general considerations to help us pray well.

1. The nature of prayer

The Catechism says that the mystery of the faith "requires that the faithful ... live from it in a vital and personal relationship with the living and true God. This relationship is prayer" (*CCC* 2558). What is prayer? Prayer is simply a loving conversation with God our father in whatever way we find natural.

One of the great modern saints, St Thérèse of Lisieux, a French Carmelite nun who died at the age of 24 in 1897, describes prayer like this: "For me, prayer is a surge of the heart; it is a simple look turned toward heaven, it is a cry of recognition and of love, embracing both trial and joy" (*Manuscrits autobiographiques*, C 25r). Another more classical description comes from an eighth century saint, St John Damascene: "Prayer is the raising of one's mind and heart to God or the requesting of good things from God" (*De fide orth.* 3, 24).

Prayer is thus a loving conversation with our father. Or a loving conversation with our brother and friend, Jesus Christ. Or with the Holy

Spirit. Or with our holy mother, Mary. Or with any of the saints for that matter. We can talk with any of them and they will raise our prayer to God. What is important, though, is not to know how to define prayer, but rather to practise it; just as it is not as important to know how a good son or daughter ought to relate to their father, as it is to be a good son or daughter.

Prayer as a gift from God

We should always remember that, in addition to our own action in seeking God in order to talk with him, prayer is first and foremost an action of God. It is a gift from God, who seeks us out and invites us to talk with him. The Catechism expresses it like this: "In prayer, the faithful God's initiative of love always comes first; our own first step is always a response. As God gradually reveals himself and reveals man to himself, prayer appears as a reciprocal call, a covenant drama" (CCC 2567). That is, even though we may experience a strong desire to stop and pray, it is God who put that desire there, because he wants to talk with us. Prayer is thus a "covenant drama", a dialogue between two persons, each of whom seeks the other moved by love.

Also important in prayer is to come to God not only with our words, but with our heart. According to Scripture, it is the heart that prays. Listen to these words of the prophet Isaiah quoted by Jesus himself: "This people honours me with their lips, but their hearts are far from me" (Is 29:13; Mt 15:8). So we should try to put our heart into our prayer, to love the God with whom we are talking, to mean what we say.

2. THE DIFFERENT FORMS OF PRAYER

What forms does prayer take? Really, it can take whatever form we want, as long as through it we are talking with God in some way. But Christian tradition has given us three main types of prayer: vocal prayer, mental prayer or meditation and contemplative prayer. We can add a fourth type: aspirations, or short phrases directed to God at any time.

Vocal prayer

The easiest and most common form of prayer is vocal prayer. This can mean two things, and the Catechism uses it in both senses. The more customary meaning is the recitation of prayers with a fixed formula, like the *Our Father, Hail Mary* and *Glory be*. The other meaning, although less common, is prayers said out loud, as distinct from those said silently in the heart.

As always, when we say vocal prayers what matters most is not the recitation of the words, but rather the disposition of the heart. We should be thinking of what we are saying and of the person with whom we are talking. In this regard St John Chrysostom writes: "Whether or not our prayer is heard depends not on the number of words, but on the fervour of our souls" (*Ecloga de oratione* 2; *CCC* 2700).

And St Teresa of Avila writes, relating vocal prayer and mental prayer: "Know that with regard to our prayer being mental or not, the difference does not consist in keeping the mouth shut; for if uttering a prayer vocally, I do attentively consider and perceive that I am speaking with God, being more intent on this thought than on the words I pronounce, then I use both mental prayer and vocal prayer together" (*Way of Perfection*, 12). This is the case, for example, with the Rosary, which is a series of vocal prayers. When we recite the *Hail Marys* while meditating on the life of Christ contained in the mysteries, we are doing both vocal prayer and mental prayer at the same time.

How important is vocal prayer? In the words of the Catechism, "Vocal prayer is an essential element of the Christian life." Consider, for example, that Jesus himself taught us to say the *Our Father* (cf. *CCC* 2701). An advantage of vocal prayer is that it is very useful for praying in groups. For example, families and other groups say Grace before and after meals, the Rosary and other prayers like the *Angelus*.

What vocal prayers should a Catholic know and use? We have already mentioned the *Apostles' Creed*, the *Our Father, Hail Mary,* and *Glory be,* all of which are said in the Rosary, as is the *Hail, Holy Queen*. Other prayers which it is good to know are the *Angelus*, the *Morning Offering*, the *Memorare*, and the *Act of Contrition*.

Meditation

The second type of prayer is meditation, often called mental prayer. If, in the usual sense, vocal prayer is prayer with a fixed formula, meditation is talking to God in our own words. Here we simply talk things over with God, saying whatever comes into our heart and mind. In this sense it is a very personal form of prayer.

What should we meditate on? We can meditate on anything: a passage from Scripture, some incident in the life and teaching of Jesus Christ, our own family life, our relationships at work, our virtues and defects, our desires to help someone come closer to God... Literally, anything. The goal of meditation, as the Catechism says, is "to make our own in faith the subject considered, by confronting it with the reality of our own life" (*CCC* 2723).

The Catechism describes meditation as "above all a quest. The mind seeks to understand the why and how of the Christian life, in order to adhere and respond to what the Lord is asking" (*CCC* 2705). That is, beginning with some question or with some truth, we seek to go deeper into it, to understand it and apply it to our life.

In order to keep the mind centred on the topic of our prayer, and as a source of ideas, we usually find books a great help. The Catechism suggests, among others, "the Sacred Scriptures, particularly the Gospels, holy icons, liturgical texts of the day or season, writings of the spiritual fathers and works of spirituality" (*CCC* 2705). Even the great saints used books as an aid in meditation. St Teresa of Avila, for example, writes:

> It would have been impossible, I think, for me to persevere during
> the eighteen years for which I had to bear this trial and these great
> aridities due to my being unable to meditate. During all these years,

except after receiving Communion, I never dared to begin to pray without a book. My soul was as much afraid to engage in prayer without one as if it were having to go and fight a host of enemies (*Life*, 4).

At the same time, we should not limit our meditation to reading. Meditation involves reflection on what we have read. As the Catechism says, "to meditate on what we read helps us to make it our own by confronting it with ourselves. Here, another book is opened: the book of life. We pass from thoughts to reality. To the extent that we are humble and faithful, we discover in meditation the movements that stir the heart and we are able to discern them. It is a question of acting truthfully in order to come into the light: 'Lord, what do you want me to do?'" (*CCC* 2706) St Isidore of Seville, a seventh century Spanish saint, offers some practical advice:

By prayers we are cleansed, by readings we are instructed; both are good, if possible to do both; if it is not possible, it is better to pray than to read. Whoever wants to be with God always, should pray frequently and read frequently. For when we pray we speak with God; but when we read, God speaks with us (cf. *Liturgy of the Hours*, Office of Readings, April 4).

In any case, the ultimate goal of meditation and, indeed, of the whole spiritual life is love, union with Christ. This is especially the role of the third type of prayer: contemplation.

Contemplation

What is contemplation? It could be defined very simply as "a gaze of love at God". It is more an activity of the heart than of the mind. The Catechism sums it up: "It is a gaze of faith fixed on Jesus, an attentiveness to the Word of God, a silent love" (CCC 2724).

How does contemplation differ from meditation? In meditation the mind is active, passing from one idea to another in order to arrive at specific conclusions, whereas in contemplation it is more quiet, more passive. Ultimately, as the Catechism says, the object of contemplation is "Jesus, and in him, the Father. We seek him, because to desire him is always the beginning of love, and we seek him in that pure faith which causes us to be born of him and to live in him. In this inner prayer we can still meditate, but our attention is fixed on the Lord himself" (*CCC* 2709).

A simple description of contemplation is given by a peasant of Ars in France who, when the Curé asked him how he prayed, replied: "I look at him [that is, at God] and he looks at me." In contemplation we might simply sit in the church and look at the crucifix, considering that Jesus loved us so much that he died on the Cross for us. Or we might look at the tabernacle, the ornate receptacle in the church beside which a lamp is always burning, where our Lord waits for us in the Blessed Sacrament of love. Or we might look at an image of Our Lady, abandoning ourselves into her motherly arms. Even though the mind may not be active, our heart is giving itself to God. The Catechism often refers to contemplation as "prayer of the heart."

What is more, contemplation is very much "prayer of love" based on our awareness of being children of our Father God. As the Catechism says: "Contemplative prayer is the prayer of the child of God, of the forgiven sinner who agrees to welcome the love by which he is loved and who wants to respond to it by loving even more. But he knows that the love he is returning is poured out by the Spirit in his heart, for everything is grace from God. Contemplative prayer is the poor and humble surrender to the loving will of the Father in ever deeper union with his beloved Son" (*CCC* 2712). Once again we see that contemplation, like every form of prayer, is a work of the Holy Spirit, who is poured out in our heart, enabling us to contemplate.

Whereas there are times when vocal prayer and meditation can be difficult, contemplation is generally easier. As the Catechism puts it, "Contemplative prayer is the simplest expression of the mystery of prayer. It is a *gift*, a grace; it can be accepted only in humility and poverty.

Contemplative prayer is a *covenant* relationship established by God within our hearts. Contemplative prayer is a *communion* in which the Holy Trinity conforms man, the image of God, 'to his likeness'" (*CCC* 2713).

This is very much what Pope John Paul II had in mind when he frequently asked the faithful to "contemplate the face of Jesus." It is very helpful to open the Gospels to the various scenes where Jesus looks at someone and to contemplate that look: his look of love towards the young rich man, his look at Peter after the three denials which made Peter go out and weep for his sins, his look at those standing around the Cross of Calvary, etc.

Aspirations

A fourth type of prayer, often not included in books on prayer, is aspirations. What are aspirations? We can describe them as brief words or phrases addressed to God. They are like darts of love, from the Latin word for aspirations *iaculata*, literally darts. They can be as simple and spontaneous as "Lord, help me" or "Lord, thank you," or "Lord, I am sorry", or "Jesus, I love you". We say them whenever the Spirit moves us, so that they can be said at any moment of the day. They are simply whatever comes to our heart in a given moment, when we find ourselves in the presence of God and want to say something to him.

St Basil says of them: "How great it is to imitate on earth the chorus of the Angels! To prepare oneself to pray at the beginning of the day and to glorify the Creator with hymns and praises. Afterwards, when the sun shines on high, full of splendour and light, to go to work with our prayer accompanying us everywhere, seasoning our works, so to speak, with the salt of aspirations" (*Epist.* II, 3). And St John Chrysostom is thinking of aspirations when he says:

> A woman who is occupied in the kitchen or sewing a garment, can always raise her thought to heaven and call on the Lord with fervour. One who goes to the square or is travelling alone, can pray

with attention. Another who is in a wine cellar, occupied in sewing some wine skins, is free to raise his soul to the Lord. If the servant cannot go to the church because he has to go to the market to buy something or to carry out other duties or to cook, he is always free to pray with attention and ardour. No place is indecorous for God (*In Anna Prophet. Hom.*, 4, 6).

As this great saint says, aspirations are a form of prayer we can use at any time, even while we are working. We simply raise our heart to God and ask him for help, or thank him or tell him we love him. Apart from the spontaneous aspirations that will come naturally to our heart, some aspirations can be taken from Scripture. The first Christians used such aspirations as: "Jesus, Son of David, have mercy on me, a sinner", "Lord, if you wish, you can heal me", "Jesus, remember me when you come into your kingdom", "My Lord and my God" and "Lord Jesus, receive my spirit". Others are part of Catholic tradition: "Jesus, Mary and Joseph, I love you, save souls;" "Jesus, I trust in you;" "O Sacred Heart of Jesus, have mercy on us;" "O Sacred Heart of Jesus, grant us peace."

It can be good to choose some aspiration at the beginning of the day and try to say it as often as possible, so that the day is punctuated by these short prayers to God. In this way we can pray at all times, whether by saying vocal prayers, stopping for a longer time for meditation or contemplation, or simply raising our heart to God through aspirations.

3. GENERAL CONSIDERATIONS

We come now to some general considerations which can help us to pray well. First of all, the place for prayer.

The place for prayer

Where should we pray? We can pray anywhere of course. But perhaps the easiest place is in a church, before the tabernacle where Our Lord is truly present in the Eucharist. Apart from being a quiet place, free from the distraction of telephones, television and perhaps children, there we are certain that Our Lord is present in his humanity and divinity, that he sees us and hears us.

We can also pray at home, in a quiet room. Here it is helpful to have some image on which to focus our attention: a crucifix, an image of Our Lady or of the Sacred Heart of Jesus, an icon, a Bible, etc. Our Lord himself invited us to pray in our home: "But when you pray, go into your room and shut the door and pray to your Father who is in secret; and your Father who sees in secret will reward you" (Mt 6:6). Also, if there is a monastery nearby, where nuns or priests live a contemplative life of prayer, it too can be a very suitable place for prayer. The peace and quiet that reign in a monastery are very conducive to prayer.

Times for prayer

When should we pray? There are some traditional times when it is always good to pray. The first of these is in the morning, when we wake up. At this time we can thank God for the rest he has given us and offer the day ahead to him. The *Morning offering* is a traditional prayer said at this time, offering the day to God. Another common time is meals. Before we begin to eat we should stop and say what is commonly called *Grace before meals*. This is a prayer asking God to bless us and the gifts we have received from his generosity.

Another traditional time for prayer is twelve noon, when we say the *Angelus*, a prayer reminding us of the angel announcing to the Blessed Virgin Mary that she is to be the mother of God. The *Angelus* can also be said at 6 in the morning and 6 in the evening. And of course we should always say some prayers before going to bed at night. We can thank God for all the blessings of the day and ask his grace for a quiet and restful night. It is a good time to make a short examination of our conscience, considering what we have done during the day, both good and bad, and ending with an act of contrition. Many people have the custom at night of saying three *Hail Marys* for their own chastity and that of others.

And then it is good to set aside some other time each day for prayer, perhaps fifteen minutes. Here we can recollect ourselves in meditation or contemplation, or perhaps say the Rosary. If we decide to do this it is important to determine when and where we will do it and then hold ourselves to our resolution. If we don't, our prayer will easily fall by the wayside. Just as we set aside regular times for meals and relaxation, we should set aside regular times to nourish our soul in prayer. It is a matter of priorities. We set aside time for whatever we consider important. Surely our relationship with God is important for us.

The Catechism is very clear: "One does not undertake contemplative prayer only when one has the time: one makes time for the Lord, with the firm determination not to give up, no matter what trials and dryness one may encounter. One cannot always meditate, but one can always enter into inner prayer, independently of the conditions of health, work or emotional state" (*CCC* 2710).

Facing difficulties

When we set out to pray, we will inevitably encounter difficulties: lack of time, lack of desire, lack of feelings, distractions... The Catechism gives us some helpful advice: "Prayer is both a gift of grace and a determined response on our part. It always presupposes effort. The great figures of prayer of the old Covenant before Christ, as well as the Mother of God, the saints, and he himself, all teach us this: prayer is a battle. Against whom? Against ourselves and against the wiles of the tempter who does all he can to turn man away from prayer, away from union with God. We pray as we live, because we live as we pray... The 'spiritual battle' of the Christian's new life is inseparable from the battle of prayer" (*CCC* 2725).

One of the difficulties everyone faces in prayer is distractions. We cannot pray for very long before our mind is attracted to something completely different. Here we should never become discouraged. We should simply accept our human limitations, ask Our Lord for pardon, and go back to the subject of our prayer. What is more, distractions may even be a good sign, as St Alphonsus Liguori says in his *Treatise on Prayer*: "If you have many distractions at prayer, that prayer of yours may well be upsetting the devil a great deal."

What is important is to persevere in our prayer. God is very happy with the effort we make, even when we think we are getting nowhere. If we continue in our prayer, we will grow in love for God our Father and we will become friends of Jesus Christ, our God, our Saviour, our friend.

In the next lesson we will consider the love of our life, Jesus Christ, true God and true man. Until then, may God bless you and fill you with his love.

QUESTIONS FOR DISCUSSION

1. Prayer can be defined and described in many different ways. How do you most like to think of it and how would you describe it to a friend who didn't know what it is?

2. Why is it so important to pray regularly? Isn't it enough to know that God is always there?

3. Mental prayer or meditation is one of the most personal forms of prayer, since in it we speak to God in our own words. Are there any particular books or ideas you have found especially helpful in doing mental prayer?

4. Why is it so important to have a regular routine of times for prayer each day, and is it a good idea to pray even when we don't feel like it?

5. Everyone has distractions when praying. What are some ways you have found helpful to deal with them?

POINTS TO REMEMBER

- We should all pray because prayer is simply a loving conversation with our Father God, who created us and loves us and has a place for us in heaven.

- The principal forms of prayer are vocal prayer, meditation, contemplation and aspirations.

- Although we should try to pray always, it is good to set aside certain times each day for prayer.

- Prayer always involves effort and so we should struggle to overcome our reluctance to pray, the lack of fervour and the distractions.

6. Jesus Christ, true God and true man

But when the time had fully come, God sent forth his Son, born of woman, born under the law, to redeem those who were under the law, so that we might receive adoption as sons (Gal 4:4-5)

Summary

At the heart of Christianity is the figure of Jesus Christ. Everyone has heard of him but who is he? Is he God or man, or perhaps both?

We begin by considering how Jesus is truly God, the second person of the Trinity, who took flesh in the womb of the Blessed Virgin Mary. We study how we know he is God, starting from what he said about himself and from his miracles and prophecies, and the consequences this has for our faith.

Then we look at what we call the Incarnation, the taking flesh of the Son of God in the womb of Mary. Here we answer the question, "How did the Son of God become man?" and we also consider why he became man.

We go on to study how Jesus is truly man like us and how his divinity and humanity are related. We also look at non-Christian historical writings that speak of his existence on earth.

Finally, we consider how we can grow in friendship with Jesus, since this is what most matters in our faith.

Welcome back to our excursion into the marvellous truths of the Catholic faith. I hope you are appreciating how rich our faith is, and how solidly grounded it is in reason as well as in the Scriptures and Tradition of the Church.

In the last lesson we studied our life of prayer, which should now be taking firm root in all of us. The more we come to know about God who is a true father, rich in mercy and kindness, the more we want to enter into a personal relationship with him. This relationship is prayer, in its different forms of vocal prayer, meditation, contemplation and aspirations.

In this lesson we will begin our study of the eternal Son of God, who took human nature in the womb of the Blessed Virgin Mary and lived on our planet two thousand years ago in order to redeem us from original sin. This, of course, is Jesus Christ. In this lesson we will consider the person of Jesus, true God and true man. In the next lesson we will study his life, death and resurrection, by which he redeemed us. But let us begin as usual with a prayer.

Heavenly Father, you so loved the world that you sent your only-begotten Son, so that all who believe in him should not perish but have eternal life. You sent your Son into the world not to condemn the world, but so that the world might be saved through him (cf *Jn* 3:16). How rich you are in mercy, how much you love us! Help us to grow in a personal and strong relationship with Jesus, your Son, our Lord, so that through him we may come to know and love you and be with you forever in heaven. We make our prayer through Christ our Lord. Amen.

In this lesson we will consider four main topics: Jesus Christ, true God; the Incarnation; Jesus Christ, true man; and friendship with Jesus Christ.

1. JESUS CHRIST, TRUE GOD

Who exactly is Jesus Christ? People have asked this question time and again down the ages, and as often as not they have received the wrong answer. But this is nothing new. The question was first posed by Jesus himself. We read it in the sixteenth chapter of St Matthew's Gospel. There Jesus asked the apostles: "Who do men say that the Son of man is?" They answered: "Some say John the Baptist, others say Elijah, and others Jeremiah or one of the prophets" (*Mt* 16:13-14). As you can see, people had been thinking about who this Jesus was, but all their answers were wrong. Then, as now, opinion polls don't always lead to the truth! Then Jesus said, "But who do you say that I am?" Simon Peter answered, "You are the Christ, the Son of the living God" (*Mt* 16:16). This of course is exactly who Jesus is. But what does this mean, "the Christ, the Son of the living God"?

The name *Christ* comes from a Greek word meaning "anointed". It is the word used by the Jews in the Old Testament to refer to the one who was to come eventually to save the people and to sit on the throne of his ancestor King David. There were many prophecies in the Old Testament about this person, whom they called by the Hebrew name Messiah, which means anointed. Jesus had come to fulfil those prophecies. He was the Christ, the anointed one, the Messiah. We see this too at the birth of Christ, when an angel announced to the shepherds in the fields nearby: "To you is born this day in the city of David a Saviour, who is Christ the Lord" (*Lk* 2:11).

And what does *Son of the living God* mean? Here we go back to our study of the Blessed Trinity. We recall that in the one God there are three divine Persons: the Father, the Son and the Holy Spirit, all equal and all existing from all eternity. When St Peter professed that Jesus was the "Son of the living God", he meant that he was the second Person of the Blessed Trinity, the Son, who had become man. That is, Jesus is truly God, a divine person. St John describes Jesus' divinity at the beginning of his Gospel, referring to the second Person of the Trinity as the Word, or *Logos* in Greek:

> In the beginning was the Word, and the Word was with God, and the Word was God. He was in the beginning with God; all things were made through him, and without him was not anything made that was made. In him was life, and the life was the light of men ...

And the Word became flesh and dwelt among us, full of grace and truth; we have beheld his glory, glory as of the only Son from the Father" (*Jn* 1:1-5, 14).

In this passage it is clear that Jesus is indeed the Son of God from all eternity: "... and the Word was God. He was in the beginning with God". Moreover, it was through the Word that the universe was created: "... all things were made through him". And finally the Word, the Son of God, "became flesh and dwelt among us". God became man. This is Jesus.

But we should ask what the name *Jesus* means. Jesus is a Hebrew name meaning "God saves". As we know, an angel appeared to Joseph, who was betrothed to Mary, and told him in a dream: "...and you shall call his name Jesus, for he will save his people from their sins" (*Mt* 1:21). Before that, the angel Gabriel had appeared to Mary to announce that she was to be the mother of God and had told her: "and you shall call his name Jesus. He will be great, and will be called the Son of the Most High; and the Lord God will give him the throne of his father David, and he will reign over the house of Jacob for ever; and of his kingdom there will be no end" (*Lk* 1:31-33). We see in the very name *Jesus* the reason for his becoming man: to save us from our sins, from both original sin and personal sin.

The other name applied to Jesus is *Lord*. We have just seen how the angel announcing the birth of Christ to the shepherds called him "Christ the Lord". What does *Lord* mean here? We recall how in Old Testament times the Jews never pronounced the divine name Yahweh. They held that name in such reverence that they didn't dare to say it. Rather they used another name for God, *Adonai*, which is translated as Lord. So when we say that Jesus is Lord we mean it in the same sense, that he is truly God. The apostle Thomas used this name when Jesus appeared in the Upper Room a week after his Resurrection and showed Thomas the marks of the wounds in his hands and side. St Thomas exclaimed, "My Lord and my God" (*Jn* 20:28), by way of professing his faith in the divinity of Christ.

We use the name *Lord* often in Christian prayers. For example, the priest says, "The Lord be with you" as a greeting in Mass, and many prayers end "through Christ our Lord". We should always understand this phrase as meaning "through Christ our God".

In the Nicene Creed, which we say in Mass on Sundays, we profess our faith in the divinity of Christ in the following words: "I believe in one Lord Jesus Christ, the Only Begotten Son of God, born of the Father before all ages, God from God, Light from Light, true God from true God, begotten, not made, consubstantial with the Father; through him all things were made." It is clear in these words that Jesus is the eternal Son of the Father, true God from true God. He is begotten by the Father, as children are begotten by their parents, and in his case he is begotten from all eternity. He is not made, that is, not created. And he is consubstantial, meaning of the same divine substance, of the same divine being as the Father. It is through him, as St John writes, that all things were made (cf. *Jn* 1:3).

Jesus himself affirms his divinity in many ways. Among them is his clear statement, "I and the Father are one." For saying this, the Jews were about to stone him "because", they said, "you, being a man, make yourself God" (*Jn* 10:30-33). And in the Last Supper he prayed to the Father: "Father, glorify me in your own presence, with the glory which I had with you before the world was made…" (*Jn* 17:5) Only if Jesus was God could he speak of the glory he had with the Father before the world was made.

He shows his divinity, among other ways, by the many prophecies he made that came true. For example, he prophesied that Peter would deny him, that Judas would betray him and especially that he himself would be put to death and would rise again on the third day. And of course Jesus showed by his many miracles that he was God. He cured lepers, the lame and even a man born blind, he raised three people from the dead, he cast out devils, he multiplied loaves and fish in order to feed thousands, he calmed storms... In short, he did what only God can do. His ultimate miracle was his own resurrection from the dead on the third day after his crucifixion. No human being could have done that. In short, Jesus is truly God. This has important consequences for us.

1. Since Jesus is God, *everything he says is true.* As he himself said: "I am… the truth" (*Jn* 14:6). Therefore, we should take to heart all his teachings as taught by the Church: on life after death, angels, the Trinity, the Real Presence in the Eucharist, the moral law, etc. Some of these teachings may be difficult to understand or to live, but we know that they are all true and we should believe them. After all, they come from God himself.

2. Being the very Son of God, *Jesus can lead us to the Father.* He said "I am the way… No one comes to the Father except through me" (*Jn* 14:6). We should therefore follow him closely and he will lead us to eternal life with the Father in heaven.

3. The Church that Jesus founded is the *Church that God himself founded.* It is not merely one more among the many religions in the world. It is God's own religion, God's own Church. We have the joy of coming into it, or of already belonging to it.

4. Since Jesus is truly God, *he always hears and answers our prayers* (cf. *Mt* 7:7-11). Therefore, we can pray to him with confidence.

2. The Incarnation

We come now to our second topic, the Incarnation. Here we answer the question, "How did the Son of God, the second Person of the Blessed Trinity become man?"

The word "incarnation", by the way, means literally "enfleshment" from the Latin word for flesh, *carnis.* As we have seen, St John writes in the first chapter of his Gospel that "the Word became flesh and dwelt among us" (*Jn* 1:14).

But how did the Word become flesh? St Luke, in the first chapter of his Gospel, gives us the answer. Some two thousand years ago, the angel Gabriel appeared to a young girl named Mary in the town of Nazareth in Galilee, in northern Israel. Mary would have been in her teens, according to the customs of the time. She was a virgin and was betrothed to a man named Joseph. Betrothal is similar to engagement today, except that the two persons were already considered to be husband and wife, even if they had not yet come to live together.

After greeting Mary with the familiar words "Hail, full of grace", the angel told her that she would conceive in her womb and would bear a son, whom she was to call Jesus (cf. *Lk* 1:28-31). Mary naturally asked how this could be since she was a virgin and intended to remain so. The angel answered: "The Holy Spirit will come upon you, and the power of the Most High will overshadow you" (*Lk* 1:35).

That is, Mary would conceive the child not by the intervention of Joseph, but by the Holy Spirit, the third Person of the Blessed Trinity. This was of course extraordinary, unprecedented. But it fulfilled the prophecy of Isaiah in the Old Testament, "Behold, a virgin shall conceive and bear a son, and shall call his name Immanuel" (*Is* 7:14). Through his conception by the Holy Spirit, Jesus is truly "Christ," that is anointed by the Holy Spirit from the first moment of his human existence. And he is truly Immanuel, which means "God with us".

Because Jesus had no human father but only his eternal divine Father, the first Person of the Blessed Trinity, he was, as the angel told Mary, truly "the Son of God" (*Lk* 1:35). And, because he was conceived by a woman and spent nine months in her womb like any other human being, he is truly man. Jesus is truly God and truly man.

As we know, Mary's response to the angel's proposal was simple and immediate: "Behold, I am the handmaid of the Lord; let it be to me according to your word" (*Lk* 1:38). With those words the divine Word, the second Person of the Blessed Trinity, took flesh in the womb of Mary. Nine months later he was born in Bethlehem.

The Church celebrates the conception of Jesus on the feast of the Annunciation on March 25 each year, and the birth of Jesus nine months later on the feast of Christmas, December 25.

We might now ask *why* the Word became flesh. The Catechism gives us four reasons.

1. The first is the most obvious. He became flesh *to save us from our sins* and reconcile us with God. As we say in the Nicene Creed, "For us men and for our salvation he came down from heaven" (cf. *CCC* 457).

2. The Word became flesh *so that we might know God's love*. In Jesus Christ we see the love of God made visible, in the flesh. St John writes the familiar words: "For God so loved the world that he gave his only Son, that whoever believes in him should not perish but have eternal life" (*Jn* 3:16; *CCC* 458).

3. The Word became flesh *to be our model of holiness*. In Jesus we see the model of humanity, the example of how we ought to live. By imitating him we grow in holiness (cf. *CCC* 459).

4. The Word became flesh *to make us participate in the divine nature*. By assuming our human nature, Jesus allows us to share in his divine nature (cf. *2 Pet* 1:4; *CCC* 460). In so doing, he made us adopted sons and daughters of God. We are not merely creatures of the creator, but children of God the Father. We have a very intimate relationship with our Father God.

To these benefits we could add that by becoming man and living amongst us, we are assured that *Jesus understands our weakness*. He too knew hunger, thirst, cold, heat, physical pain, misunderstanding, rejection, persecution and death. We can therefore pray to him in the confidence that he truly knows our human nature with all its limitations. As the *Letter to the Hebrews* says, he is "a man like us in all things but sin" (*Heb* 4:15).

3. JESUS CHRIST, TRUE MAN

We look now at our third topic, Jesus Christ, true man, and at how the divine and human natures come together in the divine person of Jesus. Notice that we speak of "the divine person of Jesus". As we have seen, Jesus is a divine person, the eternal Son of God. He is not a human person, even though he has human nature. In simple terms, he is a divine person with both a divine nature, which he had from all eternity, and a human nature which he received on taking flesh in the womb of Mary. In Jesus there is one person with two natures.

The Catechism sums it up: "The unique and altogether singular event of the Incarnation of the Son of God does not mean that Jesus Christ is part God and part man, nor does it imply that he is the result of a confused mixture of the divine and the human. He became truly man while remaining truly God. Jesus Christ is true God and true man" (*CCC* 464).

Since Jesus had human nature, he had a true human soul with a human intellect and will, as we have. By intellect, we mean a human mind, or understanding. That is, in addition to his divine intellect with its divine knowledge of all things past, present and future, he had a human intellect, which could grow in knowledge. As the Catechism explains, Christ's human knowledge "could not in itself be unlimited: it was exercised in the historical conditions of his existence in space and time. This is why the Son of God could, when he became man, 'increase in wisdom and in stature, and in favour with God and man'" (*Lk* 2:52; *CCC* 472). For example, Jesus learned Jewish prayers and customs from Mary and Joseph, he learned from Joseph how to make various objects in his workshop, he learned about the Galilean countryside, etc.

Among the objects of Christ's knowledge was what we call the Beatific Vision, the immediate vision of God which the saints have in heaven. Pope Pius XII wrote in his Encyclical *Mystici Corporis* (1943): "In virtue of the Beatific Vision which he enjoyed from the time when he was received into the womb of the mother of God, he has forever and

continuously had present to him all the members of his mystical Body
and embraced them with his saving love."

Just as Jesus had a human intellect in addition to his divine intellect,
he also had a human will in addition to his divine will. Nonetheless, his
human will was always identified with the divine will. In the words of the
Catechism, the human and divine wills in Christ cooperated in such a way
"that the Word made flesh willed humanly in obedience to his Father all
that he had decided divinely with the Father and the Holy Spirit for our
salvation" (*CCC* 475).

We see this in the Garden of Gethsemani when, considering the
suffering he is about to undergo in his passion and death, Jesus asks the
Father that he may be spared the chalice of suffering, but he concludes:
"Only as your will is, not as mine is" (*Mt* 26:39).

We should always pray like that when we are asking God to spare us
some suffering or to grant us some favour. Like Jesus we should identify
our will with that of God, and be happy to accept whatever our loving
Father chooses to give us. If we do not receive what we asked for, we can
take consolation in the fact that neither did Jesus. God the Father wanted
Jesus to suffer and die on the Cross so that he might redeem us, and he
will have a purpose in not giving us what we asked for.

Christ's historical existence

Every now and then we hear of someone who questions whether Jesus
Christ actually existed. It is helpful to know that in addition to the sacred
Scriptures, for which there are hundreds of manuscripts dating back to
the early centuries, there are also secular writings that speak of Christ.

For example, the Roman historian *Tacitus* wrote around 116 AD,
"Christians take their name from Christ who, in the reign of Tiberias,
the proconsul Pontius Pilate condemned to suffer" (*Annales* XV, 1, 4).
Suetonius, in his life of the emperor Claudius written around 120 AD,
says that Claudius expelled the Jews from Rome because of the unrest

among them "stirred up by Chresto", an obvious reference to Christ (*Vita Claudii*, XXV, 4). And *Pliny the Younger*, proconsul of Bithynia from 111 to 113 AD, in one of his letters to the Emperor Trajan wrote that "the Christians gather at dawn on a fixed day and sing a hymn to Christ as to a God" (*Epist.* X, 96).

So there is no doubt that Jesus actually existed. He truly dwelt among us, as true God and true man. The Second Vatican Council, for our great consolation, comments on his humanity: "He worked with human hands, he thought with a human mind. He acted with a human will, and with a human heart he loved. Born of the Virgin Mary, he has truly been made one of us, like to us in all things except sin" (cf. *Heb* 4:15; *GS* 22).

And faith in Jesus is essential if we are to understand ourselves and our destiny. Again we quote the Second Vatican Council:

> The Church believes that Christ, who died and was raised for the sake of all, can show man the way and strengthen him through the Spirit in order to be worthy of his destiny: nor is there any other name under heaven given among men by which they can be saved (cf. *Acts* 4:12). The Church likewise believes that the key, the centre and the purpose of the whole of man's history is to be found in its Lord and Master. She also maintains that beneath all that changes there is much that is unchanging, much that has its ultimate foundation in Christ, who is the same yesterday, and today, and forever. And that is why the Council, relying on the inspiration of Christ, the image of the invisible God, the firstborn of all creation, proposes to speak to all men in order to unfold the mystery that is man and cooperate in tackling the main problems facing the world today (*GS* 10).

4. FRIENDSHIP WITH JESUS CHRIST

As we have seen several times, what truly matters is not knowing *about* God, or *about* Jesus Christ, but entering into a personal relationship with them.

Jesus is at the heart of our faith. To be a Catholic is to know and love him, among other reasons because he knows and loves us. He loves us so much that he became man and died on the Cross for us. Therefore we should try to grow in personal friendship with him. After all, he told the apostles, and he tells each one of us, "I have called you friends" (*Jn* 15:15). We can have no better friend than Jesus, the friend who is both God and man, and who will always be there for us.

How can we grow in friendship with him? First, by *coming to know him better*. We do this by reading the Scriptures, especially the New Testament, at least a few minutes each day. We can also read other books about him: books about his life, about his suffering and death, and books about the saints, which always bring us closer to Jesus.

Second, *by dealing with him in prayer*: talking to him, listening to him, knowing that he always hears and answers us. The more we talk with him, the more we will fall in love with him. He invites us to do this: "Come to me all who labour and are heavy laden, and I will give you rest" (*Mt* 11:28).

Third, we can grow in friendship with Christ by *relating to him in the sacraments*, especially by receiving his pardon in the sacrament of Penance and Reconciliation, and by receiving him whole and entire in the sacrament of the Eucharist. There is no closer union with Christ on earth than holy Communion, where, as he says, we live in him and he lives in us (cf. *Jn* 6:56).

Thomas à Kempis sums up the importance of love for Jesus in his classic work *The Imitation of Christ*: "He who finds Jesus finds a treasure... And he who loses Jesus loses a great deal, more than if he lost the whole world. He who lives without Jesus is poor indeed, and he who is with Jesus is rich indeed" (*The Imitation of Christ*, II).

In our next lesson we will study Jesus' life, death and resurrection, especially his role as our Redeemer. Until then, may God love you and draw you ever closer to him.

QUESTIONS FOR DISCUSSION

1. What arguments do you find most convincing to show that Jesus Christ is truly God and not just a good man?

2. The fact that Jesus is truly God means that everything he says and that the Church teaches is true. How should we react when we find that some of these teachings may be difficult to understand or to live?

3. How does the fact that Jesus is truly man help you in your relationship with him?

4. Jesus in his humanity always identified his human will with the will of the Father. How does this help you, especially when you find it hard to accept the will of God in the face of difficulties in life?

5. What ways do you find especially helpful to enter into a personal friendship with Jesus?

POINTS TO REMEMBER

- Jesus Christ is not a human person but a divine person, the second person of the Blessed Trinity, who took flesh in the womb of the Blessed Virgin Mary.

- Jesus is a divine person with two natures: the divine nature which he had with the Father and the Holy Spirit from all eternity, and the human nature which he took in the womb of Our Lady.

- By his miracles, prophecies and words Jesus showed that he is truly God.

- We call Jesus' taking of flesh in the womb of Mary the Incarnation.

- We can grow in friendship with Jesus, our friend, through reading of the New Testament, prayer and the sacraments.

7. THE LIFE, DEATH AND RESURRECTION OF CHRIST

For God sent the Son into the world, not to condemn the world, but that the world might be saved through him (cf. Jn 3:16)

SUMMARY

Having studied who Jesus Christ is in his divinity and humanity, we now study the principal events in Jesus' life from his birth in Bethlehem to his Ascension into heaven and his Second Coming at the end of time.

We begin with Jesus' infancy and hidden life, by which we mean his thirty years in Nazareth before he began his three years of public life. We see how each event has something to teach us.

Then we consider the three years of Jesus' public life, during which he preached the Gospel, worked many miracles, chose the apostles and founded the Church.

We go on to study the important event of Jesus' death on the cross by which he brought about our redemption. We study in particular what we mean by redemption, why we needed to be redeemed, and whether Jesus died for all or only for some.

Finally we consider Jesus' Resurrection from the dead, his Ascension into heaven and his Second Coming at the end of time. Here we study the reality and the importance of his Resurrection from the dead, which is the definitive proof of his divinity. We also see how Jesus ascended into heaven forty days after his Resurrection, returning to the Father from whom he had come, and how he will come again at the end of time to judge the living and the dead.

Welcome back to our journey of faith. In the last lesson we studied Jesus Christ, true God and true man, and our effort to grow in friendship with him. In this lesson we will consider the life of Christ, looking at the principal events of his birth, life, death, Resurrection, Ascension into heaven and his Second Coming. We will study in particular how he redeemed us and what we mean by redemption.

But let us begin with a prayer. Heavenly Father, moved by love you sent us your only-begotten Son, the Second Person of the Blessed Trinity, to dwell among us and redeem us by his death and Resurrection. Help us to grow more and more in friendship with him, so that we can become more Christlike and so help many others to find him, love him and come through him to eternal life with you. We make our prayer through Christ our Lord. Amen.

In the Apostles' Creed we express our faith in many events in the life of Christ. In this lesson we will study these principal events in order to come to a deeper understanding of their significance in our lives. We will consider four main topics: Jesus' infancy and hidden life, his public life, his death for our redemption, and his Resurrection, Ascension into heaven and Second Coming.

Before we begin, though, we should be clear about three truths. First, Jesus Christ is not only man, but true God. Everything he does is done by his divine person, acting through his human nature. Second, Jesus' whole life is a cooperation in his work of redemption, of making up to the Father for our sins. In the words of the Catechism, "Christ's whole life is a mystery of redemption. Redemption comes to us above all through the blood of his cross, but his mystery is at work throughout Christ's entire life" (CCC 517). And third, we find in Jesus our model, so that we can imitate him in everything if we want to grow in holiness. As the Catechism puts it, "In all his life Jesus presents himself as our model. He is 'the perfect man', who invites us to become his disciples and follow him" (CCC 520).

Naturally, we cannot pretend to consider all the events of Christ's life

in one lesson. Therefore it is good to read the Gospels or a book on the
life of Christ in order to be familiar with his whole life.

1. JESUS' INFANCY AND HIDDEN LIFE

As we remember from the last lesson, Jesus was conceived in the womb
of the Blessed Virgin Mary by the power of the Holy Spirit. Nine months
later he was born in Bethlehem, a town in Judaea, not far from Jerusalem.
Because there was no room for Joseph and Mary in the inn, Jesus was
born in a stable and was laid in a manger, a feeding trough for animals
(cf. *Lk* 2:1-7). By his poverty, we can learn to be detached from earthly
things.

After he was born an angel appeared to shepherds in the fields nearby
and announced to them: "Be not afraid; for behold, I bring you good
news of a great joy which will come to all the people; for to you is born
this day in the city of David a Saviour, who is Christ the Lord" (*Lk* 2:10-
11). As we recall, this tells the shepherds that the Christ, the Messiah,
the one whom the Jews were awaiting for many centuries, had now been
born. He was their Saviour and would redeem them from their sins.

Some days later wise men came from the East to adore Jesus (cf. *Mt*
2:1-12). We celebrate their arrival on January 6 in the feast we call the
Epiphany, a word meaning "manifestation". The Church sees in these
men the representatives of the many gentiles, the non-Jews, who would
one day come to believe in Christ.

Forty days after his birth Jesus was presented to God in the temple
of Jerusalem in fulfilment of the Old Testament law. There an elderly
man named Simeon took Jesus in his arms and prophesied that he would
be a sign of contradiction and that a sword would pierce the soul of his
mother Mary (cf. *Lk* 2:34-35). Simeon was announcing that Jesus would
be put to death and that his mother Mary would have to suffer too.

When King Herod wanted to kill Jesus, because he feared him as a
rival, an angel appeared to Joseph in a dream to warn him, and so Joseph

took Mary and Jesus and fled into Egypt, where they remained until the death of Herod (cf. *Mt* 2:13-22). Jesus' departure from Egypt recalls the exodus of the Israelites from Egypt under Moses some 1200 years earlier and presents Jesus as the definitive liberator of God's people.

Jesus then lived in obedience to Mary and Joseph for some thirty years in Nazareth in what we call his hidden life. Here we can all identify with him as we too seek holiness in the ordinary circumstances of our work, family life and rest.

The Gospel of Luke records one event of these years, the fact that Jesus was taken to Jerusalem for the feast of the Passover when he was twelve and remained behind in the temple only to be found by Joseph and Mary three days later (cf. *Lk* 2:41-51). When they found him, Jesus said, "Did you not know that I must be in my Father's house"? Here he reveals his total dedication to the mission his Father God had sent him to do on earth. It is a call to all of us to do the will of God in everything.

2. JESUS' PUBLIC LIFE

When he was about thirty years of age, Jesus began his public life with his baptism by John the Baptist in the Jordan River. The Holy Spirit appeared in the form of a dove and rested on Jesus, while a voice from heaven said, "This is my beloved Son, with whom I am well pleased" (*Mt* 3:13-17). These words of God the Father announce Jesus as the Son of God, the second Person of the Blessed Trinity. Although, as God, Jesus did not need to be baptised for the remission of sins as we do, he willed to be baptised in order to sanctify the waters of Baptism forever after.

Immediately after his baptism Jesus went out into the desert where he remained for forty days without eating and was tempted by Satan three times (cf. *Mk* 1:12-13). Here, as the second Adam, Jesus made up for Adam's giving in to temptation, by resisting temptation himself. Jesus' fidelity in resisting temptation is an encouragement for us to imitate him when we are tempted. As the *Letter to the Hebrews* says, "For we have not a high priest who is unable to sympathise with our weaknesses, but one who in every respect has been tested as we are, yet without sinning" (*Heb* 4:15). The Church relives each year Jesus' forty days in the desert by the forty days of prayer, penance and works of charity in Lent.

After his forty days in the desert, Jesus began his public ministry by preaching: "The time is fulfilled, and the kingdom of God is at hand: repent, and believe in the gospel" (*Mk* 1:14-15). What do we mean by the phrase "kingdom of God", or "kingdom of heaven", which appears so often in Christ's teaching? As the glossary of the Catechism says, quoting *Romans* 14:17, the kingdom of God is "righteousness and peace and joy in the Holy Spirit." It is equivalent to life in Christ, through grace. One could also think of it as God's life-giving and redeeming rule over mankind, which one enters by becoming a disciple of Christ through Baptism.

The kingdom of God on earth is the Church. The Catechism points out that the Church is "on earth the seed and beginning of that kingdom" (*LG* 5; *CCC* 541). The kingdom of God extends beyond earth to Purgatory and to heaven as well, where it reaches its fulfilment. Christ sent out his disciples to call all people to the Church and he accomplished the coming of his kingdom by his death and Resurrection. Jesus accompanied his preaching of the kingdom with many miracles. These make it clear that the kingdom is present in him and that he is truly the promised Messiah and the Son of God.

A key moment of Jesus' public life was the founding of the Church, which we will study in more detail in the next lesson. Another important moment was his Transfiguration, the manifestation of his divinity to the apostles Peter, James and John, on Mount Tabor (cf. *Lk* 9:28-36; *Mt* 17:1-8). Here Jesus appeared in all his glory accompanied by Moses and Elijah, two figures from the Old Testament, and once again as at his Baptism the voice of the Father was heard saying, "This is my Son, my Chosen; listen to him" (*Lk* 9:35).

Having prophesied his death and Resurrection three times, Jesus went up to Jerusalem for the feast of the Passover, prepared to die there. On what we now call Palm Sunday, only five days before his death, Jesus entered Jerusalem in triumph, hailed as the Son of his ancestor King David and as the one who would bring salvation. The people shouted, "Hosanna to the Son of David! Blessed is he who comes in the name of the Lord!" (*Mt* 21:9). The Hebrew word *Hosanna* means "Save!" or "Give salvation!" Jesus entered Jerusalem in humility, riding on a donkey, inviting us too to enter into the heavenly kingdom along the way of humility.

3. JESUS' DEATH FOR OUR REDEMPTION

In the Apostles' Creed we say that Jesus "suffered under Pontius Pilate, was crucified, died and was buried". We know that Jesus was condemned to death by the Roman governor Pontius Pilate at the urging of the Jewish leaders. He was scourged and crowned with thorns, then forced to carry his cross to Mount Calvary, just outside Jerusalem. There he was nailed to the cross between two thieves, and he hung on the cross for three hours before dying. We commemorate these events on Good Friday each year and in the Sorrowful Mysteries of the Rosary.

Why did the leaders of the Jews want Jesus put to death? By his powerful preaching and his many miracles, including raising three people from the dead, Jesus had attracted many followers, and the leaders of the Jews feared that their own power would be diminished. They were always looking for opportunities to catch him out in his speech and have him say something that would provide grounds to condemn him. They were especially angered by his words and actions where he seemed to be saying that he was God. For example, he dared to forgive sins, to change the law of Moses by forbidding divorce, and to say such things as "Before Abraham was, I am" and "I and the Father are one" (*Jn* 8:58; 10:30). The leaders of the Jews did not have the humility to recognise Jesus for what he truly was and they condemned him to death as a blasphemer, "for making himself equal to God" (*Jn* 10:33).

While Jesus' death on the cross may seem a tragedy, humanly speaking, we know that through it he redeemed us from our sins. His death was thus the culmination of his life, the fulfilment of the whole purpose of his Incarnation. As the Catechism explains, "The Paschal mystery of Christ's cross and Resurrection stands at the centre of the Good News that the apostles, and the Church following them, are to proclaim to the world. God's saving plan was accomplished 'once for all' by the redemptive death of his Son Jesus Christ" (*Heb* 9:26; *CCC* 571). The word "paschal", by the way, refers to the Passover, to Jesus' death and resurrection by which he passed over to the Father.

The need for Christ to die takes us back to the original sin of Adam and Eve, which cost them and their descendants the intimate friendship with God which we call sanctifying grace, and closed the gates of heaven, so that they could not enter heaven when they died. Since then, mankind had been awaiting the coming of the one who would crush the head of the serpent, and Jesus accomplished that by his death on the Cross. This is what we mean by redemption. As the glossary of the Catechism explains: "Christ paid the price of his own sacrificial death on the cross to ransom us, to set us free from the slavery of sin, thus achieving our redemption." The word redemption comes from the Latin word *redemptio* meaning "to buy back" or "to buy again". Jesus ransomed or redeemed us from the slavery of sin, paying the price of his own life.

This had been announced by John the Baptist, who said that Jesus was "the Lamb of God, who takes away the sin of the world" (*Jn* 1:29). The Catechism explains it like this: "Man's sins, following on original sin, are punishable by death. By sending his own Son in the form of a slave, in the form of a fallen humanity, on account of sin, God 'made him to be sin who knew no sin, so that in him we might become the righteousness of God'" (*2 Cor* 5:21; *CCC* 602). Thus by his death and Resurrection, Christ reconciled us with God and opened up the gates of heaven so that all who die in God's grace and friendship could once again go to enjoy eternal life with God.

Did Christ die only for some, or for the whole of mankind? The answer is obvious. The Catechism teaches: "The Church, following the apostles, teaches that Christ died for all men without exception: 'There is not, never has been, and never will be a single human being for whom Christ did not suffer'" (Council of Quiercy (853); *CCC* 605). The Catechism cites two Scriptural texts for this statement, one of which is from St John: "... and he is the expiation for our sins, and not for ours only but also for the sins of the whole world" (*1 Jn* 2:2).

On the night before he died, in what we call the Last Supper, Jesus instituted the Eucharist, the Mass, in order to make present down the ages the sacrifice of his life and his Resurrection so that we could participate in it. We will study this more in depth when we consider the Eucharist.

After his death, Jesus' body was laid in a nearby tomb, and this was sealed with the customary large flat circular stone. Through the sacrament of Baptism we are symbolically buried with Christ in order to rise again with him to the new life of grace. As St Paul writes, "We were buried therefore with him by baptism into death, so that as Christ was raised from the dead by the glory of the Father, we too might walk in newness of life" (*Rom* 6:4).

In the Apostles' Creed we say that "He descended into hell; on the third day he rose again." What do we mean by this? While the word "hell" can imply the state where the damned suffer for all eternity, here it means rather the "realm of the dead". That is, while Jesus' body remained in the tomb, his soul went to the realm of the dead, where all the souls of the just who had died since Adam were awaiting their entrance into heaven, in order to announce to them the good news of their redemption. As the Catechism puts it, he "descended there as Saviour, proclaiming the Good News to the spirits imprisoned there" (*CCC* 632).

4. JESUS' RESURRECTION, ASCENSION AND SECOND COMING

In the Apostles' Creed we profess our faith that on the third day Jesus rose again from the dead. That is, Jesus was buried on Good Friday and on Easter Sunday morning the tomb where he had been laid was found with the stone rolled away and the body no longer there. This was seen by the holy women and later by the apostles Peter and John. That same day Jesus appeared in the flesh to Mary Magdalene, to two disciples on their way to Emmaus, to Peter and finally to all the apostles gathered in the Upper Room where they had celebrated the Last Supper. All were overjoyed to see him alive again, and they remembered that he had prophesied several times that he would rise again on the third day after his death.

If the apostles' faith was shaken by Christ's death, it was restored and strengthened by his Resurrection. In the following years the apostles would go out to many nations preaching the Resurrection of Christ, and dying for that belief. The Resurrection is a most important article of our faith. The Catechism says of it: "The Resurrection of Jesus is the crowning truth of our faith in Christ, a faith believed and lived as the central truth by the first Christian community; handed on as fundamental by Tradition; established by the documents of the New Testament; and preached as an essential part of the Paschal mystery along with the cross" (CCC 638).

What was the state of Christ's body after the Resurrection? First of all, it was the same body he had when he died. Jesus ate food with the apostles, he invited Thomas to touch him, and his body still had the wounds of the crucifixion and the piercing of his side.

At the same time, his body had the properties of a glorified body. It was not limited by space and time as we see in the fact that Jesus would suddenly appear or disappear, he appeared in the Upper Room passing through closed doors, and he was often not recognised by those who knew him intimately. In this sense he was not like the three persons he had raised from the dead – Lazarus, Jairus' daughter and the young man of Naim – who all returned to normal earthly life, until they would die again. As the Catechism explains, "Christ's Resurrection is essentially different. In his risen body he passes from the state of death to another life beyond time and space" (CCC 646).

Christ's Resurrection is very important for us. It is the definitive proof of his divinity, his ultimate miracle, and it confirms our faith in him and in all his works and teachings. At the same time, it is the principle and source of our own future resurrection. As St Paul says, "Christ has been raised from the dead, the first fruits of those who have fallen asleep" (*1 Cor* 15:20-22). That is, when we die we too can join Christ in eternal life in heaven, and our body will be resurrected to join the soul on the Last Day.

After his Resurrection, Jesus appeared frequently to the apostles over the next forty days. Then he gathered the apostles together and gave them the great mission to go out to all nations. He told them, "Go therefore and make disciples of all nations, baptising them in the name of the Father and of the Son and of the Holy Spirit, teaching them to observe all that I have commanded you; and behold, I am with you always, to the close of the age" (*Mt* 28:19-20). Immediately afterwards, he ascended into heaven and disappeared from their sight (cf. *Mk* 16:19; *Lk* 24:51).

In the Apostles' Creed we profess our belief in these events with the words "He ascended into heaven and is seated at the right hand of the Father." By the last words, we understand that Jesus, as the Son of God, takes the place of honour which he had with the Father from all eternity. In heaven Jesus, now in his humanity as well as his divinity, continues to intercede with the Father for the Church, for all humanity, for each one of us. When we pray to him, we know that he always hears us and asks the Father to give us what is best.

Finally, we say in the Apostles' Creed, "From there he will come to judge the living and the dead." Here we profess our belief that at the end of time, at the end of the world, whenever that may be, Jesus will come again in glory to judge all souls in what we call the General Judgment. We will study this in more detail when we consider the Last Things, the events that follow our death.

In the meantime, each generation of humanity lives out its life on earth, striving to do the will of God in order to deserve eternal life when they die. And since the kingdom of God is not completely fulfilled until the Last Day, we can expect trials and tribulations, at the same time as we count on the grace of God to help us remain faithful and grow in holiness.

What thoughts should we have as we consider the second coming of Christ? St Augustine suggests the following: "Let us not resist his first coming, so that we will not fear the second... For what kind of love for Christ is it to fear his coming? Are we not ashamed, my brethren? We love, and we fear that he may come. Do we really love? Or do we love our sins more?" *(Ex En. in Ps.,* Ps 95, 14, 15)

That concludes our study of Christ's life, death and Resurrection, by which he brought about our redemption. Now we live in the hope of our own resurrection to eternal life. In the next lesson we will consider the coming of the Holy Spirit, the third person of the Blessed Trinity, and the Church. In the meantime, may God fill you with his grace and help you to grow ever more in love for his Son Jesus Christ, our Lord and Saviour. God bless you.

Questions for Discussion

1. What lessons can we draw from the fact that it was God's plan for his Son to be born into a poor family and in a stable, rather than in a palace or even a house?

2. How should we respond to Jesus' love for each one of us, which led him to become man and then to suffer and die on the cross to redeem us?

3. Why do we say that the Resurrection of Christ from the dead is a most important article of our faith? What does it mean for you personally?

4. Our Lord sent the apostles out to carry his message of truth and love to all nations, and they fulfilled that command, taking the faith all over their world. How can we fulfil this command in our own circumstances today?

5. How can Christ's Ascension into heaven help us in our spiritual life?

Points to Remember

- Jesus Christ was born in a stable in Bethlehem some 2000 years ago to teach us the value of simplicity and detachment from material comforts.

- Jesus' thirty years of hidden life show us that our own ordinary life can be a continuous encounter with God.

- Jesus' death on the cross brought about our redemption, our deliverance from original sin and personal sin, opening up for us the gates of heaven.

- Jesus' Resurrection from the dead is the definitive proof of his divinity and the confirmation of our faith in him.

- At the end of time Jesus will come again to judge the living and the dead.

8. THE HOLY SPIRIT AND THE CHURCH

You are Peter and on this rock I will build my Church, and the powers of death shall not prevail against it (Mt 16:18)

SUMMARY

In this lesson we consider two important articles of the Creed: the Holy Spirit and the Church.

From our study of the Blessed Trinity we recall that the Holy Spirit is the third person of the Blessed Trinity. In this lesson we consider the coming of the Holy Spirit into the world and his role in furthering the mission of Christ.

Then we study the foundation of the Church by Jesus, beginning with the calling of the twelve apostles and the choice of St Peter to be their head. Peter is made the rock, the cornerstone, of the Church and he is given the power of the keys, with the promise that the powers of death will not prevail over the Church.

We go on to study the Church as the Mystical Body of Christ, the union of all the baptised, whether on earth, in Purgatory or in heaven, with Christ as their head.

Then we consider the Church as the People of God, looking at the role of the Pope, the bishops, priests and deacons, the lay faithful and those in the consecrated life. We also study the gift of infallibility, which is shared by the Pope and the bishops in communion with him.

Finally we consider the four marks of the Church that we profess in the Nicene Creed: that she is one, holy, catholic and apostolic.

Welcome once again to our journey into the truths of our faith. In the last lesson, as you will recall, we considered the life, death and Resurrection of Jesus Christ and our personal relationship with him. Through his death and Resurrection, Jesus redeemed us and reconciled us with the Father, opening up for us the gates of heaven. This truth fills us with hope in our own resurrection after death. If we die faithful to God, we will be with the Father, the Son and the Holy Spirit for all eternity in the happiness of heaven.

We come now to the next two articles of faith that we profess in the Apostles' Creed: the Holy Spirit and the Holy Catholic Church. These truths are very related to each other. After all, as we shall see, the Holy Spirit is the life, the soul of the Church.

But first let us pray. Heavenly Father, after your divine Son ascended into heaven, you sent the Holy Spirit upon the apostles, transforming them into bold preachers of the faith and giving life to the Church. Enkindle in us the fire of the Holy Spirit, so that we too may grow in faith and help many others to come to believe in you. We make our prayer through Christ our Lord. Amen.

In this lesson we will consider five topics: the mission of the Holy Spirit, the foundation of the Church, the mystery of the Church, the Church as the People of God, and the four marks of the Church. We begin with the mission of the Holy Spirit.

1. THE MISSION OF THE HOLY SPIRIT

In the Apostles' Creed we say, "I believe in the Holy Spirit". As we recall from our study of the Blessed Trinity, the Holy Spirit is the third divine person, coeternal, all powerful, of the same divine being and nature as the Father and the Son. "With the Father and the Son he is worshipped and glorified", we say in the Creed at Mass on Sundays. But today we will consider more the role of the Holy Spirit in what the Catechism calls "the divine economy;" that is, the sending of the Holy Spirit into the world to fulfil God's plan of salvation (cf. *CCC* 685).

The Holy Spirit is alluded to in numerous passages of the Old Testament. For example in the creation of the universe the book of Genesis tells us that the spirit of God "hovered over the waters" (*Gen* 1:2), and on creating man God breathed into him "the breath of life" (*Gen* 2:7). In the prophet Isaiah there is a significant passage that relates the Holy Spirit and the Messiah: "There shall come forth a shoot from the stump of Jesse, and a branch shall grow out of his roots. And the Spirit of the Lord shall rest upon him, the spirit of wisdom and understanding ..." (*Is* 11:1-2). Jesus will later apply another passage from Isaiah to himself: "The Spirit of the Lord God is upon me, because the Lord has anointed me to bring good tidings to the afflicted ..." (*Is* 61:1-2; *Lk* 4:18-19).

In the New Testament, as we know, the Angel Gabriel announced to Mary that the Holy Spirit would come upon her to enable her to conceive Jesus (cf. *Lk* 1:35). Then, at Jesus' Baptism in the Jordan, the Holy Spirit came down in the form of a dove (cf. *Mt* 3:16). Always, the Holy Spirit is closely associated with the work of Jesus, the Son of God. The Catechism sums it up: "From the beginning to the end of time, whenever God sends his Son, he always sends his Spirit: their mission is conjoined and inseparable" (*CCC* 743).

In the Last Supper, Jesus promises to send the Holy Spirit to the apostles and the Church. Among the things he says on that occasion are that the Spirit of truth, the other Paraclete, will be given by the Father in answer to Jesus' prayer; he will be with the Church for ever; he will remain with us and be in us; he will teach us everything and remind us of all that Christ said to us; he will lead us into all truth and will glorify Christ (cf. *Jn* 14:15-25; *CCC* 729).

Finally, the Holy Spirit comes down upon the apostles in a dramatic way on the feast of Pentecost, ten days after Jesus' Ascension into heaven. The apostles are gathered together in prayer, together with Mary and other women, when the Holy Spirit comes down in the form of tongues of fire and a great wind, moving the apostles to go out and preach Jesus and his Resurrection to the thousands of people gathered in Jerusalem for the feast. The apostles are given the gift of tongues so that they can be understood by people of many languages (cf. *Acts* 2:1-6). With this coming of the Holy Spirit, in a sense the Church is born, it comes alive and the apostles are enabled to fulfil Jesus' command to go out to all nations to baptise and teach (cf. *Mt* 28:19-20). St Luke tells us that some three thousand people were converted and baptised on that very day (cf. *Acts* 2:41). Truly, the Holy Spirit gives life to the Church.

We will study the role of the Holy Spirit in our own life in later classes, when we consider the sacraments, our moral life and prayer.

2. THE FOUNDATION OF THE CHURCH

After professing faith in the Holy Spirit we say in the Apostles' Creed, "I believe in the Holy Catholic Church". This simple statement is rich in meaning. First though, what do we mean by the Church? The word "Church", or *ecclesia* in Latin, comes from the Greek word *ek-ka-lein*, meaning to 'call out of'. It thus means a *convocation* or *assembly*. In the Greek Old Testament the word *Ekklesia* is used frequently to refer to the Chosen People of God, above all for their gathering on Mount Sinai where they received the Ten Commandments. The Church is thus the gathering of God's people. The English word *church* comes from another Greek word, *Kyriake*, which means "what belongs to the Lord" (cf. *CCC* 751).

The Church has its origin in the Old Testament People of God, the Jewish people chosen by God to prepare for the coming of the Messiah. Like the Church today, the Old Testament Jewish people had a sacrifice, which was celebrated daily, and a priesthood. The Church is thus the People of God of the New Testament, gathered together under the Pope as their head for the salvation of mankind.

The early Fathers of the Church saw the whole of creation as centred on the Church. For example, St Clement of Alexandria wrote: "Just as God's will is creation and is called 'the world,' so his intention is the salvation of men, and it is called 'the Church'" (*Paed.* 1, 6, 27).

The Church, as we know, was founded by Jesus Christ. We see this clearly in the New Testament. First Jesus chose twelve men whom he called apostles, undoubtedly to represent the twelve tribes of Israel of the Old Testament. The word apostle, by the way, comes from the Greek word *apostolos*, meaning "one who is sent." Jesus called the apostles one by one, by their names. They were Simon Peter and his brother Andrew, James and his brother John, Bartholomew, Philip, Thomas, James the Lesser, Jude, Simon the Zealot, Matthew and Judas Iscariot (cf. *Mt* 4: 18 ff; *Mt* 10:2 ff). Christ spent considerable time teaching and forming them for their mission (cf. *Mk* 4:34; *Mt* 11:1; *Mt* 13:52).

From among the twelve apostles, Jesus chose one who was to be their head. He would have special powers over the other eleven and over the whole Church. This was of course Peter. Jesus first promised Peter that he would be the head of the Church. He told him, "You are Peter and on this rock I will build my Church, and the powers of death shall not prevail against it. I will give you the keys of the kingdom of heaven, and whatever you bind on earth shall be bound in heaven, and whatever you loose on earth shall be loosed in heaven" (*Mt* 16:18-20). It is clear from the words "I will build my Church" that Jesus intended to form a new community, different from the Jewish people.

Peter was to be the rock, the foundation and source of unity of the Church. Obviously, the ultimate foundation of the Church is Christ himself, the cornerstone. It is Christ who gives the Church its stability down the ages. What is more, Peter is given "the keys of the kingdom of heaven". Keys are always seen as a symbol of authority over a building or an institution. The person who has the keys to a house has authority or dominion over it: he can enter and leave whenever he wants, welcome others into it and lock the doors to prevent others from entering. Finally, Peter is given the power to bind and loose, meaning to impose obligations and punishments, and to free people from them. Later, Jesus gives this same power to all the apostles (cf. *Mt* 18:18).

After his resurrection, Jesus conferred on Peter in a formal way the pastoral role of being head of the Church. In response to Jesus' three questions to Peter, "Do you love me more than these?" and Peter's answer in the affirmative, Jesus said "Feed my lambs…Tend my sheep… Feed my sheep" (*Jn* 21:15-17). Earlier in his ministry Jesus had said, "I am the good shepherd" and "there will be one flock and one shepherd" (*Jn* 10:11, 16). Now he is about to ascend into heaven and he entrusts the care of his flock, the Church, to Peter. Note that he does not entrust it to all twelve apostles, but only to Peter as their leader. With this role, Peter has authority over the whole flock, including the other apostles.

We see in these texts the basic structure of the Church. There is a group of twelve apostles, who will be succeeded by the bishops, and one of their number, Peter, is their head. Peter will of course be succeeded by the Popes. This divinely constituted hierarchical structure is not within the power of the Church to change.

3. THE MYSTERY OF THE CHURCH

Having seen the founding of the Church and its structure, we now look briefly at what the Catechism calls "the Mystery of the Church". Why do we call the Church a mystery? Because, in addition to the visible aspect, with people, buildings and ceremonies, the Church is also, and especially, an invisible, divine, spiritual reality, sharing in the very life of God. As the Catechism puts it, "The Church is both visible and spiritual, a hierarchical society and the Mystical Body of Christ. She is one, yet formed of two components, human and divine. That is her mystery, which only faith can accept" (*CCC* 779).

Indeed, as the Catechism says, the Church is the Mystical Body of Christ. This is a traditional way of describing the Church, and it is based on numerous texts in the New Testament. For example, St Paul says that Christ "is the head of the body, the Church" (*Col* 1:18). St Augustine is fond of referring to the Church, head and body, as the "whole Christ." He writes:

> Let us rejoice then and give thanks that we have become not only
> Christians, but Christ himself. Do you understand and grasp,
> brethren, God's grace toward us? Marvel and rejoice: we have
> become Christ. For if he is the head, we are the members; he and
> we together are the whole man ... The fullness of Christ then is the
> head and the members. But what does 'head and members' mean?
> Christ and the Church (*In Jo. Ev.* 21, 8).

Through Baptism, all the members of the Church share in the very
life of God, and they are united with one another, with Christ as their
head. This includes not only the faithful on earth, but also the souls in
Purgatory and the saints in heaven. This is a very consoling truth. All
in the Church, whether on earth, in Purgatory or in heaven, are praying
for one another and strengthening one another. No one is alone. All
form one single body, with Christ as their head. We often refer to the
Church in this sense as the Communion of Saints. It is the union, the
communion, of all the members of the Church with one another and
with Christ. It is traditional to refer to these three states of the Church as
the Church militant on earth, the Church suffering in Purgatory and the
Church triumphant in heaven.

The saints in heaven serve as our models of holiness and they
constantly intercede for those who are still on the journey to heaven,
whether on earth or in Purgatory. As the Catechism puts it, they "fix the
whole Church more firmly in holiness" (*CCC* 956). So the Church is truly
a mystery, a divine reality, the Mystical Body of Christ, a Communion of
Saints, with Christ as our head.

4. THE CHURCH, THE PEOPLE OF GOD

But the Church is not only a mystery, which is in some way invisible. It is
also the People of God. This was one of the principal ways of describing
the Church in the Second Vatican Council. Indeed, the second chapter
of the Council's Dogmatic Constitution on the Church was entitled
"The People of God."

Just as God had chosen the Israelites in the Old Testament as his very own chosen people, so now in the New Testament he forms the Church as the new People of God. God wanted to sanctify and save human beings not as individuals without any bond between them, but rather as a society, as a people, his chosen people. This people is the Church. One comes to belong to the People of God through Baptism. The head of this people is Jesus Christ, the anointed one or Messiah. And because the anointing of Christ by the Holy Spirit flows from the head into the whole body, the Church is what is called a "messianic people", an anointed people. The mission of this people is to be the salt of the earth and light of the world, in order to bring salvation to all. And its destiny is eternal life with God in heaven.

We say that the People of God is a priestly, prophetic and royal people. That is, by virtue of their Baptism all the faithful share in Christ's priestly office of being mediators between God and man. They share in his prophetic or teaching office by believing and passing on the faith to others. And they share in his royal or kingly office by helping to establish Christ's kingdom on earth through their work and their service to the poor (cf. CCC 784-786).

We also say that the Church, as the People of God, is hierarchical. By this we mean that while all are equal in dignity, there is a diversity of functions, with some having roles of authority over others. Leadership in the Church, however, is always exercised as a service to the others, just as Jesus Christ himself came "not to be served but to serve" (Mt 20:28).

Those with the mission of leading the Church are especially the Pope and the bishops. The very name "Pope", or "Papa" in some languages, means precisely "father", and so we call the Pope the "Holy Father". We should look on him as our father in the family of the Church, and pray for him as he carries out his difficult ministry as father of a family with over one billion members. The Pope, as the successor of St Peter, has authority over the whole Church, including over the bishops. It is he who appoints the bishops and through them he exercises his pastoral ministry in the Church.

In order to keep the Church true to the faith down the ages, Christ gave the Pope and the bishops a share in his own infallibility. That is, with this gift, the Pope and the bishops cannot err in their teaching in certain circumstances. In the words of the Second Vatican Council, the Pope "enjoys this infallibility in virtue of his office, when, as supreme pastor and teacher of all the faithful – who confirms his brethren in the faith – he proclaims by a definitive act a doctrine pertaining to faith or morals" (*CCC* 891). In other words, he cannot err when he proclaims a definitive teaching, one which cannot be changed, on faith or morals for the whole Church. The most obvious exercise of this gift is the proclamation of a dogma, such as the Immaculate Conception or the Assumption of the Blessed Virgin into heaven.

The bishops too, have the gift of infallibility when, "together with Peter's successor, they exercise the supreme Magisterium," above all in an Ecumenical Council, but also when scattered throughout the world. The response of the faithful to this teaching of the Pope and bishops, when they propose a doctrine "for belief as being divinely revealed" ought to be what we call the "obedience of faith" (*CCC* 891). After all, if we believe that Christ founded the Church and that he remains with it as its head down the ages, we should have faith that when the Church teaches in the name of Christ, this teaching is true and to be accepted.

Just as the Pope has authority over the universal Church, so the bishops govern the dioceses and other communities of the faithful entrusted to them. They do this in their role as pastors, or shepherds, in a spirit of service. Their leadership includes the roles of teaching, sanctifying and ruling, always under the authority of the Holy Father, and the faithful should receive their teachings and indications with sincere respect. Bishops are assisted in their pastoral ministry by priests and deacons, who have more immediate contact with the faithful entrusted to them. We will see more about priests and deacons when we study the sacrament of Holy Orders.

The main group of faithful in the Church is the lay faithful, or laity.

What is their role? In the words of the Second Vatican Council, "By reason of their special vocation it belongs to the laity to seek the kingdom of God by engaging in temporal affairs and directing them according to God's will" (*LG* 31; *CCC* 898). That is, the place where the laity carry out their mission is in the world: in the home, in the workplace, in politics, business, trade unions, the media, education, etc. There they bring Christian principles and values, striving to christianise society. Given the fact that the laity make up some 99.9% of the Church, if the Church is to fulfil her mission of announcing the Word of God so that all might be saved, it is primarily the laity who must do it. The mission of the laity is truly momentous.

Apart from the clergy – that is, bishops, priests and deacons – and the lay faithful, there is a third group of faithful in the Church: those who dedicate themselves to the service of God by a divine vocation in the celibate state. This way is known as the consecrated life or the religious life. It is characterised by the profession of poverty, chastity in celibacy and obedience, within a permanent state of life recognised by the Church (cf. *CCC* 915). Through their radical consecration to God, these women and men detach themselves from the things of this world and give witness to the life to come in heaven.

The consecrated life can take many forms: that of hermits, consecrated virgins, nuns, brothers, religious priests, members of secular institutes, societies of apostolic life, etc. The Second Vatican Council describes this great variety in a beautiful way: "From the God-given seed of the counsels a wonderful and wide-spreading tree has grown up in the field of the Lord, branching out into various forms of the religious life lived in solitude or in community" (*LG* 43).

5. The four marks of the Church

We come now to our fifth topic: the four marks of the Church. In the Nicene Creed we profess our belief in the "one, holy, catholic and apostolic Church". These four aspects, which are essential features of the Church founded by Jesus Christ, are often referred to as the "four marks" of the Church.

First, the Church is one. It is clear that Jesus wanted his Church to be one, not many. He told Peter that "on this rock I will build my Church" (*Mt* 16:18) and he said there would be "one fold and one shepherd" (*Jn* 10:16). The Catholic Church is one in many ways. It has one founder and head, Jesus Christ; one soul, the Holy Spirit; one body of teaching to be believed by all; one celebration of worship in the Mass and the sacraments; and one government under the Pope as the vicar of Christ on earth. One of the beautiful features of the Catholic Church is this unity. No matter where one goes on earth, one finds the same beliefs, the same Mass and sacraments, the same respect for the Pope. This unity expresses itself in a marvellous diversity of local traditions and cultures, which help to manifest the richness of Christ's Church within this unity.

Over the years, different communities have separated from the Catholic Church, often over doctrinal issues. This has given rise to the many different groups which call themselves Christian: Orthodox, Anglican, Lutheran, Presbyterian, Baptist, Assemblies of God, etc. These groups retain many elements of sanctification and truth, based on a common Baptism, so that Catholics look on them as brothers and sisters. And we pray that one day they may be reunited with us in the one Church of Christ. The effort to promote the unity of all Christians is called "ecumenism" or the "ecumenical movement". It is based on Christ's prayer to the Father: "That they may all be one. As you, Father, are in me and I am in you, may they also be one in us" (*Jn* 17:21).

The second mark of the Church is its holiness. The Church is holy especially because its founder, Jesus Christ, the very Son of God, is holy and because the Church is his Mystical Body. Then too the Church is holy because it calls all the baptised to a life of holiness, and offers them all the means to grow in holiness: the sacraments, the Mass, and the various forms of prayer and penance. In addition, many members of the Church down the ages have in fact lived lives of exceptional holiness and now serve as models and intercessors for the Church in heaven. The greatest of the saints is Mary, the all-holy mother of God. And the Church is holy in her teaching, which includes a demanding moral code and encourages all to seek holiness of life. Naturally, in spite of its essential holiness, the Church will always be made up of frail human beings, who commit sins. For this reason the *Credo of the People of God* of Pope Paul VI states: "The Church is therefore holy, though having sinners in her midst, because she herself has no other life but the life of grace. If they live her life, her members are sanctified; if they move away from her life, they fall into sins and disorders that prevent the radiation of her sanctity."

Thirdly, the Church is catholic, which means "universal". The Church is catholic in two senses. First, because the Church is the body of Christ and therefore has all the means of sanctification and salvation to fulfil her mission. And second, because the Church is sent out to all nations for the salvation of all people. The Church is for everyone, not just those of a particular nation, ethnic group or social class. God wants all to be saved and the Church is his instrument for that purpose.

Fourth, the Church is apostolic. That is, it is built on the foundation of the apostles and hands on the teaching it received through the apostles. The apostles entrusted to their immediate collaborators the mission of teaching, sanctifying and ruling which they had received from Christ. To this end they ordained bishops to succeed them, and so today the Church has bishops who can trace their ordination back to the apostles in an unbroken line. This is what we call apostolic succession. It guarantees the validity of priestly ordination and of the sacraments in the Church.

Summing up, it is only in the Catholic Church that we find the fullness of these four marks of the Church, even though other Christian communities have some of them, to a limited degree. In the words of the Second Vatican Council, "The sole Church of Christ which in the Creed we profess to be one, holy, catholic, and apostolic, ... subsists in the Catholic Church, which is governed by the successor of Peter and by the bishops in communion with him. Nevertheless, many elements of sanctification and of truth are found outside its visible confines" (*LG* 8).

We are privileged to be associated with the Church founded by God himself through his Son Jesus Christ. The Church has been here for 2000 years and it will last until the end of time. After all, Jesus said to the apostles: "I am with you always, to the close of the age" (*Mt* 28:20). But that privilege carries with it a responsibility to pray for all our pastors: the Pope, the bishops and priests, and for all in the Church. And to be loyal to the Church, accepting wholeheartedly her teachings and carrying out faithfully her laws. We form part of the marvellous Communion of Saints, from which we receive so much, but we must also contribute to it by our faithfulness and our zeal to help others find the fulness of truth which Christ has given us.

In the next lesson we will consider a topic very dear to all Catholics: the Blessed Virgin Mary, mother of God and our mother. Until then, may God bless you and keep you in his love.

QUESTIONS FOR DISCUSSION

1. Just as the Holy Spirit gave life to the Church on the first Pentecost, so he gives life to the Church today. What should this mean for our trust in the Church?

2. St Peter was made the head of the Church by Christ himself. In view of this how should we relate to the Pope, the Holy Father, whoever he may be?

3. Through the Communion of Saints, how can the saints in heaven help us?

4. How should Catholics receive the teachings of the Church?

5. We say that the Church is holy, even though it is made up of sinners like ourselves. In what ways is the Church holy and what should this mean for the way we live our own lives?

POINTS TO REMEMBER

- The Holy Spirit is the third person of the Blessed Trinity, who came down on the apostles in a dramatic way on the day of Pentecost.

- Jesus Christ founded a Church, the new People of God, with St Peter as the head and the apostles as the first bishops.

- The Church as the Communion of Saints is made up of the faithful on earth, the souls in Purgatory and the saints in heaven.

- Christ promised the Church the assistance of the Holy Spirit, who would keep her always in the truth.

- The Church founded by Jesus Christ is one, holy, catholic and apostolic.

9. THE BLESSED VIRGIN MARY

Hail, full of grace, the Lord is with you (Lk 1:28)

SUMMARY

Having studied the role of the Holy Spirit and the Church, we now consider the one who is the mother of the Church and our mother, the Blessed Virgin Mary. We study first the four dogmas that relate to Mary and then the fact that Mary is our mother.

The first Marian dogma is her divine motherhood, that she is the Mother of God. If Mary is the mother of Jesus, having conceived and given birth to him, and Jesus is God the Son, then Mary is the mother of God, a truth defined in the Council of Ephesus in the year 431.

The second Marian dogma is her Immaculate Conception, that by the will of God Mary was spared the stain of original sin from the moment of her conception. This truth was defined by Pope Pius IX in 1854.

The third Marian dogma is her perpetual virginity, that Mary was always a virgin: before conceiving and giving birth to Jesus, in giving birth to him and after giving birth to him. The title was given to Our Lady by the Second Council of Constantinople in 553.

The fourth Marian dogma is her bodily Assumption into heaven at the end of her earthly life, a truth proclaimed by Pope Pius XII in 1950.

Finally, we study the fact that Mary is our own mother and mother of the Church, a truth that has many implications for our spiritual life.

Welcome once again to our journey into truth. If you are considering entering the Catholic Church, or if you are already a Catholic, you are drawn by a variety of reasons. But the most important one is that this religion is true. After all, as we saw in the last lesson, the Catholic Church was founded by God himself, by Jesus Christ, who is the eternal Son of God. And everything that God teaches is true, because he knows all things and he can neither deceive nor be deceived. Jesus said of himself that he is "the way, the truth and the life" (*Jn* 14:6). It is comforting to know that everything we learn about our Catholic faith is true, and that it is the way that leads to life, eternal life with God in heaven.

In this lesson we study a topic that is very dear to all of us, because it is the topic of our mother, our heavenly mother Mary. As we will see, as he hung on the Cross, Jesus gave us his mother to be our own mother. Mary loves each of us as her own son or daughter, she is the model of the virtues and she intercedes powerfully for us in heaven. She is truly our hope, and in the words of Pope John Paul II, she gives the Church "a motherly presence" (Address, 2 May 1979).

Let us begin as usual with a prayer. Almighty God and Father, through your Son Jesus Christ you gave us the Blessed Virgin Mary to be our mother, and to accompany us by her example and intercession on our earthly pilgrimage. Help us to know her and love her, so that she can lead us more effectively to you. We make our prayer through Christ our Lord. Amen.

In this lesson we will consider five topics: Mary's divine motherhood, her Immaculate Conception, her perpetual virginity, her Assumption into heaven, and her role as mother of the Church and our mother.

1. MARY IS THE MOTHER OF GOD.

First, the Blessed Virgin Mary is the Mother of God. There are four dogmas, or defined truths of faith, about Mary. They are her divine motherhood, her Immaculate Conception, her perpetual virginity and her bodily Assumption into heaven. The most important of these is the first: that Mary is the Mother of God. The others are in relationship with this one.

The first and most obvious truth about Our Lady is that she is the mother of Jesus. As we have seen, an angel announced to Mary that the Holy Spirit would come upon her and she would give birth to a son. She immediately accepted and nine months later she gave birth to Jesus in Bethlehem. This means that Mary is the mother of Jesus. But why do we say that she is the mother of God? Do we mean that she gave birth to God the Father, or to the Holy Spirit, or to the whole Blessed Trinity? Of course not. God created Mary, not the other way around.

We say that Mary is the mother of God because she gave birth to Jesus, who is God the Son, the second person of the Blessed Trinity. In other words, Mary gave birth to God, and therefore we call her mother of God. Mary's kinswoman Elizabeth professed this truth during the visitation when, moved by the Holy Spirit, she called Mary "the mother of my Lord" (*Lk* 1:43).

St Cyril of Alexandria, commenting on this truth, writes, "I am exceedingly astounded that there could be anyone who has any doubt as to whether the Blessed Virgin should be called the Mother of God. If Our Lord Jesus Christ is God, why should the Blessed Virgin, who gave him birth, not be called the Mother of God?" *(Letter* I, 27:30)

Mary's divine motherhood was proclaimed as a dogma of faith in the Ecumenical Council of Ephesus in the year 431 against the errors of Nestorius. Nestorius, as we have seen, maintained that in Christ there were two persons, one divine and the other human, and that Mary was the mother only of the human person. His errors went very much against the belief of the people at that time, who were firmly convinced that Mary was truly the *Theotokos*, the God-bearer. It was for this reason that St Cyril of Alexandria, who attended the Council, defended the dogma in the words we have just read. Each year we celebrate the fact that Mary is the mother of God on January 1, the feast of the Divine Maternity of Mary.

2. MARY'S IMMACULATE CONCEPTION

The second great truth about Our Lady is that she was conceived immaculate in the womb of her mother, to whom tradition gives the name St Anne. This truth, also a dogma of faith, is known as Mary's Immaculate Conception. It means that Mary was never subject to original sin, as was the rest of mankind. She was immaculate, without stain of sin, from the moment of her conception.

Where did the Church get this belief about Mary? We see it first of all in the New Testament, in the account of the annunciation to Mary that she was to be the mother of God. When the angel Gabriel greeted her he called her "full of grace" (*Lk* 1:28). No other person at that time could be called "full of grace" since all were stained by original sin. The Church sees in these words that from her conception in the womb of her mother Anne, Mary was preserved free from original sin and was thus in the state of grace. In the words of the Catechism, "Through the centuries the Church has become ever more aware that Mary, 'full of grace' through God, was redeemed from the moment of her conception. That is what the dogma of the Immaculate Conception confesses, as Pope Pius IX proclaimed in 1854: 'The most Blessed Virgin Mary was, from the first moment of her conception, by a singular grace and privilege of almighty God and by virtue of the merits of Jesus Christ, Saviour of the human race, preserved immune from all stain of original sin'" (Pius IX, *Ineffabilis Deus*, 1854; *CCC* 491).

Note that the Catechism says that Mary was "redeemed" from the moment of her conception. Given the clear statement of St Paul that "just as sin came into the world through one man, and death came through sin, and so death spread to all because all have sinned" (*Rom* 5: 12), it was always the belief of the Church that original sin affected everyone, and that Christ redeemed everyone, including his mother Mary. Even great medieval theologians like St Anselm, St Bernard, St Thomas Aquinas and St Bonaventure therefore argued against the Immaculate Conception of Mary on the grounds that it exempted her from the universality of redemption. It was the Franciscan Duns Scotus, who died in 1308, who reasoned that Christ could redeem his mother in an anticipated way, from the very moment of her conception. Her Immaculate Conception thus demonstrates Christ's redemptive power.

In order to understand this, the following example is helpful. If a person falls into a pit and is pulled out, he is said to have been saved from the pit. But if someone catches him and holds him back before he falls in, again he can be said to have been saved from the pit. This was the case with Our Lady. She too needed to be redeemed from original sin, but she was redeemed before she became subject to it, from the moment of her conception.

What is more, it is very fitting that Mary was never subject to original sin. Since through her offspring Jesus, she was to crush the head of the evil one, as prophesied to Eve in the book of Genesis (cf. *Gen* 3:14), it was fitting that she not be herself subject to the devil; that is, that she be free from original sin. Also, since she was to bear the very Son of God in her womb, it was fitting that she be a "worthy vessel" for such an exalted role and therefore immaculate, free from all stain of sin. It is fitting, therefore, that God enriched her with gifts appropriate to such a role.

The dogma of Mary's Immaculate Conception was proclaimed by Pope Pius IX in 1854. It is significant that 24 years earlier, in Paris in 1830, St Catherine Labouré had a vision of Our Lady standing on a globe surrounded by the words "O Mary conceived without sin, pray for us who have recourse to thee". This is the image on what has come to be known as the "miraculous medal." In 1854 Pope Pius IX proclaimed the dogma and four years after that, in 1858, Our Lady appeared to St Bernadette Soubirous at Lourdes and identified herself: "I am the Immaculate Conception." It is as if Our Lady herself wanted to confirm the truth of her Immaculate Conception. Millions of people visit the shrine of Lourdes, in southern France, every year and many miraculous cures have taken place there over the years.

We celebrate the feast of Mary's Immaculate Conception each year on December 8. Nine months later, on September 8, we celebrate the feast of Mary's birth.

While it is not a dogma of faith, the Church also teaches that Mary remained free from all personal sin throughout her life. She was able to do this by a special grace of God, as the Council of Trent teaches: "No justified person can for his whole life avoid all sins, even venial sins, except on the ground of a special privilege from God such as the Church holds was given to the Blessed Virgin" (DS 833). Confirming this belief Pope Pius XII, in his encyclical *Mystici Corporis* in 1943, said that Mary "was immune from all sin, personal or inherited."

3. MARY'S PERPETUAL VIRGINITY

The third Marian dogma is her perpetual virginity. That is, Mary was "ever virgin." She was a virgin in three different moments: before giving birth to Jesus, in giving birth, and after giving birth.

Virgin before the birth

As regards the first aspect, we remember that when Mary asked the angel how she could bear a son when she was a virgin, the angel answered her: "The Holy Spirit will come upon you" (*Lk* 1:35). From the beginning the Church has taught, as in the Apostles' Creed, that Jesus "was conceived by the Holy Spirit." As the Catechism says, "From the first formulations of her faith, the Church has confessed that Jesus was conceived solely by the power of the Holy Spirit in the womb of the Virgin Mary, affirming also the corporeal aspect of this event: Jesus was conceived 'by the Holy Spirit without human seed'" (Council of the Lateran (649)). As a witness to the faith of the early Church, St Ignatius of Antioch around the year 107 wrote to the Church in Smyrna that Jesus was "truly born of a virgin" (*CCC* 496).

The angel also told St Joseph, referring to Mary, that "that which is conceived in her is of the Holy Spirit" (*Mt* 1:20). The Church sees in this virginal conception the fulfilment of the promise given through the prophet Isaiah: "Behold, a virgin shall conceive and bear a son" (*Is* 7:14).

Virgin in the birth

So Mary was a virgin in conceiving Jesus without the intervention of St Joseph. But she was also a virgin in the act of giving birth. The Catechism says, quoting the Second Vatican Council: "The deepening of faith in the virginal motherhood led the Church to confess Mary's real and perpetual virginity even in the act of giving birth to the Son of God made man. In fact, Christ's birth 'did not diminish his mother's virginal integrity but sanctified it' (*LG* 57; *CCC* 499).

The Fathers of the Church used such analogies as the rays of the sun passing through glass without breaking it, Christ emerging from the sealed tomb and passing through closed doors, and so on, to explain how Jesus could pass through the virginal body of his mother without rupturing it. In any case it would have been a miraculous event. St Augustine says that "in such things the whole ground of the mystery is the might of Him who permits it to happen" (*Ep.* 137).

Virgin after the birth

As regards the third aspect of Mary's virginity – that she had no carnal relations with St Joseph and no more children after Jesus – this too has been the constant faith of the Church. What are we to make then of the reference in the Scriptures to Jesus' "brothers and sisters"? (*Mk* 3:31-35; 6:3) The Catechism answers: "The Church has always understood these passages as not referring to other children of the Virgin Mary. In fact James and Joseph, 'brothers of Jesus', are the sons of another Mary, a disciple of Christ, whom St Matthew significantly calls 'the other Mary' (*Mt* 13:55; 28:1). They are close relations of Jesus, according to an Old Testament expression" (*CCC* 500).

As regards the biblical expression that Jesus was Mary's "first-born son" (*Lk* 2:7), the expression "first-born" in no way implies that Mary had more children afterwards. The first-born son had certain rights and duties in Jewish law and so it was customary to refer immediately to the first son as the first-born, even before other children, if they came at all, were born.

Another argument in favour of Jesus not having had brothers or sisters is his own entrusting of his mother into the keeping of St John at Calvary. "Behold your mother" (*Jn* 19:27) he said to John. If Jesus had brothers or sisters he would surely have entrusted his mother to them.

In any case the Tradition of Mary's perpetual virginity is constant, and St Basil remarks: "The friends of Christ do not tolerate hearing that the Mother of God ever ceased to be a virgin" (*Hom. in S. Christi generationem*, 5). And St Augustine, representing the faith of the early Church, writes that Mary "remained a virgin in conceiving her Son, a virgin in giving birth to him, a virgin in carrying him, a virgin in nursing him at her breast, always a virgin" (*Serm.* 186, 1; *CCC* 510).

The title "perpetual virgin" was given to Mary by the fifth ecumenical council, held at Constantinople in 553. The early Church represented Mary's three-fold virginity in icons by depicting her with three stars: one on each of her shoulders and one over her forehead.

4. MARY'S ASSUMPTION INTO HEAVEN

That brings us to the fourth dogma of Mary: her bodily Assumption into heaven at the end of her earthly life. The faith of the Church is that on the completion of her life, Mary was assumed body and soul into heaven, without her body decaying in a tomb.

This truth was defined as a dogma of faith by Pope Pius XII in 1950. The Pope proclaimed: "Mary, the immaculate perpetually Virgin Mother of God, after the completion of her earthly life, was assumed body and soul into the glory of Heaven" (Apost. Const. *Munificentissimus Deus; CCC* 966). Note that in this brief sentence, Pope Pius makes reference to the other three Marian dogmas: that Mary was immaculate, perpetually virgin and Mother of God.

Even though the proclamation of the Assumption is relatively recent, the belief of the Church in Mary's assumption is very ancient. In the East, at least since the sixth century, and in Rome since the end of the seventh century the Church celebrated the feast of the Dormition of Mary. The object of the feast was originally the falling asleep, or death, of Mary but soon the idea of the incorruptibility of her body and its assumption into heaven appeared. In the texts of the liturgy and the writings of the Fathers of the eighth and ninth centuries, the idea of the bodily assumption is clearly affirmed.

A question many people ask is whether Mary died before being assumed into heaven. By using the phrase "at the conclusion of her earthly life", the Pope did not enter into the question of whether Mary actually died. There was a difference of opinion among the Fathers of the Church on this point, although the most probable opinion is that Mary did die, since even her Son Jesus died. Some of the Church Fathers, among them St John Damascene and St Gregory of Tours, give an account of her death and subsequent assumption.

The Catechism explains the significance of Our Lady's assumption by saying: "The Assumption of the Blessed Virgin is a singular participation in her Son's Resurrection and an anticipation of the resurrection of other Christians" (*CCC* 966). It is as if, as the good mother she is, Mary went ahead to prepare the way for her children.

5. MARY IS OUR MOTHER AND MOTHER OF THE CHURCH

We know that when Jesus was hanging on the Cross, he said to his mother, referring to St John: "Woman, behold, your son!" And then he said to St John: "Behold, your mother!" (*Jn* 19:26-27). The tradition of the Church has always understood these words as applying not only to St John, but to all the beloved disciples of Jesus; that is, to all the baptised.

Through Baptism we can all call God our Father, Jesus our brother and Mary our mother.

St John goes on to say in his gospel: "And from that hour the disciple took her to his own home" (*Jn* 19:27). Having been given Our Lady as his mother, St John immediately took her into his heart and into his care, and Mary began to look after the apostles. St Luke relates in the *Acts of the Apostles* how, after Our Lord's Ascension into heaven, the apostles returned to the upper room in Jerusalem where they "devoted themselves to prayer, together with the women and Mary the mother of Jesus" (*Acts* 1:14). Mary was there with the apostles, praying for the coming of the Holy Spirit who had overshadowed her in the Annunciation.

In this way Mary began to exercise her motherly role and so it was fitting that Pope Paul VI in 1964 declared her "Mother of the Church" (cf. *CCC* 963). As the mother of Christ, who is the head of the Church and the "first-born among many brethren" (*Rom* 8:29), Mary is naturally mother of all the members of the Mystical Body of Christ. She is Mother of the Church. As our mother and mother of the Church, she never ceases to intercede for us before the Father. We ask her to do this when we say in the Hail Mary, "Pray for us, sinners, now and at the hour of our death."

Mary's intercession is all powerful, for she is the greatest of all the saints, the closest to God. She is mother of God the Son, daughter of God the Father and spouse of God the Holy Spirit. Because of her closeness to God, she shares in some way in God's omnipotence, and the tradition has called her *omnipotentia supplex*: supplicating omnipotence. So we can entrust our prayers to her with the confidence that they will always be heard. We say in the beautiful Marian prayer, the Memorare: "Remember, O most gracious Virgin Mary, that never was it known that anyone who fled to thy protection, implored thy help, or sought thy intercession, was left unaided."

As the greatest of the saints, Mary is also the "model of the virtues", as the Second Vatican Council called her (cf. *LG* 65). We do well therefore to strive to imitate her when we want to grow in any virtue, especially such important virtues as faith, docility to the will of God, charity, humility and fortitude.

Mary is truly Mother of the Church, and our mother. She constantly shows herself to be a mother. It is only right, then, that we should love her and live out the fourth commandment: "Honour your father and mother." This love for Mary is solidly grounded in Scripture. After all, God himself praises Mary through the angel Gabriel in the Annunciation: "Hail, full of grace, the Lord is with you" (*Lk* 1:28). Then in the visitation, Mary's kinswoman Elizabeth, moved by the Holy Spirit, praises her: "Blessed are you among women, and blessed is the fruit of your womb" (*Lk* 1:42). Finally, Mary herself prophesies: "All generations will call me blessed" (*Lk* 1:48), foreseeing the devotion that would be rendered to her down the ages. Surely she has been the object of more artworks, hymns, poems and books than any other woman in history.

We can show our devotion to Mary in many ways. The Marian devotion *par excellence* is of course the Rosary, in which we contemplate the life of Christ as seen through the eyes of his mother. Mary herself urged everyone to say the Rosary in her apparitions at Lourdes, in France, in 1858 and Fatima, in Portugal, in 1917. Then too we can say the many other Marian prayers, such as the Hail Mary; the Hail, Holy Queen; the Memorare; Mary's own prayer the Magnificat; and the Angelus, in which we consider the annunciation of the Angel to Mary and her response, bringing about the Incarnation of God as man. What is important, in any case, is to have a personal love for Mary. After all, Jesus gave her to us as our mother and we would be offending him if we did not honour his mother and ours.

In the next lesson we will conclude our study of the Creed by looking at what we call the Last Things: those final realities of death, judgment, hell, Purgatory and heaven. Until then, may God bless you and keep you in his love.

QUESTIONS FOR DISCUSSION

1. The fact that Mary is the Mother of God gives her great power when she intercedes for us in heaven, as it did at the wedding feast of Cana. What should this mean for our confidence in praying to her?

2. Are there any lessons for us in the fact that Our Lady was preserved free from all stain of sin throughout her life?

3. How would you answer a friend who says that Mary had other children after Jesus, because the Bible says so?

4. What can we learn from Our Lady's bodily Assumption into heaven?

5. If Mary is our mother, how should we relate to her in our spiritual life?

POINTS TO REMEMBER

- As the mother of Jesus, who is true God, the Blessed Virgin Mary is the mother of God.

- By a special grace, Mary was preserved from original sin from the moment of her conception through what is called the Immaculate Conception.

- Mary was a virgin all her life: before giving birth, in giving birth and after giving birth to Jesus.

- On completing her life, Mary was assumed body and soul into heaven.

- Mary is our mother, given to us by Jesus from the cross, and we should show her special love

10. THE LAST THINGS

I am the resurrection and the life; he who believes in me, though he die, yet shall he live, and whoever lives and believes in me shall never die (Jn 11:25-26)

SUMMARY

We come now to the end of our study of the Creed, where we profess our belief in life everlasting. It is a topic that has come to be called the Last Things.

We begin by considering the Christian meaning of death, with the hope of everlasting life that follows it. Then we study what we call the particular judgment, the personal judgment of each soul by God immediately after death, where we will see ourselves as God sees us and we will know our eternal destiny.

After the judgment we consider hell, the state of eternal suffering and separation from God for those who do not repent of their serious sins at the end of life. Then we study Purgatory, the state of suffering combined with great happiness for those who die in the grace of God but are not perfectly purified of their sins. This is followed by a study of heaven, the state of supreme, definitive happiness for those who die in God's grace and are perfectly purified.

Our last topic is the end of the world, which includes the resurrection of the body, the second coming of Christ, the general judgment and the new heavens and new earth.

Welcome once again to our journey into the beauty of truth, the truth of the Catholic faith. I hope you are enjoying this excursion into the richness of the faith that has been lived and handed on for two thousand years.

In the last lesson we studied Our Lady, the mother of God and our mother. Mary accompanies us on our earthly journey and she shows us the way to eternal life. In this lesson we will conclude our study of the Creed with a consideration of what awaits us at the end of life. It is a topic that has come to be called the Last Things: death, judgment, hell, Purgatory, heaven and finally the end of the world. So fasten your seat belt, sit back, relax and prepare yourself for a fascinating journey into what God has prepared for those who love him.

As usual, we will begin with a prayer. Heavenly Father, in your goodness you have made us in your own image and likeness, giving us an immortal soul destined to eternal life with you. Help us to understand the true meaning of life and death so that we can live as you want and come with you to the fulness of joy, both here and hereafter. We make our prayer through Christ our Lord.

In this lesson we will consider six topics. The first of course is death itself, followed by the particular judgment, hell, Purgatory, heaven and finally the end of the world, which includes the second coming of Christ, the last judgment and the new heavens and new earth. This consideration can be very helpful in examining how we live our life, so that we do not waste it and we prepare well for the eternal life that awaits us. After all, we have just one life to live and our eternal destiny depends on how we live it.

1. THE CHRISTIAN MEANING OF DEATH

Our first topic is death itself and its Christian meaning. We know that we human beings do not live for ever, at least not on this earth. We come into existence through the love of our parents and at some point we will die. The body will be buried or perhaps cremated, but the soul will live on, for it is spiritual and immortal. As we remember, death is one of the consequences of the original sin of our first parents.

Death for many people is a frightening thought, one they would prefer not to deal with. But for those who have faith, especially for

Christians, death should hold no fear. It is the completion of our life on earth, which is but a preparation for the fulness of life which awaits us in heaven. Death is the threshold we must cross in order to enter into eternal life with God. It fills us with hope. In the words of the Catechism, "We firmly believe, and hence we hope that, just as Christ is truly risen from the dead and lives for ever, so after death the righteous will live for ever with the risen Christ, and he will raise them up on the last day" (*CCC* 989).

Jesus, by his own death and Resurrection, transformed death into a blessing. For those who die in the love of God it is the passing from earthly life, with its joys and sorrows, to eternal life, where all is joy. St Paul writes: "For to me to live is Christ, and to die is gain" (*Phil* 1:21). Elsewhere he writes: "If we have died with him, we will also live with him" (*2 Tim* 2:11). The saints too had a very positive attitude to death. St Teresa of Avila writes: "I want to see God and, in order to see him, I must die" (*Life*, Ch 1). And St Thérèse of Lisieux: "I am not dying; I am entering life" (*The Last Conversations*; *CCC* 1011). St Ignatius of Antioch, on his way to Rome to be martyred in the year 107, likened death to giving birth to himself:

> It is better for me to die in Christ Jesus than to reign over the ends of the earth. Him it is I seek – who died for us. Him it is I desire – who rose for us. I am on the point of giving birth ... Let me receive pure light; when I shall have arrived there, then shall I be a man. Here and now, as I write in the fulness of life, I am yearning for death with all the passion of a lover. Earthly longings have been crucified; in me there is left no spark of desire for worldly things, but only a murmur of living water that whispers within me, 'Come to the Father'" (*Ad Rom* 6,1- 9,3).

Does the Catholic Church believe in reincarnation? No, we have just one life here on earth to work out our salvation. The Catechism makes it very clear: "When 'the single course of our earthly life' (*LG* 48) is completed, we shall not return to other earthly lives: 'It is appointed for men to die once' (*Heb* 9:27). There is no 'reincarnation' after death" (*CCC* 1013).

In view of the uncertainty of how long we will live, the fourth century Father of the Church St Athanasius offers some wise advice: "You do not know at what hour death is going to come, whether during sleep or during the day. Be prepared therefore so that when it comes, you may go forth to receive it like the wise virgins, with oil in your lamps, that is, with good works. Never forget that you must leave this world; keep death before your eyes each day" (*De virginitate,* 23).

2. THE PARTICULAR JUDGMENT

Immediately after death, the soul goes before the judgment seat of God to find out its eternal destiny. We call this the *particular judgment,* the judgment of each soul individually, to distinguish it from the *general judgment,* which is the judgment of all souls together at the end of time. We should have very clear that after death there is no opportunity to repent and change our mind. We must repent in this life.

Jesus himself tells us that he will be our judge: "For as the Father has life in himself, so he has granted the Son also to have life in himself, and has given him authority to execute judgment, because he is the Son of man... I can do nothing on my own authority; as I hear, I judge; and my judgment is just, because I seek not my own will but the will of him who sent me" (*Jn* 5:26-27, 30). It is a great consolation to know that our judge will be Jesus himself, who lived among us and shared our human nature. He understands our weakness. But, as he says, his judgment will be just. St Teresa of Avila writes: "It will be a great thing at the hour of death to realise that we shall be judged by One whom we have loved above all things" (*Way of Perfection*).

In this judgment, all of our life will come to light: the many good things we have done, but also our sins and other failings. St Paul seems to be describing it when he writes to the Corinthians: "It is the Lord who judges me. Therefore do not pronounce judgement before the time, before the Lord comes, who will bring to light the things now hidden in darkness and will disclose the purposes of the heart. Then every man will receive his commendation from God" (*1 Cor* 4:4-5).

In order to be prepared for the judgment, we should strive always to do the will of God, which is how we show that we love him, for it is on this that we will be judged. St John of the Cross writes: "At the evening of life, we shall be judged on our love" (*Dichos*, 64). And we should be very sincere before God in our prayer and examination of conscience, acknowledging our sins and repenting of them. Then there will be no surprises in the judgment.

Immediately after the judgment, the soul enters into the state of its reward or punishment, going to heaven, Purgatory or hell. In order to finish in heaven, let us first consider hell and then Purgatory.

3. HELL

What do we mean by hell? We mean the place or state of eternal punishment, consisting in two principal forms of suffering: the pain of loss, of being separated forever from the God who loves us and for whom we were made, and also the pain of sense, likened in the Scriptures to fire. Jesus himself speaks often of hell, using such expressions as "the unquenchable fire", the "furnace of fire", and the "eternal fire" (*Mk* 9:43; *Mt* 13:49-50; *Mt* 25:41). Included in the pain of sense are remorse of conscience and the torment of demons and other souls, who all hate each other. But the worst pain is that of being separated from God forever. Hell, in short, is a state of unimaginable suffering, and it is forever.

Who goes to hell? The answer is simple: those who at the end of life are not sorry for their serious sins. In other words, those who reject God. The Catechism makes it very clear: "To die in mortal sin without repenting and accepting God's merciful love means remaining separated from him for ever by our own free choice. This state of definitive self-exclusion from communion with God and the blessed is called 'hell'" (*CCC* 1033). Notice that anyone who goes to hell does so *by his own free choice*, refusing to accept God's merciful love. Notice too that hell is forever, a state of *definitive* self-exclusion from God.

We might be inclined to ask how a good God could punish anyone for all eternity. The answer is simple. God doesn't want anyone to go to hell. He became man and died on the cross in order to save us, to save every one of us. St Paul writes that God our saviour "desires all men to be saved and to come to the knowledge of the truth" (*1 Tim* 2:4). If someone goes to hell, it is not God who sends him there. The person himself chooses it by not repenting of his sins. God is a good and merciful father who made us free and who respects our free choices, even when we reject him and hurt ourselves. The then Cardinal Ratzinger, later Pope Benedict XVI, explains:

> God never, in any case, forces anyone to be saved. God accepts
> man's freedom. He is no magician, who will in the end wipe out
> everything that has happened and wheel out his happy ending. He
> is a true father; a creator who assents to freedom, even when it is
> used to reject him. That is why God's all-embracing desire to save
> people does not involve the actual salvation of all men. He allows
> us the power to refuse. God loves us; we need only to summon
> up the humility to allow ourselves to be loved" (*God is Near Us*,
> Ignatius 2003, pp. 36-37).

If we make good use of the graces God gives us through his Church, if we struggle to avoid sin and go frequently to the sacraments of the Eucharist and Penance, we can be very confident of going to heaven. And we do well to remind others of these important truths. It is helpful too to consider the topic of hell in our meditation from time to time, for, as St Thomas Aquinas says, "Those who in their meditation often go down to hell during life will not easily go down there at death" (*In Symb.*). And always, the reason for doing good should not be fear of hell but rather love: to respond to the love God has shown us first, striving to please our loving Father.

4. PURGATORY

If hell is not the likely destiny of someone who lives a good life, Purgatory is always a distinct possibility. What is Purgatory? It is a place or state of purification after death of souls who die in the grace of God but who are not yet perfectly purified of all their sins and the consequences of their sins. The souls in Purgatory suffer greatly, but they are exceedingly happy because they are assured of heaven and their suffering purifies their soul so that it can go to heaven. In answer to the question of who goes to Purgatory, the Catechism says: "All who die in God's grace and friendship, but still imperfectly purified, are indeed assured of their eternal salvation; but after death they undergo purification, so as to achieve the holiness necessary to enter the joy of heaven" (*CCC* 1030).

The Catechism speaks of "the holiness necessary to enter the joy of heaven". What sort of holiness is necessary? The answer is complete holiness, where there is no stain of sin whatever on the soul. After all, the soul is going to enter into the presence of God, where all is light, love, purity, holiness. The soul must be completely pure, with the wedding garment of holiness. The *Letter to the Hebrews* speaks of the "holiness without which no one will enter heaven" (*Heb* 12:14) and the Book of Revelation says that "nothing unclean can hope to enter" (*Rev* 21:27). Traditionally the Church has taught that the soul needs to be purified of three things:

1. *Temporal punishment* due to sin; every sin harms the Mystical Body and must be atoned for through good deeds, penance, indulgences, etc. This punishment is called *temporal*, because it is undergone in time, either on earth or in Purgatory, and is thus distinguished from the *eternal punishment* of hell.

2. *Attachments and bad habits* caused by sin; for example, attachment to material things or to one's reputation or situation in life.

3. *Lack of sorrow for venial sin;* one cannot enter heaven with lack of sorrow for any sin, even venial.

Pope Benedict XVI speaks of the suffering of Purgatory as coming through the encounter of the soul with the love of Christ. In his encyclical *Spe Salvi* he writes: "This encounter with [Christ], as it burns us, transforms and frees us, allowing us to become truly ourselves... His gaze, the touch of his heart heals us through an undeniably painful transformation 'as through fire'. But it is a blessed pain, in which the holy power of his love sears through us like a flame, enabling us to become totally ourselves and thus totally of God... The pain of love becomes our salvation and our joy" (*SS*, 47).

From the earliest times, the Church has believed in Purgatory and has offered prayers and Masses for those who have died, asking God to take them quickly to heaven. Already at the end of the second century Tertullian speaks of the custom of offering Mass on the anniversary of their death for those who have died: "We offer the sacrifice for the deceased on the anniversary as on their birthday" (*De cor. mil.* 3). And St Isidore of Seville, who died in 636 AD, goes so far as to say: "To offer the sacrifice [of the Mass] for the repose of the faithful departed is a custom observed all over the world. For this reason we believe that it is a custom taught by the very Apostles" (*On ecclesiastical offices*, 1).

In view of the reality of Purgatory, we should do all we can in this life to make up for our sins through good deeds, acts of self-denial, prayer and indulgences, so that we may be as pure as possible when we die and may even avoid Purgatory altogether. And we should always pray very much for those who have died, so that they may be released from their sins and go to heaven as soon as possible. We should never take it for granted that anyone, no matter how good they were, has gone straight to heaven. If we pray for the faithful departed, we can be confident that

God, in his mercy and justice, will ensure that there will be people to pray for us after we die, should we find ourselves in Purgatory.

5. HEAVEN

This brings us to the final state that, we pray, will be our own destiny: the eternal happiness of heaven. What is heaven? The Catechism answers: "This perfect life with the Most Holy Trinity – this communion of life and love with the Trinity, with the Virgin Mary, the angels and all the blessed – is called 'heaven.' Heaven is the ultimate end and fulfilment of the deepest human longings, the state of supreme, definitive happiness" (*CCC* 1024). This description takes us back to those familiar words of St Augustine: "You have made us for yourself, and our heart is restless until it rests in you" *(Conf.* 1, 1, 1). In heaven, the heart rests, for it has found the object of its longing: communion with the God who is love. This happiness, as the Catechism says, is supreme. It is not like the limited, even though great, happiness we know on earth. It is supreme, maximum. And it is definitive, not like the passing happiness that comes and goes here below. Heaven is forever.

In addition to communion with God, with each of the three divine persons of the Trinity, the soul will enjoy the presence of the Blessed Virgin Mary, of the angels and of all the blessed. Among the blessed, in addition to all the saints we have heard about and perhaps taken as our patrons, will be the loved ones we knew on earth: our family members, friends, and acquaintances. One cannot imagine or describe the joy of heaven. Even St Paul, who had a vision of heaven, could only write: "no eye has seen, nor ear heard, nor the heart of man conceived, what God has prepared for those who love him" (*1 Cor* 2:9). This contemplation of God, as he is, "face to face" (*1 Cor* 13:12) the Church calls the "beatific vision" (cf. *CCC* 1028).

Pope Benedict XVI describes heaven like this: "[Eternal life] would be like plunging into the ocean of infinite love, a moment in which time – the before and after – no longer exists. We can only attempt to grasp the idea that such a moment is life in the full sense, a plunging ever anew into the vastness of being, in which we are simply overwhelmed with joy" (Enc. *Spe Salvi*, n. 12).

6. THE END OF THE WORLD

That brings us to our final topic, the end of the world. Scripture sometimes refers to it as the "day of the Lord" or "the last day". The end of the world involves a number of realities: the resurrection of the body, the second coming of Christ, the general judgment and the new heavens and new earth.

In the Apostles' Creed we profess our belief in "the resurrection of the body". This is a truth revealed in the Scriptures. St Paul writes: "If the Spirit of him who raised Jesus from the dead dwells in you, he who raised Christ Jesus from the dead will give life to your mortal bodies also through his Spirit who dwells in you" (*Rom* 8:11). Jesus himself spoke of it in his discourse on the Eucharist: "He who eats my flesh and drinks my blood has eternal life, and I will raise him up at the last day" (*Jn* 6:54). And the Catechism teaches: "God, in his almighty power, will definitively grant incorruptible life to our bodies by reuniting them with our souls, through the power of Jesus' Resurrection" (*CCC* 997). The body will be incorruptible, no longer subject to decay, and it will be, in the words of St Paul, a "spiritual body" (*1 Cor* 15:44).

As we know, when we die, our body stays behind on earth and decays while our soul continues to live, going to hell, Purgatory or heaven. At the end of time, the body will be raised and reunited with the soul, thus reintegrating the whole person. In this way the body will share in the joy or suffering of the person for all eternity, just as it shared in the person's sins and good deeds in this life.

The end of the world will also involve the second coming of Christ in glory to judge the living and the dead in what we call the Last Judgment or the general judgment. The Church's understanding of the Last Judgment is that all who have ever lived will be gathered together in the presence of Christ, who will judge them all, so that everyone can see what judgment the others have received. It will be here especially that the justice and mercy of God will be revealed. Naturally, those who have already been judged in the particular judgment will not see that judgment changed, but others will now be able to see it.

Jesus himself announces it: "When the Son of Man comes in his glory, and all the angels with him, he will sit down upon the throne of his glory, and all nations will be gathered in his presence, where he will divide men one from the other, as the shepherd divides the sheep from the goats... And they will go away into eternal punishment, but the righteous into eternal life" (*Mt* 25:31-32, 46). The Catechism describes it like this: "In the presence of Christ, who is Truth itself, the truth of each man's relationship with God will be laid bare. The Last Judgment will reveal even to its furthest consequences the good each person has done or failed to do during his earthly life" (*CCC* 1039).

The expression "to its furthest consequences" gives food for thought. The good we do in life, and also the evil, has effects which can go on for generations after we die. For example, the help we give to someone who converts to the Catholic Church and then raises their children in the faith, goes on for many generations, when their children marry and bring up their own children in the faith. These "furthest consequences" of our actions will come to light in the Last Judgment. The Catechism says of this: "We shall know the ultimate meaning of the whole work of creation and of the entire economy of salvation and understand the marvellous ways by which his providence led everything towards its final end" (*CCC* 1040).

As to when the world will end, only God knows. The Catechism says: "The Last Judgment will come when Christ returns in glory. Only the Father knows the day and the hour; only he determines the moment of its coming. Then through his Son Jesus Christ he will pronounce the final word on all history" (*CCC* 1040).

Finally, the last day will inaugurate what St Peter calls "new heavens and a new earth" (cf. *2 Pet* 3:13). The Catechism teaches that "at the end of time, the Kingdom of God will come in its fullness ... [and] the universe itself will be renewed" (*CCC* 1042). The Second Vatican Council says that the "universe itself, which is so closely related to man and which attains its destiny through him, will be perfectly re-established in Christ" (*LG* 48).

What will the new heavens and new earth be like? St Augustine explains that the properties of the new earth will be suited to the immortal existence of the transfigured human body, just as the present world is suited to the mortal body (cf. *City of God*, 20, 16). What this means in practical terms we cannot know but, as the Catechism says quoting St Paul, "It will be the definitive realisation of God's plan to bring under a single head 'all things in [Christ], things in heaven and things on earth'" (*Eph* 1:10; *CCC* 1043).

That brings us to the end of our study of the Creed. In the next lesson we will begin our study of the liturgy and especially the sacraments, by which we celebrate and draw life from the mystery of Christ. Until then, may God bless you and fill you with his love.

QUESTIONS FOR DISCUSSION

1. How should a Christian look upon death, which holds out so much fear for people without faith?

2. How can we live in such a way that we have no fear of facing Our Lord in the particular judgment when we die?

3. What must we do so that we have a good chance of avoiding Purgatory and going straight to heaven when we die? How can we help the souls in Purgatory?

4. What aspects of heaven make it so desirable to go there?

5. What do you find consoling about the general judgment at the end of time?

POINTS TO REMEMBER

- Death for a person of faith, is the passing from this life to eternal life with God and so it should fill us with hope.

- Immediately after death, we will be judged by God on the whole of our life in what we call the particular judgment.

- Hell is a state of eternal punishment and separation from God reserved for those who do not repent of their serious sins at the end of life.

- If we die in God's grace but are not perfectly purified of our sins and the effects of sin, we will be purified in the state of suffering and happiness called Purgatory.

- Heaven is the state of supreme, definitive happiness with God, Our Lady, the angels and the saints reserved for those who are perfectly purified of their sins.

- At the end of time Christ will come again to raise our bodies to be reunited with our souls and to judge the living and the dead in the general judgment.

11. The Liturgy and the Sacraments

Holy, holy, holy is the Lord of hosts; the whole earth is full of his glory (Is 6:3)

Summary

We now begin the first of five lessons based on Part Two of the Catechism, which deals with the liturgy and the sacraments.

We start by studying the meaning and role of the liturgy, which is the public worship offered to God by the Church. It is an action of Christ himself as head of the Mystical Body along with his body the Church.

Then we look at the use of signs and symbols in the liturgy. Since we are composed of body and soul it is fitting that our worship of God enter through our senses, and so the liturgy uses material things: gestures, silence, colours and even smells.

We go on to consider the liturgical year, the succession of different themes and feast days that characterise the various seasons of the year. It is important to have a basic understanding of the year so that we derive more benefit when attending Mass and other ceremonies.

Lastly, we begin our study of the sacraments by considering the number and nature of the sacraments, their efficacy and some general characteristics they all have in common.

Welcome once again to our journey into the truths of the Catholic faith. Having studied in the previous lessons the principal truths contained in the Creed, we now turn to the way the Church lives out and celebrates those truths in the liturgy and the sacraments. Without the grace of the sacraments, it would be extremely difficult to be faithful to God.

But let us begin as usual with a prayer. Heavenly Father, you so loved the world, this world that became separated from you through the original sin of our first parents, that you sent your Divine Son to dwell among us and redeem us by his suffering, death and glorious resurrection. We celebrate this mystery of love and we receive the benefits of it in the liturgy and the sacraments. Help us to understand the meaning of this mystery so that we can participate more fully in it and be led to a deeper communion with you, both in this life and in the next. We make our prayer through Christ our Lord. Amen.

In this lesson we begin our study of the second part of the Catechism, which is entitled "The celebration of the Christian mystery". The Catechism explains: "The second part of the Catechism explains how God's salvation, accomplished once for all through Christ Jesus and the Holy Spirit, is made present in the sacred actions of the Church's liturgy (Section One), especially in the seven sacraments (Section Two)" (*CCC* 15).

In these next five lessons, we will study the way we celebrate what we call the Paschal mystery of Christ; that is, his passion, death and resurrection by which he redeemed us and united us with the Father. First we will study the liturgy and the sacraments in general, and then each of the sacraments in particular.

In this lesson we look at four main topics: the meaning and role of the liturgy, the use of signs and symbols, the liturgical year, and the sacraments in general.

1. THE MEANING AND ROLE OF THE LITURGY

We have been using the word "liturgy" but we should clarify what we mean by the term. The word comes from the Greek word *leitourgia*, meaning a public work or a service on behalf of the people. In the Church the word liturgy means the public and official prayers and rites of the Church, or more simply the public worship that the Church offers to God (cf. CCC 1069). Among the acts of the liturgy are the Mass, the celebration of the sacraments, Exposition and Benediction with the Blessed Sacrament, the rite of funerals, and the Liturgy of the Hours, also known as the Divine Office or breviary.

Why does the Church have a liturgy? Every religion has some form of public worship, consisting in prayers and other rituals, often involving sacrifices, some form of temple and some form of priesthood. The Catholic Church's worship carries out God's plan for the salvation of the world, brought about by Christ's passion, death and resurrection. The Church thus celebrates in the liturgy "above all the Paschal mystery by which Christ accomplished the work of our salvation" (CCC 1067). In other words, the purpose of the liturgy is to celebrate, make present and pass on to souls the fruits of the redemption brought about by Christ through his death and Resurrection. It is a most perfect form of worship, involving the traditional elements of prayers, rituals, the sacrifice of the Mass, the priesthood and a church in which the liturgy is celebrated. And most importantly, it is Christ himself who gives us the main elements of the liturgy.

The liturgy is not merely a human act, the action of the Church's ministers and lay faithful. It is primarily an action of Christ himself. Quoting the Second Vatican Council, the Catechism says that in the liturgy "full public worship is performed by the Mystical Body of Jesus Christ, that is, by the Head and his members." As an action of Christ and the Church it is therefore "a sacred action surpassing all others. No other action of the Church can equal its efficacy by the same title and to the same degree" (SC 7; CCC 1070). The liturgy, then, is primarily an action of Christ together with his Mystical Body the Church, and it is this that gives it its efficacy.

There are two principal goals or directions of the liturgy. They are the worship of God, rising up in what can be considered an "ascending" direction, and the sanctification of men, a "descending" direction. Every liturgical rite involves these two goals or directions. Thus the Catechism refers to the liturgy as "this great work in which God is perfectly glorified and men are sanctified" (*CCC* 1089).

As regards the importance of the liturgy in the life of the Church, the Second Vatican Council teaches: "The liturgy is the summit toward which the activity of the Church is directed; it is also the font from which all her power flows" (*SC* 10). That is, all the activity of the Church is directed towards bringing souls into immediate contact with God, as happens especially in such liturgical acts as the Mass and the sacraments. And it is from these liturgical acts that all the power of the Church flows into her members.

An important feature of the liturgy is that it reminds us of the preparation of the Jewish people for the coming of Christ by taking us back to the Old Testament and incorporating certain elements of Old Testament worship. Among them are the reading of Old Testament texts, praying the psalms, and recalling Old Testament realities and persons that prefigured and were fulfilled in Christ. Among them are the flood and Noah's ark which prefigured Baptism; the Exodus, a figure of our liberation from sin; the manna, a figure of the Eucharist, etc. Especially in Advent and Lent the liturgy recalls these great events of salvation history.

Moreover, the liturgy derives much of its structure and content from the Jewish liturgy. For example, the emphasis on Sacred Scripture, on prayer of praise and intercession for the living and the dead, and on the appeal to God's mercy are all fundamental to Jewish worship. The Liturgy of the Hours or breviary, which is based on the recitation of the psalms, and other liturgical texts have a parallel in Jewish prayer, as do the Eucharistic Prayers of the Mass and especially the Paschal Triduum leading up to Easter, which is based on the Jewish Passover (cf. *CCC* 1096). Moreover, the first part of the Mass, the Liturgy of the Word, is structured on the Jewish synagogue service, just as the second part, the Liturgy of the Eucharist, fulfils and perfects the sacrifices carried out in the Temple in Jerusalem.

Another important aspect of the liturgy is that it is a participation in the heavenly liturgy where the angels and saints constantly praise God. The Book of Revelation in different places describes the liturgy of heaven with God seated on a throne, the Lamb representing Christ, and the river of life representing the Holy Spirit. Taking part in this heavenly liturgy are all the heavenly powers, all of creation, the people of the Old and New Testaments represented by the 24 elders, the new People of God represented by the 144,000, especially the martyrs, the Mother of God represented by the woman, and finally a "great multitude" beyond all counting (*Rev.* 7:9; *CCC* 1137-38). As the Catechism puts it, "It is in this eternal liturgy that the Spirit and the Church enable us to participate whenever we celebrate the mystery of salvation in the sacraments" (*CCC* 1139).

We express this participation in the heavenly liturgy in the Mass at the end of the Preface when we say, for example, "In our joy we sing to your glory with all the choirs of angels: Holy, Holy, Holy..." Moreover our participation in the liturgy spurs us on to be one day in heaven where we will participate in the heavenly liturgy with the angels and saints. As the Catechism puts it, "venerating the memory of the saints, we hope for some part and fellowship with them" (*CCC* 1090). It is very consoling to know that it is not only the people gathered in the particular church that are celebrating the liturgy, but the whole Church, including the angels and saints in heaven.

For this reason it is important that the liturgy be well performed so that it truly lifts up our soul to heaven. Liturgical ceremonies carried out with dignity and reverence, with appropriate music, in a suitably decorated church can be truly uplifting and helpful in reminding us of the liturgy of heaven.

2. SIGNS AND SYMBOLS

We come now to our second topic, the use of signs and symbols in the liturgy. The Catechism says that a sacramental celebration "is woven from signs and symbols" whose meaning is rooted in creation and in human culture (*CCC* 1145). Since we humans are composed of both body and soul, it is fitting that we participate in the ceremonies not only with our soul but also with our bodily senses. These signs and symbols are of different types.

First of all there are signs of the human world. God speaks to man through creation in such symbols as light and darkness, wind and fire, water and earth, etc., which reveal something of the Creator. Also, man uses signs taken from social life such as washing and anointing, breaking bread and sharing the cup, which can express the presence of God and man's gratitude to his Creator. The liturgy uses these signs and symbols as signs of grace and of the new creation in Christ Jesus (cf. *CCC* 1146-49).

Then there are signs taken from the Old Testament, among them the anointing and consecration of kings and priests, the laying on of hands, sacrifices and above all the Passover. Next come signs used by Christ himself to make known the mysteries of the Kingdom of God. They include the use of water, spittle and mud, the laying on of hands, etc.

Finally there are sacramental signs, which are often taken from creation, social life and the Old Covenant, but purified in order to symbolise spiritual realities: the pouring of water in Baptism, the anointing with oil in Confirmation, Holy Orders and the Anointing of the Sick, the use of bread and wine in the Eucharist, etc.

Another type of sign used in the liturgy is postures and gestures. They express our inner dispositions in an external way. For example, standing denotes alertness and readiness to act, as for example during the proclamation of the Gospel and the Creed in Mass. Kneeling expresses our humility before the greatness of God. Bowing and genuflecting are both signs of reverence and humility before God. Then too we use gestures such as making the sign of the cross and folding our hands.

We should not forget the symbolism of silence, which is called for in different parts of the Mass, and after the reading of Scripture and the homily in other ceremonies as well. It indicates our prayerful recollection in the presence of God.

An important use of signs in the liturgy is colour, seen especially in the colour of the vestments, or garments, worn by the priest and in the decoration of various items in the church, including the altar and the tabernacle. Each colour has its own symbolism. White is the colour of joy and is used in ceremonies with a festive character. Green is the colour of life and is used on Sundays during what is known as Ordinary Time throughout much of the year. Red, the colour of blood and fire, is used on the feasts of the apostles and martyrs and on the feast of Pentecost, when the Holy Spirit came down on the apostles in the form of tongues of fire. And violet, or purple, is the colour of penance and is used in the penitential seasons of Advent and Lent.

Even the sense of smell is used in the liturgy. We see it, for example, in the use of incense, whose smoke and fragrance rise up, symbolising our prayer and sacrifice rising to God; in the pleasant fragrance of flowers on special occasions; and in the sacred Chrism, the oil mixed with an aromatic substance such as balsam or perfume, used in Baptism, Confirmation and Holy Orders.

3. THE LITURGICAL YEAR

That brings us to our third topic, the liturgical year. It is good to understand that over the course of the year the character of the Church's liturgical ceremonies changes, corresponding to the nature of each season. This is what we call the "liturgical year". The liturgical year in the Eastern rites of the Catholic Church varies somewhat from that in the Latin or Roman rite, which is used by most of the Church. What follows is the liturgical year of the Roman rite.

While the calendar year begins on January 1 and the financial year in many places on July 1, the liturgical year begins on the first Sunday of Advent. Advent, which means "coming", is the season leading up to

Christmas, when we celebrate the coming of Christ into the world on December 25. Advent begins on the fourth Sunday before Christmas and extends up to the day before Christmas. Thus it varies in length from year to year, being longest when Christmas falls on a Sunday. Advent is a season of hope and expectation, and the liturgical colour is violet.

From Christmas to the feast of the Baptism of the Lord is the season of Christmas, or Christmastide. It includes a number of special feast days, including those of the Holy Family, the Divine Maternity of Mary and the arrival of the magi to adore the Christ child on Epiphany. The Baptism of Christ is celebrated either on January 13, a week after Epiphany which is celebrated on January 6, or, where Epiphany is celebrated on the Sunday closest to January 6, on the following day. It is a season of rejoicing and the colour is white.

Next comes the first part of what is known as Ordinary Time, celebrating in general Christ and the saints, where the liturgical colour is green, the colour of life. This first part focuses especially on the childhood of Christ and can vary in length, depending on the date of Easter.

After some weeks of Ordinary Time comes Lent, a time of penance in preparation for the greatest feast in the liturgical year, Easter, which celebrates the Resurrection of Christ. Lent always begins on a Wednesday, known as Ash Wednesday, and consists of the following six and a half weeks until the Saturday before Easter Sunday. There are 40 days of penance in Lent, excluding Sundays, commemorating Our Lord's 40 days of prayer and fasting in the desert. Lent is a season of penance and the colour of the vestments is violet.

After the penitential season of Lent the Church celebrates Easter Sunday, which in the words of the Catechism is "not simply one feast among others, but the 'Feast of feasts', the 'Solemnity of solemnities'" (*CCC* 1169). With Easter Sunday, the Church begins the period of seven weeks of rejoicing known as the Easter season, or Eastertide. It is characterised by the frequent use of the word "Alleluia", meaning "Praise the Lord". The colour is of course white. The Easter season ends on the feast of Pentecost, the seventh Sunday after Easter, celebrating the coming of the Holy Spirit on the apostles.

The Monday after Pentecost begins the second part of Ordinary Time, which extends until the Saturday before the first Sunday of Advent. This period focuses on Christ's public life and his preaching of the Kingdom of God. The liturgical colour is green. The last Sunday of Ordinary Time is the feast of Christ the King. A week later is the first Sunday of Advent, and so the cycle begins again. As is to be expected, on feast days throughout the year the appropriate liturgical colour is used for the vestments and other decorations.

4. THE SACRAMENTS IN GENERAL

That brings us to our final topic, the sacraments in general. Here we look at what all the sacraments have in common and particular aspects of some of the sacraments. But first we should answer the question, what is a sacrament? We know that when we use the word sacrament we are referring to such rites as Baptism, Confirmation and the Eucharist and that there are seven sacraments. But what do they all have in common? In the traditional definition given in children's catechisms, a sacrament is an outward sign instituted by Christ to give grace. The definition has three elements.

First there is an outward sign, by which we mean there is some ceremony that can be perceived by the senses. It consists in words and gestures that signify the grace that the sacraments confer on the recipient. For example, in Baptism there is the pouring of water while reciting certain words, signifying the cleansing of the soul from sin. Since man is composed of body and soul, Christ wanted us to be able to see and hear the ceremonies through which he grants us his grace and to have the certainty that we have received that grace.

Second, the sacraments have been instituted by Christ. They were not instituted by the Church over the course of the centuries but rather by Christ himself, during his life on earth. It is true that it took several centuries for the Church, reflecting on the different ceremonies it was conducting, to discern that there were seven that all conferred on the recipient the grace they signified, and it came to call them sacraments. But the sacraments were instituted by Christ, not by the Church.

Third, the sacraments give or confer the grace they signify. That is, they give the recipient a share in God's own life, a gift we call *sanctifying grace*. They also give what we call *sacramental grace*, a special grace proper to each sacrament. Sacramental grace is like a new orientation of the person toward the purpose of the sacrament. It is described by the Catechism as "the grace of the Holy Spirit, given by Christ and proper to each sacrament" (*CCC* 1129). For example, the sacrament of Matrimony gives the spouses the assurance of all the actual graces, or divine helps, they will need throughout their marriage to be faithful to their commitments to each other.

In all the sacraments the outward sign of words and gestures signifies the grace conferred. For example, as we said, in Baptism the pouring of water signifies the washing of the soul from sin and the conferring of new life on the soul. In Confirmation, the anointing with oil signifies the strengthening of the soul for spiritual battle, and in Holy Orders the laying on of hands by the bishop signifies the granting of the gift of the Holy Spirit.

The sacraments efficaciously confer the grace they signify, by the very power of the sacrament itself. We say, in the traditional Latin phrase, that the sacraments give grace *ex opere operato*, that is by the power of the work performed. In other words, it is Christ himself who efficaciously grants the grace whenever a sacrament is administered. It is not the minister of the sacrament, nor much less the recipient who confers the grace but the sacrament itself. The recipient could put an obstacle to the reception of grace, for example by receiving the Eucharist unworthily, but the sacrament still retains its power to give grace. The grace symbolically flows like a fountain from the open side of Christ as he hangs on the cross.

Nonetheless, the fruitfulness of the sacrament also depends on the dispositions of the recipient. For example, in the sacrament of Penance the penitent would receive more or less grace depending on his or her dispositions of sorrow, purpose of amendment, humility, etc. And in Holy Communion a person receiving the sacrament with greater fervour and love will receive proportionately more grace and merit. For this reason, it is important to prepare well to receive any sacrament and to ask God for the grace to have the proper dispositions.

Which are the seven sacraments? The *Catechism of the Catholic Church* divides them into three groups. First come the three sacraments of Christian initiation: Baptism, Confirmation and the Eucharist. Then two sacraments of healing: Penance and the Anointing of the Sick. And finally two sacraments at the service of communion: Holy Orders and Matrimony.

Three of the sacraments give, in addition to grace, what we call "character", which is like an indelible seal on the soul marking the person forever. These sacraments are Baptism, where the character marks the person as a Christian; Confirmation, where it seals him as an adult in the faith, prepared to witness to the truth; and Holy Orders, where the character seals the man forever as a minister of Christ. Because of this indelible seal, these three sacraments can never be repeated. As regards the effects of character, the Catechism says that it remains in the Christian "as a positive disposition for grace, a promise and guarantee of divine protection, and as a vocation to divine worship and to the service of the Church" (*CCC* 1121). It is significant that all three of these sacraments, and only these three, involve an anointing with the oil of chrism, a holy oil consecrated by the bishop mixed with an aromatic substance like balsam or perfume.

All the sacraments have a proper minister and a recipient. The minister is the person who performs the sacramental rite and this person varies with the different sacraments. For example, the ordinary minister of Baptism is a priest or deacon, but in certain circumstances a lay person can baptise. The minister of Holy Orders is a bishop and the minister of Matrimony is the spouses themselves. We will study this in more detail when we consider each of the sacraments. To confer the sacrament validly, the minister must follow the prescribed rite for the sacrament and must have the intention of doing what the Church does in that particular sacrament.

The recipient should be properly instructed in the purpose of the sacrament, and should have the proper dispositions and faith in the efficacy of the sacrament. The Catechism teaches: "The purpose of the sacraments is to sanctify men, to build up the Body of Christ and, finally, to give worship to God. Because they are signs they also instruct. They not only presuppose faith, but by words and objects they also nourish, strengthen, and express it. That is why they are called 'sacraments of faith'" (SC 59; CCC 1123). Indeed, the more we receive the sacraments, especially the Eucharist and Penance, which we can receive often, the more our faith grows.

That concludes our study of the liturgy and the sacraments in general. In the next lesson we will study Baptism and Confirmation, the first two sacraments of Christian initiation. Until then, may God bless you and lead you gently through the week.

QUESTIONS FOR DISCUSSION

1. We use the word liturgy often in this course and in the life of the Church. If a friend asked you what it means, how would you answer?

2. Why does the Church have liturgical ceremonies and why are they important for us?

3. What signs and symbols in the liturgy do you find particularly expressive?

4. Why do you think Christ instituted the sacraments in the form of outward signs in order to communicate his grace to us?

5. The sacraments are very important in our spiritual life and their fruitfulness depends in part on the way we receive them. In view of this, how should we prepare ourselves to receive them?

POINTS TO REMEMBER

- The liturgy is the public worship that the Church offers to God through her head Jesus Christ.

- Through the liturgy God is glorified and men are sanctified.

- Among the principal acts of the liturgy are the Mass, the sacraments, Benediction with the Blessed Sacrament and the Divine Office or breviary.

- The sacraments are visible signs instituted by Christ to give grace.

- There are seven sacraments: Baptism, Confirmation, Eucharist, Penance, Anointing of the Sick, Holy Orders and Matrimony.

12. Baptism and Confirmation

Go therefore and make disciples of all nations, baptising them in the name of the Father and of the Son and of the Holy Spirit (Mt 28:19)

Summary

In this lesson we study the first two sacraments of Christian initiation: Baptism and Confirmation, which lay the foundations of our spiritual life.

We begin by considering the meaning of Baptism, which is the first sacrament we all receive and which frees us from original sin and initiates us into the life of God and the Church.

Then we consider the effects of Baptism, which are symbolised by the use of water and the other visible aspects of the rite. Here we also see how the Catholic Church looks on baptised Christians of other denominations.

From there we go on to study the minister and the various ceremonies of the rite of Baptism, which are rich in symbolism and meaning. We also study the role of godparents or sponsors.

Finally we consider the sacrament of Confirmation, which confirms the grace received in Baptism. We see the history of the sacrament and how Confirmation came to be separated from Baptism, with which it was joined in the early Church. We also consider the minister of Confirmation and how the sacrament is administered, along with the effects of the sacrament and the age at which it is administered.

Welcome once again to our journey of discovery into the marvellous truths of the Catholic faith. In the last lesson, as you recall, we began the second part of our journey, studying the liturgy and the sacraments. We saw how the liturgy is the public worship that Christ, together with his Mystical Body the Church, offers to the Father and how it is through the liturgy, among other ways, that God sanctifies us. We also saw how among the acts of the liturgy are the seven sacraments, the outward signs which Christ gave the Church in order to confer his grace on us, and how the liturgy makes present the Paschal mystery of Christ's death and resurrection. In this lesson we will study the first two sacraments of Christian initiation: Baptism and Confirmation.

Let us begin with a prayer. Heavenly Father, you created us to know, love and serve you on earth in order to be happy with you forever in heaven. You gave us the Church and the sacraments to strengthen us in truth, love and grace for this journey. Help us to understand the great gift that you have bestowed on us in the sacraments, and to respond to this gift by a life of true holiness. We make our prayer through Christ our Lord. Amen.

In this lesson we will study four main topics: the meaning of Baptism, the minister and ceremonies of Baptism, the effects of Baptism and the sacrament of Confirmation.

1. THE MEANING OF BAPTISM

The first three sacraments an adult receives on entering the Church are Baptism, Confirmation and the Eucharist, and for this reason they are called sacraments of Christian initiation. The Catechism says that they "lay the foundations of Christian life" and that, in resemblance to our human birth and growth, "the faithful are born anew by Baptism, strengthened by the sacrament of Confirmation, and receive in the Eucharist the food of eternal life" (CCC 1212).

The first sacrament we all receive is Baptism, whether as infants or on entering the Church as adults. Through it we come to share in God's own life and to belong to his Mystical Body, the Church. The Catechism says:

"Holy Baptism is the basis of the whole Christian life, the gateway to life in the Spirit *(vitae spiritualis ianua)*, and the door which gives access to the other sacraments. Through Baptism we are freed from sin and reborn as sons of God; we become members of Christ, are incorporated into the Church and made sharers in her mission" (*CCC* 1213).

The Catechism goes on to say that "Baptism is the sacrament of regeneration through water and in the word" (*CCC* 1213). Regeneration means rebirth. It is an apt term because in Baptism the soul passes from the state of original sin, where it is deprived of divine life and is in some way spiritually dead, to the state of grace where it receives a sharing in divine life. This rebirth is brought about through the pouring of or immersion in water, accompanied by the words of the sacrament.

The word Baptism comes from a Greek word meaning to plunge or immerse. The immersion in water symbolises the person's burial with Christ in the tomb, and his or her rising up with Christ to new life. St Paul describes it like this: "Do you not know that all of us who have been baptised into Christ Jesus were baptised into his death? We were buried therefore with him by baptism into death, so that as Christ was raised from the dead by the glory of the Father, we too might walk in newness of life" (*Rom* 6:3-4).

In the early Church Baptism was called by different names. St Gregory of Nazianzus, a Father of the Church, explains these names:

> Baptism is God's most beautiful and magnificent gift ... We call it gift, anointing, enlightenment, garment of immortality, bath of rebirth, seal, and most precious gift. It is called *gift* because it is conferred on those who bring nothing of their own; *grace* since it is given even to the guilty; *Baptism* because sin is buried in the water; *anointing* for it is priestly and royal as are those who are anointed; *enlightenment* because it radiates light; *clothing* since it veils our shame; *bath* because it washes; and *seal* as it is our guard and the sign of God's Lordship" (*Oratio*, 40, 3-4; *CCC* 1216).

As we know, Jesus himself was baptised by St John the Baptist in the

Jordan River. Naturally, being God, Jesus had no original sin and he had not committed any personal sins so he did not need to be baptised. He did it, as he himself said, "to fulfil all righteousness" (*Mt* 3:15); that is, as an act of humility and self-emptying. Also, by being baptised, Jesus in a sense sanctified the waters of Baptism for ever after. The Preface of the Mass for the feast of St John the Baptist speaks of "waters made holy by the one who was baptised."

Just before his Ascension into Heaven, Jesus gave the apostles the mission to baptise, telling them: "Go, therefore and make disciples of all nations, baptising them in the name of the Father and of the Son and of the Holy Spirit, teaching them to observe all that I have commanded you" (*Mt* 28:19). This text gives us not only the command to baptise but also the form of words to be used, words which have never varied in the history of the Church.

From the time of the apostles, it was through Baptism that people were initiated into the life of the Church. This included children, of whom the Catechism says: "The practice of infant Baptism is an immemorial tradition of the Church. There is explicit testimony to this practice from the second on, and it is quite possible that, from the beginning of the apostolic preaching, when whole 'households' received baptism, infants may also have been baptised" (*CCC* 1252).

Because of the importance of Baptism, the *Code of Canon Law* says that "parents are obliged to see that their infants are baptised within the first few weeks" (Can. 867). What about the salvation of infants who have died without being baptised? The Catechism answers: "The Church can only entrust them to the mercy of God, as she does in her funeral rites for them. Indeed, the great mercy of God who desires that all men should be saved, and Jesus' tenderness toward children which caused him to say: 'Let the children come to me, do not hinder them,' (*Mk* 10:14) allow us to hope that there is a way of salvation for children who have died without Baptism" (*CCC* 1261). That is, the Church holds out the hope of their salvation, but she cannot be absolutely certain of it.

Therefore the Catechism goes on to say: "All the more urgent is the Church's call not to prevent little children coming to Christ through the gift of holy Baptism" (*ibid*).

If these infants do not go to heaven, where do they go? They would go to a place or state where they would be immensely happy, although without seeing God face to face, as in heaven. This is the state that has traditionally been called *Limbo*. One would hope, though, for example, that in the case of the miscarriage of a child whose parents have had all of their children baptised, God would take the child to heaven, as he would in so many other and possibly all cases.

2. THE EFFECTS OF BAPTISM

What effects does this sacrament have? The use of water symbolises the two principal effects. First of all, we use water for washing and in Baptism it symbolises the cleansing of the soul from all sins, both original and personal. As we know, all human beings are born in the state of original sin, and so from the beginning, the Church has baptised both children and adults to free them from this sin, which would prevent their entry into heaven. But it is not only original sin, but personal sins too of adults that are washed clean in the waters of Baptism. For this reason, an adult about to be baptised does not need to be absolved of their sins beforehand in the sacrament of Penance. The Baptism itself forgives all their sins.

And even more, all the temporal punishment owing for their sins is erased. We know that every sin has as a consequence what the Catechism calls "an unhealthy attachment to creatures" (*CCC* 1472), and this must be made up in some way either on earth or in Purgatory. Baptism erases the whole of this temporal punishment. The Catechism sums it up: "By Baptism all sins are forgiven, original sin and all personal sins, as well as all punishment for sin. In those who have been reborn nothing remains that would impede their entry into the Kingdom of God, neither Adam's sin, nor personal sin, nor the consequences of sin, the gravest of which is separation from God" (*CCC* 1263).

While Baptism erases all sin and temporal punishment, it does not take away some of the effects of original sin. For example, we still have such effects as suffering, sickness and death, weakness of character and disorder in the passions. There remains too the inclination to sin that Tradition calls concupiscence, or metaphorically, 'the tinder for sin', *fomes peccati* in Latin. But we should always remember that this inclination to sin is not itself sinful and, as the Council of Trent teaches, it "cannot harm those who do not consent but manfully resist it by the grace of Jesus Christ" (*DS* 1515; *CCC* 1264).

The second main effect of Baptism is the infusion of divine life into the soul. This effect too is symbolised by the use of water, since water is necessary for life. In Baptism the person receives a sharing in the very life of God which we call sanctifying grace. As the name indicates, this grace truly sanctifies – it makes us holy. As effects of sanctifying grace, we become children of God and heirs of heaven, the Blessed Trinity comes to dwell in our soul and, in the words of St Peter, we are made sharers in the divine nature (cf. *2 Pet* 1:4). In a word, the soul is lit up by the life of God now within it, symbolised by the lighted candle given to the newly baptised person. Given the great holiness we receive in Baptism, we are all called to develop that gift by a struggle to grow in love for God, in holiness, throughout our lives.

Along with sanctifying grace, Baptism infuses in the soul the three theological virtues of faith, hope and charity, which enable us to believe, hope and love God. It also gives the moral virtues of prudence, justice, fortitude and temperance, and the seven gifts of the Holy Spirit, which we will consider in a later lesson. These virtues and gifts make up what the Catechism calls "the whole organism of the Christian's supernatural life" (*CCC* 1266). Just as we have a natural organism, with a body and soul, an intellect and will, and the emotions, enabling us to perform human actions, so we have a supernatural organism, with the life of grace, the infused virtues and the gifts of the Holy Spirit, enabling us to carry out actions which are supernaturally meritorious before God.

Another important effect of Baptism is the seal, or character, it impresses on the soul. This seal remains forever and stamps the Baptised person as a Christian, as one belonging to Christ. Because of this seal, God will always recognise the person as a Christian, even if he or she leaves the Church and joins some other faith community. And, of course, because of this seal, the sacrament of Baptism cannot and need not be repeated. For this reason, a person who has been validly baptised in another Christian community and who wishes to enter the Catholic Church is not baptised in the ceremony of reception into the Church.

How does the Catholic Church look on other baptised Christians? Following the Second Vatican Council, it teaches that "Baptism constitutes the foundation of communion among all Christians", and that non-Catholic Christians "are put in some, though imperfect, communion with the Catholic Church. Justified by faith in Baptism, [they] are incorporated into Christ; they therefore have a right to be called Christians, and with good reason are accepted as brothers by the children of the Catholic Church" (cf. UR 3; CCC 1271). After the Council it has become common to refer to other Christians as our "separated brethren", a term that emphasises our union in the same family.

Another effect of Baptism is that it makes us members of the Church, the great family of God with Christ as its head. As members of the Church we are in communion with all the other members, helping one another by our prayer and support on our journey to heaven. And we share in all the rights and duties of members of the Church, including the right to receive the other sacraments, to be formed in the faith and to receive the other spiritual helps of the Church. As for our responsibilities, through Baptism we share in the threefold mission of Christ, as priest, prophet and king. That is, all the baptised have the mission to worship God and to be mediators between God and others (the priestly role), to teach and pass on the faith to others (the prophetic role) and to help establish Christ's kingdom on earth (the kingly role). And of course we have a duty to respect and obey the Church's leaders, especially the Pope and the bishops, and to follow the Church's laws.

3. THE MINISTER AND CEREMONIES OF BAPTISM

The ordinary minister of Baptism, that is, the one who performs the ceremony, is a bishop or priest and, in the Latin Church, also a deacon. But in case of necessity, anyone can baptise, even a lay person. All that is required in this case is that they have the intention of doing what the Church does and that they pour the water and pronounce the correct words.

The ceremonies of Baptism are rich in meaning. At the beginning the one to be baptised is marked with the sign of the cross on the forehead, indicating the grace of the redemption which Christ won for us by his cross. Then comes the reading of texts from the Bible. a principal part of all the sacraments. Its purpose is to enlighten and instruct those present, especially those to be baptised, so that they can later respond with the profession of faith. The exorcisms pronounced over the candidate signify the liberation from sin and from the power of the devil brought about by the sacrament. This is followed by the anointing with the oil of catechumens, signifying cleansing and strengthening, after which the candidate renounces Satan and recites the Profession of Faith.

The blessing of baptismal water is a prayer of what we call *epiclesis*, asking God the Father through his Son to send the power of the Holy Spirit on the water so that those who are baptised may be born of water and the Spirit. The essential rite of Baptism itself, signifying and bringing about death to sin and entry into the life of the Trinity, is performed either by triple immersion in water, symbolising entry into the tomb with Christ and rising with him, or by pouring water three times over the person's forehead. At the same time the minister says the name of the person followed by, "I baptise you in the name of the Father, and of

the Son, and of the Holy Spirit." In the Eastern rites the candidate faces
East, that is towards the rising sun of Christ, and the minister says: "The
servant of God, N, is baptised in the name of the Father, and of the Son,
and of the Holy Spirit."

After the Baptism comes the anointing with sacred chrism, the
perfumed oil consecrated by the bishop on Holy Thursday. It signifies
the gift of the Holy Spirit given to the newly baptised person, who
has become a Christian, that is, one 'anointed' by the Holy Spirit and
incorporated into Christ, who is himself the anointed one. While in the
Eastern Churches the anointing of the infant with chrism is the sacrament
of Chrismation or Confirmation, in the Roman liturgy this anointing
will be followed years later by a second anointing with chrism in the
sacrament of Confirmation. In the baptism of adults, this anointing with
chrism is the sacrament of Confirmation.

Then the person is given a white garment, which symbolises that the
person has 'put on Christ' (*Gal* 3:27), has been clothed in him and been
given new life in him. He or she is also given a candle, lit from the Easter
candle, which signifies that Christ has lit up the person's soul and he or
she is called to be the "light of the world" (*Mt* 5:14). As a new child of
God, the baptised person then recites the prayer of the children of God,
the *Our Father*.

In the Eastern Churches the infant is now given Holy Communion,
whereas in the Latin Church the ordering of Baptism to the Eucharist is
expressed by bringing the baptised child to the altar for the praying of
the *Our Father*. In the Baptism of adults, the newly baptised adult will
receive Holy Communion at the proper time in the Mass. The ceremony
concludes with the solemn blessing, including a special blessing of the
mother in the baptism of infants.

Each person to be baptised is to have at least one godparent or
sponsor, with the special responsibility of assisting the newly baptised
person to live in accordance with their faith and to grow in it throughout
their life. For this reason the sponsor is to be a Catholic, at least sixteen

years of age, who has been confirmed, has received the Eucharist and who lives a life in keeping with this important role.

4. THE SACRAMENT OF CONFIRMATION

This brings us to the second sacrament of Christian initiation: Confirmation. The name comes from the role of the sacrament in completing or confirming the grace received in Baptism. As regards the purpose of the sacrament, the Catechism says that "by the sacrament of Confirmation, [the baptised] are more perfectly bound to the Church and are enriched with a special strength of the Holy Spirit. Hence they are, as true witnesses of Christ, more strictly obliged to spread and defend the faith by word and deed" (*CCC* 1285). It used to be said that Confirmation makes the recipients "soldiers of Christ" so that, strengthened by the Holy Spirit, they are prepared to witness to the faith. Just as the Holy Spirit came down on the apostles at Pentecost and transformed them into bold preachers of the faith (cf. *Acts* 2:1-4), so in Confirmation the Holy Spirit strengthens the person to spread and defend the faith.

Since the beginning of the Church, the sacrament has been conferred by the laying on of hands. Very early too, in order to signify the gift of the Holy Spirit, an anointing with the perfumed oil of chrism was incorporated into the rite, and it has continued ever since. This anointing with chrism highlights the name "Christian", which means belonging to Christ, the anointed one. The Eastern Churches call this sacrament *Chrismation*, or anointing with chrism.

In the first centuries, Confirmation was generally administered by the bishop in the same ceremony as Baptism. But as the Church grew and it became difficult for the bishop to be present at all Baptisms, the two sacraments became separated. In the West, Confirmation is now reserved to the bishop in a later ceremony, while in the East the priest performing the Baptism also confirms the person, using chrism consecrated by a bishop. Thus the original minister of Confirmation is the bishop.

The bishop is the ordinary minister today for the Confirmation of Catholics who were baptised as infants. But for those entering the Church as adults, the priest baptising them or receiving them into the Church also confirms them. Naturally, where the adult comes from a community which has valid sacraments, such as the Orthodox, the person is not confirmed again. In danger of death, any priest can administer Confirmation, even to infants, since the Church wants all her children to be strengthened by the Holy Spirit for their departure from this world.

In the ceremony of Confirmation, after the bishop or priest extends his hands over those to be confirmed to call down the Holy Spirit, he lays his hand on each person's head and anoints the forehead with chrism, saying, "Be sealed with the Gift of the Holy Spirit." In the Eastern Churches of Byzantine rite the more significant parts of the body are also anointed: the eyes, nose, ears, lips, chest, back, hands and feet, each anointing accompanied by the words, "the seal of the gift of the Holy Spirit" (cf. *CCC* 1300). The rite concludes with the sign of peace, signifying the union of the Confirmed person with the bishop and with all the faithful.

As regards the effect of Confirmation, the Catechism says it is "the special outpouring of the Holy Spirit as once granted to the apostles on the day of Pentecost" (*CCC* 1302). In general, Confirmation gives an increase and deepening of baptismal grace. It strengthens the grace of divine sonship, unites us more firmly with Christ, increases the gifts of the Holy Spirit, renders our union with the Church more perfect, and gives a special strength of the Holy Spirit to spread and defend the faith by word and action as true witnesses of Christ.

Like Baptism, Confirmation imprints on the soul an indelible spiritual seal, or character which, in the words of the Catechism, "is the sign that Jesus Christ has marked a Christian with the seal of his Spirit by clothing him with power from on high so that he may be his witness" (*CCC* 1304). As Christ was marked with his Father's seal – "For it is on him that God the Father has set his seal" (*Jn* 6:27) – so Christians are marked with the seal of the Father to carry on Christ's mission. In this sense St Paul writes to the Corinthians: "It is God who establishes us with you in Christ and has commissioned us; he has put his seal on us and given us his Spirit in our hearts as a guarantee" (2 *Cor* 1:21-22). Because this seal is indelible, Confirmation can only be received once.

Because Confirmation is a sacrament of initiation, every baptised person should be confirmed. But when? In the East, as we have seen, infants are anointed immediately after their Baptism. In the West, two traditions have arisen. One sees children confirmed before they make their first Communion in order to preserve the proper order of the sacraments of initiation. The other has them confirmed somewhat later, towards the end of primary school. Both traditions are acceptable. In danger of death, any child should be confirmed.

That concludes our study of Baptism and Confirmation. In the next lesson we will study the third sacrament of Christian initiation, the Holy Eucharist, which is the central sacrament around which the others revolve. In the meantime, may God bless you and keep you in his love.

QUESTIONS FOR DISCUSSION

1. The sacrament of Baptism has many effects. Which of them seem most important to you?

2. Why do you think the Church has from the beginning baptised newly born infants, when they are unaware of what is happening to them?

3. What aspects of the rite of Baptism do you find particularly expressive?

4. What is the importance of the character, or seal, impressed on the soul by Baptism?

5. Why do you think Christ instituted a separate sacrament of Confirmation, in addition to the sacrament of Baptism? What does Confirmation do for the soul?

POINTS TO REMEMBER

- Baptism, Confirmation and the Eucharist are the three sacraments of Christian initiation.

- Through Baptism we are freed from sin and reborn as children of God, and we become members of Christ and his Church.

- Because of the importance of Baptism, parents are to have their children baptised within the first few weeks after birth.

- Baptism, like Confirmation and Holy Orders, impresses an indelible seal on the soul known as character.

- All of the baptised share in the threefold mission of Christ as priest, prophet and king.

- The sacrament of Confirmation binds us more perfectly to the Church and strengthens us with the Holy Spirit to be effective witnesses of Christ.

13. The Holy Eucharist

I am the living bread which came down from heaven; if any one eats of
this bread, he will live for ever; and the bread which I shall give for the life
of the world is my flesh (Jn 6:51)

Summary

We come now to the third sacrament of Christian initiation, the
Eucharist. The Eucharist is the source and summit of the Christian
life and the centre of the whole sacramental system. All the other
sacraments prepare for and revolve around it.

We begin by studying the institution of the Eucharist by Jesus
Christ during the celebration of the Jewish Passover in what we call
the Last Supper. We see how the very words Christ used, and which
we still use in the Mass, make clear that the Eucharist makes present
the sacrifice of Christ on the cross.

Then we consider the sacrifice of the Mass itself, its history,
structure and parts, and its relationship with the sacrifice of the cross.

From there we go on to study the Real Presence of Christ in the
Eucharist, the truth that the Eucharist is not bread or wine, but truly
Jesus Christ himself. We consider some of the consequences of this
truth, and the importance of Eucharistic adoration.

Lastly, we study the sacrament of Holy Communion, where Jesus
gives himself as food for our soul. We consider how we should
prepare to receive Our Lord in the Eucharist and how often we may
and should receive him.

Welcome once again to our journey into truth, the beautiful truth of

155

the Catholic faith. The more we discover on this journey the more we become convinced that the Catholic Church is truly the work of God. It is the work of the Blessed Trinity through Jesus Christ, who called himself "the Way, the Truth and the Life" (*Jn* 14:6). Jesus is the only way to the Father, he teaches us the truth, and he communicates his life to us through the sacraments. In the last lesson we studied the first two sacraments of Christian initiation: Baptism and Confirmation. Now we consider the third, the sacrament of the Eucharist, the central sacrament from which the Church draws its strength.

Let us begin, as usual with a prayer. Heavenly Father, out of love for us sinners, you sent your eternal Son to take human nature, to dwell amongst us, and to restore us to union with you through his suffering and death on the Cross. On the night before he died, he instituted the Eucharist, to make his sacrifice present down the ages and to give us himself, the bread of life, as nourishment for our soul. Help us to understand and love the Eucharist and to participate in it often, so that through it we may be more united with the Mystical Body of Christ and with you. We make our prayer through Christ our Lord. Amen.

The Second Vatican Council called the Eucharist the "source and summit of the Christian life" (*LG* 11). Indeed, the Eucharist is the centre of the whole sacramental system and it should be the centre of our spiritual life too. For whereas the other sacraments give us grace, the Eucharist gives us the very source of grace, Christ himself. In the words of the Catechism, "The other sacraments, and indeed all ecclesiastical ministries and works of the apostolate, are bound up with the Eucharist and are oriented toward it. For in the blessed Eucharist is contained the whole spiritual good of the Church, namely Christ himself, our Pasch" (*PO* 5; *CCC* 1324).

We should make clear that when we use the name Eucharist we are referring to three distinct but related realities. The Eucharist is at one and the same time the sacrifice of Christ on Calvary made present in the

Mass, it is the sacrament of Holy Communion, and it is the Real Presence of Christ abiding in the tabernacle for our prayer and adoration.

In this lesson we will study four topics: the institution of the Eucharist, the Mass, the Real Presence and Eucharistic adoration, and Holy Communion.

1. THE INSTITUTION OF THE EUCHARIST

Jesus instituted the Eucharist in what we call the Last Supper on the night before he died on the Cross. He was celebrating with the apostles for the last time the Jewish feast of Passover. We recall that in the Passover the Jews celebrated, and continue to celebrate today, their deliverance from slavery in Egypt, when Moses led them to freedom in the thirteenth century before Christ. In the plan of God that first Passover was intended to be a figure of, and a preparation for, the definitive Passover when Christ would free all mankind from the slavery of sin by his death on the Cross. It was thus fitting that he should institute the Eucharist in the Passover on the night before he died, as a way of perpetuating the sacrifice of the Cross down the ages and allowing us to share in it. The Gospels of Matthew, Mark and Luke, and the first letter of St Paul to the Corinthians all relate the institution of the Eucharist.

In the Last Supper, after taking bread, giving thanks and breaking it, Jesus said, "This is my body which is given for you. Do this in remembrance of me." And likewise the cup after supper, saying, "This cup which is poured out for you is the New Covenant in my blood" (*1 Cor* 11:23-26).

When Jesus says, "This is my body" he means just that. After the words he had pronounced over it, the bread was no longer bread but the very body of Christ. And when he adds, "which is given for you", he is referring to the fact that he would give up his body as a sacrifice on the cross the following day. Likewise, he says of the wine that it is no longer wine but "the New Covenant in my blood". He adds, "which is poured out for you", referring to the shedding of his blood on the cross the following day as a sacrifice for our sins. In saying, "Do this in remembrance of me" he is instructing the apostles to continue to celebrate the Eucharist down the ages. Implied in these words is his giving the apostles the power to change bread and wine into his body and blood; that is, giving them the sacrament of Holy Orders, which we will study later.

Thus Jesus gave the Jewish Passover its definitive meaning. As the Catechism puts it, "Jesus' passing over to his father by his death and Resurrection, the new Passover, is anticipated in the Supper and celebrated in the Eucharist, which fulfils the Jewish Passover and anticipates the final Passover of the Church in the glory of the kingdom" (CCC 1340). Here we see how the Eucharist both looks back to the Jewish Passover, which it fulfils, and forward to the final Passover of the Church in heaven, which it anticipates.

From then on, the apostles and later the bishops and priests have continued to celebrate the Eucharist, which we now call the Mass. The *Acts of the Apostles* record how the first Christians in Jerusalem "devoted themselves to the apostles' teaching and fellowship, to the breaking of bread and the prayers" (*Acts* 2:42). The "breaking of bread" was how they referred to the Eucharist, since in it the priest breaks the bread, as Christ did in the Last Supper.

The *Acts* also explain that the first Christians met for the Eucharist "on the first day of the week" (*Acts* 20:7), that is on Sunday, the day of the Resurrection. Whereas the Jews celebrated Saturday, the Sabbath, as their day of rest in order to worship God, the first Christians, from the very beginning, began to celebrate on Sunday.

2. THE MASS

From the very beginning, the Church has celebrated the Eucharist, or the Mass, everywhere with the same fundamental structure. We see this in a lengthy description of the Mass written by St Justin Martyr in the middle of the second century (cf. *CCC* 1345). He describes how the Mass begins with a series of readings from the prophets of the Old Testament and the apostles. Then the priest gives a commentary, or homily, on the readings, exhorting the people to put them into practice. This is followed by prayers for all in the Church, what today we call the general intercessions or Prayer of the Faithful. After this comes the sign of peace, which today we have before Communion.

St Justin describes even the collection, taken up for the benefit of the poor and needy (cf. *CCC* 1351). Then the gifts of bread, water and wine are brought to the priest who offers them to God and says a long prayer, that today we call the Eucharistic prayer. The people answer "Amen" at the end of this prayer. Then comes Communion, administered by the deacons both to those present and to those unable to attend (cf. *CCC* 1345).

Since the beginning, the Mass has consisted of two main parts: the liturgy of the Word with the opening prayers, the readings, the homily, the profession of faith and general intercessions; and the liturgy of the Eucharist, with the presentation of the gifts, the Eucharistic Prayer and Communion. Together these two parts form "one single act of worship" (*SC* 56). No matter where we go in the world, we will find the Mass celebrated with this same structure, even though the language, some of the prayers and the hymns may vary considerably according to local custom and to the different rites.

The Catechism teaches that from the time of the apostles "down to our own day the celebration of the Eucharist has been continued so that today we encounter it everywhere in the Church with the same fundamental structure. It remains the centre of the Church's life" (*CCC* 1343). This is the beauty of our Catholic faith. The Church goes back to Jesus Christ and the apostles, and we have been celebrating Mass in essentially the same way from the very beginning. And we celebrate it in that same way everywhere in the world. The Catholic Church is truly universal.

If we ask "What exactly is the Mass?" the answer is clear. The Mass is the very same sacrifice of Christ on Calvary made present on the altar. As the Catechism says, quoting the Council of Trent, "The sacrifice of Christ and the sacrifice of the Eucharist are *one single sacrifice*: 'The victim is one and the same: the same now offers through the ministry of priests, who then offered himself on the cross; only the manner of offering is different'" (*DS* 1743; *CCC* 1367). The manner of offering is different in that Christ does not actually shed his blood in the Mass as he did on the cross. Thus when we attend Mass we should remember that we are not just at a gathering of the local community. We are present at Calvary, where Jesus offers himself once and for all to the Father for the forgiveness of our sins. That is, the Mass does not repeat the sacrifice of Christ, but rather makes it present. In the words of the Catechism, "The Eucharist is the memorial of Christ's Passover, the making present and the sacramental offering of his unique sacrifice" (*CCC* 1362). St Paul alluded to this in his description of the institution of the Eucharist: "For as often as you eat this bread and drink the chalice, you proclaim the Lord's death until he comes" (*1 Cor* 11:26).

The Mass is the sacrifice of Christ but it is also the sacrifice of the Church, his Mystical Body. The Catechism explains: "In the Eucharist the sacrifice of Christ becomes also the sacrifice of the members of his Body. The lives of the faithful, their praise, sufferings, prayer, and work, united with those of Christ and with his total offering, and so acquire a new value" (*CCC* 1368). This thought can be very helpful in our spiritual life. We can offer all our prayers, works, joys and sufferings in union with the Mass so that they take on a new meaning and value.

Traditionally we are taught that the Mass is offered for four principal ends or purposes. It is at the same time a sacrifice of praise to the Father, a sacrifice of thanksgiving for all God's gifts, a sacrifice of atonement in reparation, or sorrow, for our sins, and a sacrifice of petition, asking God for all our needs. Since it is the action of Christ himself, the Mass is the Church's most powerful prayer. It is of infinite value. Whenever we have special intentions of any type, the best way to pray for them is through the Mass.

3. THE REAL PRESENCE AND EUCHARISTIC ADORATION

As we have seen, when Christ instituted the Eucharist in the Last Supper he said to the apostles on giving them the bread he had just blessed, "This is my body which is given for you." And likewise with the cup, "This cup which is poured out for you is the New Covenant in my blood" (*1 Cor* 11:23-26; *CCC* 1339). This is one of the most awesome truths of our faith, the Real Presence of Christ in the Eucharist.

Christ had announced this truth some time before, in the synagogue of Capernaum in his long discourse on the Eucharist. Among other things, he said on that occasion: "Very truly I tell you, unless you eat the flesh of the Son of Man and drink his blood, you have no life in you; he who eats my flesh and drinks my blood has eternal life, and I will raise him up at the last day" (*Jn* 6:53-54). Naturally the thought of eating Jesus' flesh and drinking his blood left his listeners shocked and puzzled, and even some of his disciples left him as a result (cf. *Jn* 6:66). But he was clearly inviting the people to eat his flesh and drink his blood.

In the Last Supper Jesus instituted the Blessed Eucharist, giving the apostles his flesh to eat and his blood to drink under the appearance of bread and wine. That the Eucharist is truly the body and blood of Christ has been the faith of the Church from the beginning. Some twenty years after Christ's death and resurrection St Paul expressed this belief, writing to the Corinthians: "The cup of blessing that we bless, is it not a sharing in the blood of Christ? The bread that we break, is it not a sharing in the body of Christ?" (*1 Cor* 10:16) And in the following chapter he writes: "Whoever, therefore, eats the bread or drinks the cup of the Lord in an unworthy manner will be answerable for the body and blood of the Lord" (*1 Cor* 11:27). So Scripture is clear that the Eucharist is truly Our Lord's body and blood, not just a symbol.

Following on these passages, numerous Fathers of the Church testify to the Church's belief in the Real Presence. As early as the beginning of the second century, St Ignatius of Antioch wrote: "Be resolved to celebrate one Eucharist only; for there is only one flesh of our Lord Jesus Christ and only one chalice for unification with his blood" (*Ad Phil.* 4). In the middle of the second century St Justin wrote of the Eucharist: "We receive this not as ordinary bread and ordinary drink; ... the food over which thanksgiving has been made ... is both flesh and blood of that same incarnate Jesus" (*Apol.* 66, 2). And at the end of that century, St Irenaeus of Lyons wrote that "the bread over which thanksgiving is pronounced, is the body of the Lord and the chalice of his blood" (*Adv. haer.*, IV 18, 4).

In short, the belief in the Real Presence of Christ in the Eucharist was universal, accepted by all. Indeed, the Council of Trent in the sixteenth century could say: "Because Christ our Redeemer said that it was truly his body that he was offering under the species of bread, it has always been the conviction of the Church of God, and this holy Council now declares again, that by the consecration of the bread and wine there takes place a change of the whole substance of the bread into the substance of the body of Christ ..." (*DS* 1642; *CCC* 1376).

We must understand what we mean by this belief. We mean that after the Consecration of the Mass, when the priest pronounces the words of Christ in the Last Supper, the bread is no longer bread, but the body of Christ, and the wine is no longer wine, but the blood of Christ. The appearances remain those of bread and wine but the substance, the nature, has been changed into the body and blood of Christ. This change is called *transubstantiation*, meaning literally change of substance. It is brought about by Christ himself, acting through the priest. St John Chrysostom explains: "It is not man that causes the things offered to become the Body and Blood of Christ, but he who was crucified for us, Christ himself. The priest, in the role of Christ, pronounces these words, but their power and grace are God's" (*Prod. Jud.* 1:6; *CCC* 1375).

As we have been saying, we call this the Real Presence of Christ in the Eucharist. The Catechism explains: "This presence is called 'real' – by which is not intended to exclude the other types of presence as if they could not be 'real' too, but because it is presence in the fullest sense: that is to say, it is a *substantial* presence by which Christ, God and man, makes himself wholly and entirely present" (*CCC* 1374).

It is because of our faith in the Real Presence of Christ in the Eucharist that we genuflect, that is we go down on one knee, when passing in front of the tabernacle in the church, where Christ is present. And we bow, or genuflect, before receiving Christ in Communion. In the words of the Catechism, "The Catholic Church has always offered and still offers to the sacrament of the Eucharist the cult of adoration, not only during Mass, but also outside of it, reserving the consecrated hosts with the utmost care, exposing them to the solemn veneration of the faithful, and carrying them in procession'" (Paul VI, *MF* 56; *CCC* 1378). Adoration, of course, is the form of worship reserved for God alone.

Likewise, we observe silence in church, since it is truly the house of God, and we want to respect the desire of others to pray to Our Lord in the tabernacle. And wherever possible, we try to make a visit to the Blessed Sacrament, as we call it, in order to keep Our Lord company and to pray to him for all our intentions. The easiest place to pray is a church where Jesus is truly present. He invites us to do this: "Come to me all you who labour and are heavy laden, and I will give you rest" (*Mt* 11:28).

Many parishes and communities offer an opportunity for the people to pray and worship Our Lord in what is called Eucharistic adoration. That is, the host is exposed to view on the altar for a period of time in what is called a monstrance, a beautiful gold or silver vessel in the centre of which the host can be seen. Often this adoration concludes with the priest blessing everyone present with the monstrance in what is known as Benediction with the Blessed Sacrament. It is clear that Christ truly blesses those who honour him by praying before him in Eucharistic adoration, and he will be quick to answer their prayers.

In the Blessed Sacrament we have Christ present among us, the same Christ who loved us to the end and gave his life for us. Pope John Paul II, in his Letter *Dominicae Cenae* (1980) on the Eucharist, encourages us to express our devotion to Our Lord in the tabernacle: "The Church and the world have a great need for Eucharistic worship. Jesus awaits us in this sacrament of love. Let us not refuse the time to go to meet him in adoration, in contemplation full of faith, and open to making amends for the serious offences and crimes of the world. Let our adoration never cease" (*CCC* 1380).

We should know that the Blessed Sacrament remains in the tabernacle, not only so that the people can go there to pray and to adore Our Lord, but also so that Communion can be taken to the sick or given to people who request it outside Mass.

4. HOLY COMMUNION

This brings us to our final topic, the sacrament of Holy Communion, where Jesus gives himself to us as food for our soul. He invites us to receive him as he invited the apostles in the Last Supper: "Take, eat; this is my body" (*Mt* 26:26). He had said in the synagogue of Capernaum, "Truly I say to you, unless you eat the flesh of the Son of man and drink his blood, you have no life in you" (*Jn* 6:53). Through the reception of Communion the Mass is, in the words of the Catechism, "the sacrificial memorial in which the sacrifice of the cross is perpetuated and the sacred banquet of communion with the Lord's body and blood ... To receive Communion is to receive Christ himself who has offered himself for us" (*CCC* 1382).

How should we receive Our Lord in Communion? Taking into account that we are receiving Jesus himself, in the fulness of his humanity and divinity, we should prepare ourselves very well. St Paul writes to the Corinthians: "Whoever, therefore, eats the bread or drinks the cup of the Lord in an unworthy manner will be guilty of profaning the body and blood of the Lord" (*1 Cor* 11:27). For this reason the Catechism reminds us: "Anyone conscious of a grave sin must receive the sacrament of Reconciliation before coming to Communion" (*CCC* 1385). That is, if we have committed a mortal sin, it is not sufficient to make an act of contrition; we must confess our sins in the sacrament of Penance before receiving Communion.

This is a practice that has been lived in the Church from the very beginning. St Justin, in his *Apology* written to the Roman Emperor around the middle of the second century, explains that only baptised Christians who truly believe in the Church's teachings and are living in accordance with them may receive Communion. He writes: "We call this food Eucharist, and no one may take part in it unless he believes that what we teach is true, has received baptism for the forgiveness of sins and new birth, and lives in keeping with what Christ taught" (*Apol.* 1, 66, 1-2; *CCC* 1355).

Even when we have prepared well for Communion, we are still in some sense unworthy to receive Our Lord. As the Catechism teaches, "Before so great a sacrament, the faithful can only echo humbly and with ardent faith the words of the Centurion: 'Lord, I am not worthy that you should enter under my roof, but only say the word and my soul will be healed'" (cf. *Mt 8:8*; CCC 1386). We recognise these words as those said by the priest on holding up the host just before Communion in Mass. So we should try to receive Our Lord with the greatest possible faith and humility, considering ourselves always unworthy to receive him. But in his mercy and love, he gives himself to us, and actually cleanses us from venial sins through Communion itself (cf. *CCC* 1393). Rather than a reward for the virtuous, Communion should be seen as a remedy for weakness.

As part of our preparation, we are required to abstain from all food and drink, except water and medicine, for one hour before receiving Communion (cf. *CCL* can. 919 §1). This is not difficult, taking into account that not so long ago the required fast was from midnight the night before. In addition, as the Catechism explains, "Bodily demeanour (gestures, clothing) ought to convey the respect, solemnity, and joy of this moment when Christ becomes our guest" (*CCC* 1387). Most clubs and restaurants have a minimum standard of dress as a condition for entry, and we should not dress any less formally to attend Mass and receive Our Lord in Communion.

How often should we receive Communion? We are obliged to receive Communion at least once a year, if possible during the Easter season. But, as the Catechism explains, "the Church strongly encourages the faithful to receive the holy Eucharist on Sundays and feast days, or more often still, even daily" (*CCC* 1389). After all, we pray in the Our Father, "Give us this day our daily bread." It is good to know too that we can receive Communion up to twice a day, so long as the second time is within the celebration of Mass (cf. *CCL* can. 917).

That concludes our study of the Blessed Sacrament of the Eucharist, the source and summit of the Church's life. In the next lesson we will study the two sacraments of healing: Penance and the Anointing of the Sick. Until then, may God bless you and fill you with his love.

QUESTIONS FOR DISCUSSION

1. Why is the Eucharist so important that we call it the source and summit of Christian life?

2. The Mass has been celebrated in essentially the same way since the Church's earliest days. What does this mean for you?

3. If someone asked you what the Mass is, how would you answer?

4. What arguments would you use to convince a friend that the Eucharist is truly the body and blood of Christ and not just a symbol?

5. In view of the fact that in Holy Communion we receive Jesus Christ himself, how should we prepare to receive this sacrament?

POINTS TO REMEMBER

- The Eucharist is at one and the same time the sacrifice of the Mass, the sacrament of Holy Communion and the Real Presence of Jesus Christ in the tabernacle.

- Christ instituted the Eucharist in the Last Supper when he said, "This is my body, which is given for you" and "This cup which is poured out for you is the New Covenant in my blood".

- The Mass is the sacrifice of Christ on Calvary made present on the altar.

- We call the change of bread and wine into the body and blood of Christ transubstantiation.

- By the Real Presence we mean that the Eucharist is truly the body and blood of Christ, not just a symbol of him.

- We should prepare well to receive holy Communion by being in the state of grace, observing the fast of one hour, and having a deep faith and humility.

14. Penance and the Anointing of the Sick

Receive the Holy Spirit. If you forgive the sins of any, they are forgiven;
if you retain the sins of any, they are retained (Jn 20:22-23)

Summary

In this lesson we study the two sacraments of healing: Penance and the Anointing of the Sick.

We begin by looking at the institution of the sacrament of Penance, which took place on the evening of the first Easter Sunday, when Christ rose from the dead.

Then we study various aspects of confession itself, particularly the three acts of the penitent: contrition, confession and satisfaction.

Then we study the numerous effects of the sacrament, which include not only forgiveness of our sins but also the important effects of grace, the increase of the infused virtues, reconciliation with the Church, and always peace and joy.

We go on to consider the nature and effects of indulgences, which are closely connected with the sacrament of Penance.

Lastly, we study the second sacrament of healing, the Anointing of the Sick.

Welcome once again to our journey into truth, our excursion into the wonderful truths of the Catholic faith. I hope you are enjoying our journey and are becoming more and more convinced of the beauty of the faith taught to us by Jesus Christ.

In the last lesson we studied the Eucharist, the central sacrament in the constellation of seven sacraments instituted by Jesus Christ. In this lesson we will study what the *Catechism of the Catholic Church* calls the sacraments of healing. They are the sacraments of Penance and the Anointing of the Sick.

Let us begin, as usual, with a prayer. Heavenly Father, you know our desire to love you with our whole heart, soul, mind and strength, and our eagerness to be with you forever in heaven. You also know our human weakness – our many failings and sins. Help us to appreciate the great value of the sacraments of Penance and the Anointing of the Sick, by which you heal us and strengthen us for the battles ahead so that we may serve you faithfully until the end and be with you forever in heaven. We make our prayer through Christ our Lord. Amen.

In this lesson we will study six topics: the institution of the sacrament of Penance, the confession of sins, the effects of the sacrament, indulgences, the Anointing of the Sick and the effects of the anointing.

1. THE INSTITUTION OF THE SACRAMENT OF PENANCE

One of the first issues in relation to the sacrament of Penance is its name. How are we to call it? We used to call it simply confession or the sacrament of Penance. Then it became the sacrament of Reconciliation. In the Catechism, the article on this sacrament is entitled "The Sacrament of Penance and Reconciliation". The Catechism also says that it is called the sacrament of conversion and the sacrament of forgiveness (cf. *CCC* 1423-24). I like to refer to it also as the sacrament of mercy and the sacrament of joy. So we can call it whatever we want: the sacrament of Confession, Penance, Reconciliation or the sacrament of Penance and Reconciliation. People will always understand what we mean. For the sake of simplicity, here we will call it the sacrament of Penance, as does the *Code of Canon Law*, by the way.

The sacrament of Penance is one of the great treasures of the Church, a treasure that we should seek and use often. Through it God forgives our sins and fills us with his grace. Our Lord gave it to the apostles on the very evening of his resurrection as the first fruits, so to speak, of his death and resurrection. St John tells us how Jesus appeared to the apostles in the Upper Room on that first Easter Sunday and said, "Peace be with you". Then "he breathed on them, and said to them, 'Receive the Holy Spirit. If you forgive the sins of any, they are forgiven; if you retain the sins of any, they are retained'" (*Jn* 20:21-23). We see in these words how the Holy Spirit, who is our advocate and the love between the Father and the Son, is associated with this sacrament. Just before the priest absolves our sins in the sacrament, he says that God "sent the Holy Spirit among us for the forgiveness of sins."

We also see implied in the words of institution the need to confess our sins individually to the priest. Only if the priest hears our sins can he can judge whether to forgive them or to retain them. It would be very rare that the priest did not forgive our sins but it could happen if it was clear that we were not sorry and not resolved to try to avoid committing them again.

Since Christ gave the power to forgive sins to the apostles, only a bishop or a priest who has faculties from a bishop or religious superior can administer the sacrament of Penance validly. We can always assume that the priest hearing our confession has these faculties.

Jesus gave us the sacrament of Penance because he knew we needed it. It responds to some of the deepest needs of the human person. First, it responds to the fact that we all sin. St John reminds us in his first letter: "If we say we have no sin, we deceive ourselves, and the truth is not in us." He goes on to say, "If we confess our sins, [God] is faithful and just, and will forgive our sins and cleanse us from all unrighteousness" (*1 Jn* 1:8-9). Second, the sacrament responds to our deep-seated need to tell someone what we have done, whether good or bad. We all experience this need, but often when we tell others what we have done, they go and tell others and soon everyone knows our most intimate life. Likewise they may give us bad advice. In the sacrament of Penance we have the opportunity to tell God through the priest what we have done. The priest tells no one and, what is more, he gives us good advice in addition to forgiving our sins. And third, we have a need to hear with our ears that we are forgiven, and this happens when the priest pronounces the words of forgiveness, "I absolve you from your sins". We leave the sacrament freed of the burden of sin, at peace with God and the Church, and full of joy, eager to begin again. The sacrament of Penance is truly a great treasure.

2. The confession of sins

We come now to the confession itself and how it is done. In simple terms, we confess our sins to the priest, who listens carefully, judges whether we are truly sorry, gives us some advice and a penance to perform, and then absolves our sins on behalf of God and the Church. The Catechism explains: "Sin is before all else an offence against God, a rupture of communion with him. At the same time it damages communion with the Church. For this reason conversion entails both God's forgiveness and reconciliation with the Church, which are expressed and accomplished liturgically by the sacrament of Penance and Reconciliation" (*CCC* 1440).

As the Catechism says, sin is an offence against God and hence only God can forgive it. For this reason Christ instituted the sacrament of Penance so that we could confess our sins to God through the priest and hear his forgiveness through the priest. The power to forgive sins in God's name was given to the priest when he was ordained. It is an exercise of the power of "binding and loosing" given by Christ to the apostles. Christ had said, "Truly, I say to you, whatever you bind on earth shall be bound in heaven, and whatever you loose on earth shall be loosed in heaven" (*Mt* 18:18). When the priest absolves, or looses, our sins, they are forgiven in heaven and we are reconciled both with God and with the Church. It is truly an act of liberation from sin. There are three acts of the penitent: contrition, confession and satisfaction.

Contrition

First, contrition. In preparing for confession, the first thing we must do is examine our conscience, considering all the sins we have committed and would like to confess, so that we can be sorry for them. This sorrow, also called contrition, is an essential act of the penitent. Without it, we cannot be forgiven.

The Catechism defines contrition as: "sorrow of the soul and detestation for the sin committed, together with the resolution not to sin again" (*CCC* 1451). Note that the resolution not to sin again, sometimes called purpose of amendment, is an essential aspect of contrition. Without it, the person would not be truly sorry. At the same time, the resolution not to sin again does not require that the person be certain of not sinning again. No one can have that certainty. All that is required is the resolution to try not to sin again.

Contrition can be of two forms, perfect and imperfect, depending on the motive for sorrow, not on its intensity. Perfect contrition is sorrow of love, for having offended God who is worthy of all our love. The Catechism explains: "Such contrition remits venial sins; it also obtains forgiveness of mortal sins if it includes the firm resolution to have recourse to sacramental confession as soon as possible" (*CCC* 1452). For those unfamiliar with these terms, venial sins are lesser sins and mortal sins are serious ones which destroy the life of grace in the soul. As the Catechism says, if a person who has committed a mortal sin says an act of perfect contrition and has the resolution to go to confession as soon as possible, he regains immediately the state of grace, even if he cannot receive communion until he has gone to sacramental confession (cf. *CCC* 1457).

Imperfect contrition, or attrition, arises from a spiritual motive less perfect than the love of God. In the words of the Catechism, "it is born of the consideration of sin's ugliness or the fear of eternal damnation and the other penalties threatening the sinner (contrition of fear)" (*CCC* 1453). By itself, imperfect contrition cannot obtain the forgiveness of grave sins, but it disposes us to obtain forgiveness in the sacrament of Penance (cf. *CCC* 1453). So when we go to confession we must have at least imperfect contrition.

Confession

The second act of the penitent is confession. Here we tell the priest all the sins we wish to confess. The Catechism explains that this confession "even from a simply human point of view, frees us and facilitates our reconciliation with others. Through such an admission man looks squarely at the sins he is guilty of, takes responsibility for them and thereby opens himself again to God and to the communion of the Church in order to make a new future possible" (*CCC* 1455).

Which sins must we confess? The Catechism answers: "All mortal sins of which penitents after a diligent self-examination are conscious must be recounted by them in confession, even if they are most secret and have been committed against the last two precepts of the Decalogue" (*CCC* 1456). The last two precepts of the Decalogue, or the Ten Commandments, forbid sins of thought against the virtues of chastity and detachment from material things. If someone knowingly withholds a mortal sin in confession, not only does he not receive forgiveness for any other sins confessed, but he commits a new sin of sacrilege by misusing the sacrament. Quoting St Jerome, the Catechism says: "For if the sick person is too ashamed to show his wound to the doctor, the medicine cannot heal what it does not know" (*In Eccl.* 10, 11; *CCC* 1456). In addition, it is traditionally taught that mortal sins must be confessed in species and number. For example, it is not sufficient to say "I have sinned against chastity". The species – fornication, adultery, etc. – must also be mentioned, as well as the approximate number of times the sin has been committed.

Must venial sins be confessed? The Catechism answers: "Without being strictly necessary, confession of everyday faults (venial sins) is nevertheless strongly recommended by the Church. Indeed the regular confession of our venial sins helps us form our conscience, fight against evil tendencies, let ourselves be healed by Christ and progress in the life of the Spirit. By receiving more frequently through this sacrament the gift of the Father's mercy, we are spurred to be merciful as he is merciful" (*CCC* 1458).

Given the sensitivity and confidentiality of confession, the Church requires the priest, under very severe penalties, to observe absolute secrecy regarding the sins he has heard in confession. This confidentiality, which admits of no exceptions, is called the "sacramental seal" (cf. *CCC* 1467). As a result, even in court under oath a priest may never reveal what he has heard in confession. So we can have absolute confidence that the priest will never reveal to anyone what we have told him in confession.

How often should we go to confession? Given the many graces that come from this sacrament, it is good to go regularly, for example once a month. Pope John Paul II, in an address in 1981 said that frequent confession "has always accompanied the ascent to holiness in the Church" (*Address,* 30 January 1981). We can be sure that all the saints went frequently to confession, and we are all called to holiness.

Satisfaction

The third act of the penitent is to do some acts of prayer or penance proposed by the priest. Since our sins have offended God and harmed his Mystical Body the Church, it is only right that we need to do something to make up in some way for the harm we have caused. For this reason after we have confessed our sins the priest will ask us to say some prayers or do some acts of penance or charity. This is called making satisfaction or expiating our sins. The Catechism explains that it "can consist of prayer, an offering, works of mercy, service of neighbour, voluntary self-denial, sacrifices, and above all the patient acceptance of the cross we must bear. Such penances help configure us to Christ, who alone expiated our sins once for all. They allow us to become co-heirs with the risen Christ, 'provided we suffer with him" (*Rom* 8: 17; *CCC* 1460). We should do this penance or satisfaction as soon as possible after we leave the confessional.

3. THE EFFECTS OF THE SACRAMENT

The sacrament of Penance has many important effects. The first is reconciliation with God if we were separated from him by mortal sin. If we were already in the state of grace, this grace will be increased. The sacrament also reconciles us with the Church, which we have harmed by our sins. It takes away, or remits, the eternal punishment incurred by mortal sins, so that we would not have to go to hell. It remits at least some of the temporal punishment owing for our sins, both mortal and venial. It gives, in addition to sanctifying grace, sacramental grace to strengthen us in the spiritual life and to help us avoid falling again into the sins we have confessed. It gives us an increase of the infused virtues of faith, hope and charity, prudence, justice, fortitude and temperance, and of the Gifts of the Holy Spirit. With the soul now completely cleansed of sin and filled with grace, we make a new beginning in the spiritual life and we are spurred on along the way of holiness. As a consequence, confession fills us with immense peace and joy. Again we see what a treasure this sacrament is.

4. INDULGENCES

A topic closely associated with the sacrament of Penance is that of indulgences. Indulgences, like the sacrament itself, help to make up for some or all of the temporal punishment owing for our sins. What is an indulgence? The Catechism answers: "An indulgence is a remission before God of the temporal punishment due to sins whose guilt has already been forgiven, which the faithful Christian who is duly disposed gains under certain prescribed conditions through the action of the

Church which, as the minister of redemption, dispenses and applies with authority the treasury of the satisfactions of Christ and the saints" (Paul VI, Apost. Const. *Indulgentiarum doctrina,* Norm 1; *CCC* 1471).

That is, from the great spiritual treasury of the merits of Jesus Christ, Our Lady and the saints, the Church grants the remission of some or all of the temporal punishment owing for our sins, provided we carry out certain acts. The Church can do this by virtue of the power of binding and loosing granted by Christ to the apostles (cf. *Mt* 18:18). If the indulgence removes all of the temporal punishment it is called a *plenary* indulgence, and if it removes only part it is called a *partial* indulgence. We can gain indulgences for ourselves and we can also apply them to the dead, that is to the souls in Purgatory (cf. *CCC* 1471).

The Church grants indulgences when we carry out certain prescribed acts as a way of spurring us on to works of devotion, penance and charity. Most of the commonly known prayers we say carry with them a partial indulgence, as does offering our work to God. And we can gain a plenary indulgence by such acts as saying the Rosary in family or in a church, making the Way of the Cross in a church where the stations are erected, and doing a half hour of prayer before the Blessed Sacrament. To gain any indulgence we must be in the state of grace – that is, not in the state of mortal sin – and to gain a plenary indulgence we must receive Communion and go to confession some days before or after, pray for the intentions of the Pope, and abhor sin, even venial sin. We can gain indulgences even if we are unaware of them, as long as we have the habitual intention of gaining them. Indulgences are an expression of the Church's motherly care for her children and they are very helpful in our journey to heaven.

5. THE ANOINTING OF THE SICK

That brings us to the second of the two sacraments of healing, the Anointing of the Sick. Christ knew the weakness of our human condition and how we sometimes experience anxiety and fear in the face of serious illness and death, and so he gave the Church a sacrament to strengthen us in those difficult moments. He alluded to it when he said of his disciples: "In my name ... they will lay their hands on the sick, and they will recover" (*Mk* 16:17-18). In another passage St Mark mentions the use of oil in the sacrament, describing how the disciples "anointed with oil many that were sick and healed them" (*Mk* 6:12-13).

From the beginning the Church has had a special rite for the anointing of the sick. St James describes it: "Is any one among you sick? Let him call for the elders of the Church, and let them pray over him, anointing him with oil in the name of the Lord; and the prayer of faith will save the sick man, and the Lord will raise him up; and if he has committed sins, he will be forgiven" (*Jas* 5:14-15). The Tradition of the Church has recognised in this rite one of the seven sacraments, and in both East and West from ancient times the Church has had the practice of anointing the sick with blessed oil.

For whom is the sacrament intended? In the words of the Catechism, "The Anointing of the Sick 'is not a sacrament for those only who are at the point of death. Hence, as soon as anyone of the faithful begins to be in danger of death from sickness or old age, the fitting time for him to receive this sacrament has certainly already arrived'" (*SC* 73; *CCC* 1514). So while the sacrament is not only for those at the point of death, neither is it for people who are merely sick. They must be in danger of death through sickness or old age. The Church has another rite of the blessing of the sick for those who are not seriously ill.

The sacrament may be received as often as necessary. As the Catechism explains, "Each time a Christian falls seriously ill, he may receive the Anointing of the Sick, and also when, after he has received it, the illness worsens" (*CCC* 1529), so a person may receive the sacrament more than once even in the same illness. What is more, as the Catechism says, "It is fitting to receive the Anointing of the Sick just prior to a serious operation. The same holds for the elderly whose frailty becomes more pronounced" (*CCC* 1515).

Who is the minister of this sacrament? Only bishops and priests can administer it. This has been the practice from the beginning, following St James' exhortation to call for the elders, that is, the presbyters or priests. Pastors should instruct the faithful on the benefits of the sacrament, and the sick should be encouraged to ask for it and to be properly prepared to receive it. When a person becomes seriously ill and especially when there is danger of death, a priest should always be called to administer the sacrament, no matter at what time of day or night. The church community, represented by members of the person's family, friends, and other parishioners, are encouraged to be present.

How is the sacrament celebrated? As regards place it may be celebrated in a home, a hospital or a church, wherever the sick person is. If possible, it is fitting to celebrate it within a Mass. It may be preceded by the sacrament of Penance and followed by the sacrament of the Eucharist. The full rite includes a Liturgy of the Word, with readings from Scripture and prayers. The priest in silence lays his hands on the sick person, praying over him or her, and then anoints the person with oil on the forehead and hands. The oil has usually been blessed by the bishop, but in case of necessity the priest may bless oil himself for the particular occasion.

6. THE EFFECTS OF THE ANOINTING

The Anointing of the Sick produces many benefits. It gives strength, peace and courage to endure in a Christian way the suffering of illness or old age, including the strength to overcome discouragement in the face of death. If the sick person is unconscious or otherwise unable to confess his sins, the sacrament forgives sins. It can restore the person to health, if God wishes to grant this for the salvation of the person's soul. It unites the sick person with the passion of Christ, allowing him to participate in Christ's work of salvation. It unites the person with the Church, which prays for him, and the sick person in turn contributes to the sanctification of the Church through the grace of the sacrament.

Finally, it prepares the person to pass over to eternal life, completing the identification of the person with Christ which began in Baptism.

If the person is dying, he or she may receive Communion with the special prayers for the dying known as viaticum. This final reception of the Eucharist fulfils Christ's words, "He who eats my flesh and drinks my blood has eternal life, and I will raise him up at the last day" (*Jn* 6:54). The Catechism sums this up, saying that "just as the sacraments of Baptism, Confirmation, and the Eucharist form a unity called 'the sacraments of Christian initiation,' so too it can be said that Penance, the Anointing of the Sick and the Eucharist as viaticum constitute at the end of Christian life 'the sacraments that prepare for our heavenly homeland' or the sacraments that complete the earthly pilgrimage" (*CCC* 1525). Let us pray that we will all be able to die well, receiving these sacraments to hasten us on our final passover to the house of the Father.

That concludes our study of the two sacraments of healing. In the next lesson we will complete our consideration of the sacraments, looking at the two sacraments at the service of communion: Holy Orders and Matrimony. Until then, may God bless you and lead you gently through the week.

QUESTIONS FOR DISCUSSION

1. We learned that the sacrament of Penance is a great treasure. What particular aspects of the sacrament do you find most attractive?

2. People coming into the Church as adults sometimes find confession somewhat difficult. What thoughts can help to overcome this difficulty?

3. Non-Catholics sometimes accuse us of sinning wilfully, going to confession and then going back to commit the same sins again. How can we make sure that this is not the case?

4. We don't hear much about indulgences these days but they are still very much part of the life of the Church. How would you explain to a friend what they are and why they are so beneficial?

5. Why is it so important to call a priest to anoint a person who is dying?

POINTS TO REMEMBER

- Penance and the Anointing of the Sick are the two sacraments of healing.

- Christ gave the Church the power to forgive sins on the evening of his Resurrection when he told the apostles, "If you forgive the sins of any, they are forgiven".

- The three acts of the person going to confession are contrition, confession of sins and satisfaction.

- Contrition always involves the resolution to try not to sin again.

- An indulgence is the remission before God of part or all of the temporal punishment owing for sins granted by the Church to those who carry out certain prescribed acts.

- The Anointing of the Sick strengthens those who are in danger of death through sickness or old age.

15. Holy Orders and Matrimony

I remind you to rekindle the gift of God that is within you through the laying on of my hands (2 Tim 1:6)

Summary

In this lesson we study the two sacraments at the service of communion: Holy Orders and Matrimony.

We begin by studying the nature of Holy Orders, through which men are ordained to continue Christ's ministry down the ages, whether as bishops, priests or deacons. We see how all these ministries are to be seen as a task of service.

We then look at the three degrees of the sacrament. Even though there is only one sacrament, it is received in the three degrees of deacon, priest and bishop. We study here the responsibilities of those in each of the three orders.

Then we look at some aspects of the ceremony of ordination for each of the three orders, including the minister and recipient of ordination, and the effects of the ordination.

We go on to study the sacrament of Matrimony, considering first the fundamental role of marriage in the plan of God and the nature of marriage as a covenant. We look too at the essential properties of marriage, which are unity, indissolubility and openness to life.

Finally we consider various aspects of the marriage rite and the effects of the sacrament.

Welcome once again to our journey into truth and our study of the sacraments. In the last lesson we considered the two sacraments of healing – Penance and the Anointing of the Sick – and today we will study the two sacraments at the service of communion – Holy Orders and Matrimony. These two sacraments help to build up and unite the Body of Christ.

Let us begin with our usual prayer. Heavenly Father, you call us to communion with you through the Church, the Mystical Body of your son Jesus. You build up that body by bringing children into the world through the family united in marriage, and you order it and sanctify it through the bishops, priests and deacons who have become your ministers through the sacrament of Holy Orders. Help us to give thanks for these sacraments and to pray for all those united in marriage and for our clergy, that they may be faithful and fruitful in their role of bringing souls to you. We make our prayer through Christ our Lord. Amen.

The sacraments of Holy Orders and Matrimony, as the Catechism says, are at the service of the communion of the Church in that "they confer a particular mission in the Church and serve to build up the People of God" (*CCC* 1534). In this lesson we will look at six topics: the nature of Holy Orders, the three degrees of Holy Orders, the celebration and effects of Orders, marriage in God's plan, the properties of marriage, and the celebration and effects of marriage.

1. THE NATURE OF HOLY ORDERS

A good way to understand the sacrament of Holy Orders is to consider that Jesus Christ entrusted to the apostles the ministry of teaching, sanctifying and ruling, which he had exercised himself, so that these ministries would continue in the Church until the end of time. We see a suggestion of this in his final words to the apostles before he ascended into heaven: "Go therefore and make disciples of all nations, baptising them in the name of the Father and of the Son and of the Holy Spirit, teaching them to observe all that I have commanded you; and behold, I am with you always, to the close of the age" (*Mt* 28:19-20). This ministry has been carried out ever since by bishops, priests and deacons, who receive their power through the sacrament of Holy Orders. As an overview of the sacrament, the Catechism says: "Holy Orders is the sacrament through which the mission entrusted by Christ to his apostles continues to be exercised in the Church until the end of time: thus it is the sacrament of apostolic ministry. It includes three degrees: episcopate, presbyterate, and diaconate" (*CCC* 1536).

The sacrament is called Holy Orders because, through it, the person being ordained enters the order of diaconate, priesthood or episcopate in the Church and is given the sacred power to carry out the duties of that order. The power is conferred by the laying on of hands by a bishop, with the corresponding prayer. And just as Christ came not to be served, but to serve and to give his life as a ransom for many (cf. *Mt* 20:28), so the sacred minister has the task of serving the Church in the name and in the person of Christ (cf. *CCC* 1591). Sacred ministry is very much a task of service, as the very name ministry suggests.

2. THE THREE DEGREES OF HOLY ORDERS

As we have said, Holy Orders is exercised in three degrees: those of bishop, priest and deacon, and this has been the case since the beginning of the Church. The degrees of bishop and priest are a participation in the priesthood of Christ, the head of the Church, and that of deacon is intended to help and serve the bishops and priests. All three degrees are received through the one sacrament of Holy Orders.

As regards bishops, the Catechism says: "Amongst those various offices which have been exercised in the Church from the earliest times the chief place, according to the witness of tradition, is held by the function of those who, through their appointment to the dignity and responsibility of bishop, and in virtue consequently of the unbroken succession going back to the beginning, are regarded as transmitters of the apostolic line" (*LG* 20; *CCC* 1555). The first bishops were the apostles themselves, and they passed on their ministry to their successors by laying their hands on them. This has continued down to the present day, in what is known as apostolic succession, and because of it bishops today have the same power Christ first conferred on the apostles.

Although all three degrees of Holy Orders constitute one sacrament, the fullness of the sacrament is received by bishops. The Catechism, quoting the Second Vatican Council, says that the bishops, "in an eminent and visible manner, take the place of Christ himself, teacher, shepherd, and priest, and act as his representative" (*LG* 21; *CCC* 1558). Thus it can be properly said that bishops, like the Pope, are "vicars of Christ" (cf. *LG* 27). Bishops are usually the head of a particular body of the faithful, such as a diocese, and are responsible for the spiritual welfare of the people entrusted to them.

Who appoints bishops? Because bishops have the role of uniting the people not only with God but also with the Holy Father and the universal Church, the Pope himself always intervenes, usually by appointing the bishop himself, but in some cases by confirming a candidate chosen in some other way, such as an election (cf. *CCC* 1559). In addition to his pastoral care of the diocese or other body of the faithful entrusted to him, the bishop also bears responsibility for the universal Church, in union with the Holy Father and the other bishops throughout the world. He exercises this responsibility, for example, in an ecumenical council, a gathering of the world's bishops called by the Pope to discuss certain topics. He also exercises it in meetings of the bishops of a whole country or other region, known as an Episcopal Conference.

The second degree of Holy Orders is that of priests. It is clear that bishops by themselves cannot attend directly to the pastoral care of all the faithful entrusted to them. For this reason, from the beginning the bishops ordained priests, known as "co-workers" of the bishops, to assist them in their ministry. Priests, like bishops, share in the threefold ministry of Christ in teaching, sanctifying and shepherding the people, and like bishops, they act "in the person of Christ the head" (*PO* 2; *CCC* 1563).

We see priests exercising their ministry in our parishes, where they say Mass, hear confessions, visit and anoint the sick, administer the sacraments of Baptism and Marriage, give instructions and coordinate the work of the whole parish. Without them, we would not have the Eucharist and the other sacraments, and we would not have the instruction in the faith that they give us in homilies and classes.

The third degree of Holy Orders is that of deacons, who since the beginning have been ordained to serve the Church in various ministries. The Catechism describes their various roles: "Among other tasks, it is the task of deacons to assist the bishop and priests in the celebration of the divine mysteries, above all the Eucharist, in the distribution of Holy Communion, in assisting at and blessing marriages, in the proclamation of the Gospel and preaching, in presiding over funerals, and in dedicating themselves to the various ministries of charity" (cf. *LG* 29; *CCC* 1570). It is also the role of deacons to administer Baptism solemnly, to take the Eucharist as viaticum to the dying and to administer sacramentals.

While in the past we were perhaps used to thinking of a deacon as someone on the way to becoming a priest, the Second Vatican Council restored the permanent diaconate, something the East has always had. It can be conferred on married men and it constitutes "an important enrichment for the Church's mission" (*LG* 29; *CCC* 1571). Priests are helped greatly in their parish work if they have a permanent deacon to carry out the many roles we have just mentioned.

3. THE CELEBRATION AND EFFECTS OF ORDERS

How is the sacrament of Holy Orders celebrated? First of all, the minister of the sacrament is always and only a bishop. The bishop, of course, must be validly ordained, meaning that he can trace his own ordination back in an unbroken line to the apostles. When a bishop is being ordained, it is customary for the ordaining bishop to have two other bishops with him as co-consecrators.

The person to be ordained must be a baptised man. The Church has never ordained women, following a constant tradition going back to the beginning of the Church, a tradition followed also by the Orthodox. This is in no way to say that women are of lesser dignity than men, for the highest person in heaven after God is a woman, the Blessed Virgin Mary. In 1994 Pope John Paul II issued an Apostolic Letter entitled *Ordinatio sacerdotalis* in which he discussed briefly the reasons why the Church has never ordained women and he went on to declare that "the Church has no authority whatsoever to confer priestly ordination on women and that this judgment is to be definitively held by all the Church's faithful" (n .4). The Holy See later clarified that this was an irrevocable, infallible teaching, so that the matter is no longer open to discussion.

While in the Eastern rites of the Catholic Church, and in the Orthodox Churches, married men can be ordained priests, in the Latin Rite priests are required to be celibate. This follows, among other reasons, the fact that Christ himself was celibate with the Church as his bride, and the priest represents Christ. The Church admits to the vocation of priesthood only men who have the calling to celibacy, just as she admits to the vocation of nun or brother only a woman or man with the same calling. We should acknowledge that there are a small number of married priests in the Latin Rite, who were married ministers in some other denomination before becoming Catholics and then being ordained priests.

The essential rite of ordination in all three degrees is the bishop's laying of hands on the head of the ordinand with a specific prayer of consecration asking God for the outpouring of the Holy Spirit and his gifts proper to each ministry (cf. *CCC* 1573). Among the additional rites of the ceremony in the Latin Church are the presentation and election of the ordinand, the instruction by the bishop, the examination of the candidate and the litany of the saints. After the anointing of the hands with chrism in the ordination of a bishop or priest, the person being ordained is given the symbols or instruments of his ministry. These are the book of the Gospels, a ring, mitre and crosier in the case of a bishop; a paten and chalice for a priest; and the book of the Gospels for a deacon.

As regards the effects of the sacrament, Holy Orders confers an indelible spiritual character, configuring the recipient to Christ the priest. For this reason, the sacrament cannot be conferred only for a time, and it cannot be repeated. In addition to the usual sanctifying grace, the infused virtues and gifts of the Holy Spirit, Holy Orders confers a special sacramental grace, of which the Catechism says: "The grace of the Holy Spirit proper to this sacrament is configuration to Christ as Priest, Teacher, and Pastor, of whom the ordained is made a minister" (*CCC* 1585). This sacramental grace assists the ordained minister with all the actual graces he will need throughout his life to be faithful and fruitful in his ministry.

Summing up the dignity and beauty of the priesthood St John Vianney, the Curé of Ars, says: "The priest continues the work of redemption on earth ... If we really understood the priest on earth, we would die not of fright but of love ... The priesthood is the love of the heart of Jesus" (*CCC* 1589). We should pray for all bishops, priests and deacons, that they will be holy and dedicated to their ministry in the name of Christ, and that God will continue to call many men to the ministry.

4. MARRIAGE IN GOD'S PLAN

We come now to the last of the seven sacraments, Matrimony, or Marriage. In some sense marriage comes first, not as a sacrament but as a natural institution, since it existed since Adam and Eve, and it is through marriage that we receive life and are able to receive the other sacraments. Marriage is not a merely human institution, as if devised by man by common agreement. Rather, it is written in the very nature of man by God his creator. The Second Vatican Council says of it: "The intimate community of life and love which constitutes the married state has been established by the Creator and endowed by him with its own proper laws ... God himself is the author of marriage" (*GS* 48, §1).

So fundamental to human nature is marriage between a man and a woman that it has existed in all civilisations and cultures. And it is fundamental to the well-being of society. The Second Vatican Council teaches: "The well-being of the individual person and of both human and Christian society is closely bound up with the healthy state of conjugal and family life" (*GS* 47 §2). It is obvious to all that when family life is not healthy, multiple problems arise in the whole of society. The family is, as it were, the basic cell of society, and when the cells are unhealthy, so is the body. Conversely, when families are united and happy, the whole of society benefits.

We are accustomed to refer to marriage as a covenant; that is, as a bond or agreement between two persons who give themselves to each other. What they exchange in marriage is not their time, their talents, their goods or their services, but themselves. The very words of the exchange of consent in the wedding ceremony express this personal self-giving: "I take you to be my lawfully wedded wife", or "husband". The marriage covenant is a reflection on earth of God's covenant relationship with his people. In the Old Testament we see especially in the prophets how God takes his people as his bride (cf. *Hos* 2:19-20; *Is* 62:5).

In the New Testament, this covenant is renewed and fulfilled in Christ's covenant with the Church, where Christ is the bridegroom and the Church is his bride (cf. *Mk* 2:19-20; *2 Cor* 11:2; *Eph* 5:25-27). Through their loving fidelity to each other, spouses show their children and the world Christ's unconditional love and faithfulness to his Church. Jesus performed his first miracle at a wedding in Cana, and the Church attaches great importance to his presence there. As the Catechism puts it, the Church "sees in it the confirmation of the goodness of marriage and the proclamation that thenceforth marriage will be an efficacious sign of Christ's presence" (*CCC* 1613).

5. THE PROPERTIES OF MARRIAGE

What are the essential properties of marriage? The Catechism mentions three. It says: "Unity, indissolubility, and openness to fertility are essential to marriage" (*CCC* 1664). All these properties stem from the properties of Christ's covenant with the Church, and also from the very nature of true love.

Unity

The first property is unity, by which we mean that Christian marriage is a union of one man and one woman, to the exclusion of all others. Just as Christ the bridegroom has only one Church as his bride, so Christians have only one spouse. And true love is a total self-giving of one person to another, to the exclusion of all others. This excludes polygamy, where a man has more than one wife. Among other reasons, as Pope John Paul II explains, polygamy "is contrary to the equal personal dignity of men and women who in matrimony give themselves with a love that is total and therefore unique and exclusive" (*FC* 19).

What is more, the spouses are so united in marriage that they come together in a one-flesh union. In the words of Christ, "they are no longer two, but one flesh" (*Mt* 19:6). It is a union not only of bodies but first and foremost of minds and hearts. As Pope John Paul II puts it, the spouses "are called to grow continually in their communion through day-to-day fidelity to their marriage promise of total mutual self-giving" (*FC* 19). They are helped in this by their communion in Jesus Christ through the sacrament of Matrimony, through their prayer and through receiving the Eucharist together.

Indissolubility

The second property of marriage is indissolubility, by which we mean that the bond of marriage of two baptised Christians cannot be broken: it is indissoluble. Just as Christ's covenant with his Church is forever, so Christian spouses pledge to remain faithful "until death do us part". Indeed, the deepest reason for fidelity in marriage is found in the fidelity of God to his covenant, in that of Christ to his Church, a fidelity to which the spouses witness by their own fidelity. What is more, it is the very nature of true love that it wants to be forever, everlasting. As the Catechism puts it, "Love seeks to be definitive; it cannot be an arrangement 'until further notice'" (CCC 1646).

Therefore, Christian marriage excludes divorce. Christ was very clear on this: "Whoever divorces his wife and marries another, commits adultery against her; and if she divorces her husband and marries another, she commits adultery" (Mk 10:11-12). When his disciples asked Jesus why Moses then had allowed divorce, he answered that it was because of the hardness of their hearts, but that from the beginning marriage was meant to be forever: "What therefore God has joined together, let not man put asunder" (Mk 10:5-9). We should remember that in the Old Testament marriage was not a sacrament, it did not give grace, so that it was harder for spouses to stay together. But in making marriage a sacrament, Christ gave Christian couples all the graces they would need to stay together all their lives and make their love grow.

The Second Vatican Council gives three reasons why marriage is indissoluble: "for the good of the partners, of the children, and of society" (GS 48 § 1). It is clear that the partners want their marriage to last and the Church's teaching on indissolubility gives them confidence that it will. It is also abundantly clear that children are far better off when their parents stay together than when they split up. Children always suffer when their parents divorce. And it is obvious that when there are many divorces the whole fabric of society is weakened and many social ills result.

Naturally, if there are serious difficulties in the relationship, the Church allows couples to separate, although it encourages them to resume married life if the cause for the separation ceases (cf. CCL, Can. 1153).

Openness to life

The third essential property of marriage is its openness to life. Indeed, if the spouses were intentionally to exclude children, their marriage would not be valid. It is obvious that marriage and married love were intended by God as the way to bring new life into the world. It is through the loving one-flesh union of husband and wife that children come into the world, just as it is through Christ's covenant with his Church that children are born into the Church through Baptism. And it is the nature of true love to want to perpetuate that love through the children that result from it. We refer to this reality with the awesome word "procreation", since it is the cooperation of the spouses with God in bringing a new human being into existence, a human being destined for eternal life with God. The Second Vatican Council teaches: "By its very nature the institution of marriage and married love is ordered to the procreation and education of the offspring and it is in them that it finds its crowning glory" (*GS* 48 §1, 50).

The Council goes on to say: "Children are the supreme gift of marriage and contribute greatly to the good of the parents themselves..; wishing to associate them in a special way in his own creative work, God blessed man and woman with the words: 'Be fruitful and multiply' (*Gen* 2:18). Hence, true married love and the whole structure of family life which results from it, without diminishment of the other ends of marriage, are directed to disposing the spouses to cooperate valiantly with the love of the Creator and Saviour, who through them will increase and enrich his family from day to day" (*GS* 50 §l).

But the spouses' role does not stop with bringing children into the world. They are also called to educate them. In the words of the Catechism, "The fruitfulness of conjugal love extends to the fruits of the moral, spiritual, and supernatural life that parents hand on to their children by education. Parents are the principal and first educators of their children" (cf. *GE* 3; *CCC* 1653).

6. THE CELEBRATION AND EFFECTS OF MARRIAGE

That brings us to our final topic: the celebration of marriage and its effects. Since Christ sealed his covenant with the Church on the cross by shedding his blood, the "blood of the covenant", it is fitting that when two Catholics marry they do so within the Mass, which makes present the sacrifice of Calvary. In this way they can also receive Communion, sharing in the Body and Blood of Christ which unites them with Christ and with one another.

The minister of the sacrament of Matrimony is the spouses themselves, who give and take each other, thereby conferring the sacrament on one another. The role of the priest or deacon is to receive their exchange of consent on behalf of the Church. For the validity of the marriage, the spouses must marry before a priest or deacon and two witnesses, or they must receive permission from the bishop to marry before some other minister.

The marriage rite consists in the spouses first answering questions about their intentions in entering marriage, after which they exchange consent, promising to be faithful to each another "until death do us part" or "all the days of my life". It is their consent that, so to speak, "makes the marriage", so that if either partner were to withhold consent, there would be no marriage (cf. (*CCL*, can. 1057 § 1; *CCC* 1626). Then comes the blessing of the rings, which are a sign of the spouses' everlasting love and fidelity. When the wedding takes place in Mass, the blessing of the spouses takes place after the Our Father and before Communion.

When a Catholic marries a non-Catholic there is usually no Mass, and the rite of marriage takes place within a Liturgy of the Word, with prayers, readings and a homily. All the parts of the marriage rite are still celebrated.

It is important to know that the spouses receive the sacrament of Matrimony, with all the corresponding graces, only when both spouses are baptised, even though one of them is a baptised Christian of some other denomination. If one of them is not baptised, neither spouse receives the sacrament, but having celebrated their marriage before God and his Church, they can count on all the help from God they will need to live out their marriage commitments. And should the non-baptised spouse later be baptised, both will receive the grace of the sacrament of Matrimony.

As regards the effects of the sacrament, the spouses receive sanctifying grace, the infused virtues and gifts of the Holy Spirit, as well as the special sacramental grace to strengthen them in loving fidelity to their marriage commitments. And once the marriage has been consummated by an act of marital intimacy, the sacrament gives rise to a bond between the spouses that cannot be broken by any human power. As we have seen, through their fidelity to each other the spouses are a sign to the world of God's unconditional love and fidelity to his people.

That concludes our study of the sacraments. In the next lesson we will begin our study of our moral life in Christ, Part III of the Catechism. Until then, may God bless you and keep you in his love.

QUESTIONS FOR DISCUSSION

1. If someone asked you why we need priests in the Church how would you answer?

2. Deacons have had an important role in the Church from the time of the apostles but their role is not always understood and appreciated. What are some of the duties of deacons?

3. Why is stable marriage and family life so important for the life of society?

4. The essential properties of marriage – unity, indissolubility and openness to life – are all consequences of true love. Why is this so?

5. Why is openness to life an essential characteristic of Christian marriage?

POINTS TO REMEMBER

- Holy Orders and Matrimony are the two sacraments at the service of communion.

- Holy Orders is the sacrament through which men are ordained to carry out the ministry of Christ as bishops, priests and deacons.

- The sacrament of Holy Orders is conferred by a bishop through the laying on of hands and a prayer of consecration.

- Although the institution of marriage has existed from the beginning, Christ gave it a special dignity and strengthened it by instituting the sacrament of Matrimony.

- The three essential properties of marriage are unity, indissolubility and openness to life.

- The minister of the sacrament of Matrimony is the spouses themselves.

16. The dignity of the human person

God created man in his own image, in the image of God he created him;
male and female he created them (Gen 1:27)

Summary

Having studied the Creed and the sacraments, we now begin the study of our moral life in Christ, Part Three of the Catechism. This is a most important part, since our earthly and eternal happiness depend on whether we live our lives as God wants. In this lesson and the next we look at some basic principles of moral life in general and then we go on to study specific moral precepts, following the Ten Commandments.

We begin by considering the basis of our dignity as human beings, created in the image and likeness of God and called to eternal life with him. This in turn reminds us of the vocation of everyone to seek holiness, that is to love God and to strive to do his will.

We go on to study what we mean by human freedom and the responsibility for our actions that goes with it. After this we study the three aspects that determine the morality of human acts: the moral object of what we choose, the intention for which we do the act, and the circumstances.

Then we consider the divine moral law, which is God's plan for our happiness and flourishing. It is shown to us in two ways: through our human reason as the natural law, and through revelation as what we call the divine positive law. Lastly, we study the five so-called precepts of the Church, which are Church laws that indicate a basic minimum to be lived if we are to be faithful Catholics.

A warm welcome once again to our journey into truth, our excursion into the marvellous truths taught by Jesus Christ and passed on to us by the Church. In this lesson we begin our study of our moral life in Christ, which is contained in Part III of the *Catechism of the Catholic Church*. The study of our moral life is very important since it concerns how we live, and it is how we live that determines whether we will find the happiness we seek in this life and the eternal happiness to which God has called us in the next.

The more we live "in Christ", in his love, sharing in his own life through grace, doing what pleases him and avoiding what offends him, the happier we will be and the more we will make those around us happy. After all, God does want us to be happy. Christ himself said: "I have said these things to you so that my joy may be in you, and that your joy may be complete" (*Jn* 15:11).

Let us begin with a prayer. Heavenly Father, you have sent your eternal Son into the world to be the way, the truth and the life, to show us the way to happiness both here and hereafter. Help us to learn the truth he teaches about the moral life, so that we may follow his way and come to eternal life with you. We make our prayer through Christ our Lord. Amen.

The Catechism follows the traditional way of presenting the study of morality, beginning with the consideration of moral life in general, including such topics as the dignity of the human person, freedom and responsibility, conscience, sin and the passions. It then goes on to consider particular moral questions, following the Ten Commandments. In this lesson and the next we will look at various issues of morality in general, and then in the following ones we will study the Ten Commandments.

In this lesson we will study five main topics: human dignity and the call to holiness, freedom and responsibility, the morality of human acts, the divine moral law and the precepts of the Church.

1. HUMAN DIGNITY AND THE CALL TO HOLINESS

We recall from our study of the creation of man the words from the book of Genesis: "God created man in his own image, in the image of God he created him, male and female he created them" (*Gen* 1:27). We saw that man is created in the image of God in that he has a spiritual soul, with an intellect capable of knowing God and a free will with which to love him. The Catechism says: "Of all visible creatures, only man is 'able to know and love his creator.' He is 'the only creature on earth that God has willed for its own sake', and he alone is called to share, by knowledge and love, in God's own life ... This is the fundamental reason for his dignity" (*GS* 12, 24; *CCC* 356). That is, animals cannot know and love their creator. Only man, through his intellect and will, can do this, coming to share in God's own life, both here and hereafter. This is the fundamental reason for the dignity of every human being.

What is more, man, unlike the animals, is called to eternal life with God, and we must use our freedom wisely in order to achieve that goal. Pope St Leo the Great, in a homily for Christmas in the fifth century, speaks of the dignity of the human person and of the sort of life we ought to live. He says, "Christian, recognise your dignity and, now that you share in God's own nature, do not return to your former base condition by sinning. Remember who is your head and of whose body you are a member. Never forget that you have been rescued from the power of darkness and brought into the light of the Kingdom of God" (*Sermo 21 in nat. Dom.*, 3; CCC 1691).

And St John Eudes exhorts us to live in such a way as to be very united with Jesus Christ: "I ask you to consider that our Lord Jesus Christ is your true head, and that you are one of his members. He belongs to you as the head belongs to its members; all that is his is yours: his spirit, his heart, his body and soul, and all his faculties... And so he longs for you to use all that is in you, as if it were his own, for the service and glory of the Father" (*Tract. de admirabili corde Jesu*, 1, 5; CCC 1698). Indeed, the more united with Jesus Christ we are through our prayer and actions, the more we will use all our faculties as Jesus did for the service of God the Father. This is holiness and this is happiness.

Everyone wants to be happy but many do not know how to find it. They think that by accumulating goods, by becoming wealthy, by being successful in the world's eyes, they will be happy. But experience teaches us that this is not the way. Many of the wealthiest and most successful people are very unhappy. The authentic happiness we all seek can be found only in living close to God, who is the infinite good and the source of true happiness. St Augustine expresses it beautifully in his *Confessions*: "How is it, then, that I seek you, Lord? Since in seeking you, my God, I seek a happy life, let me seek you so that my soul may live, for my body draws life from my soul and my soul draws life from you" (*Conf.* 10, 20). And of course we all remember those other familiar words of St Augustine, "Lord, you made us for you and our heart is restless until it rests in you" (*Conf.* 1, 1, 1). They remind us that if we want to be truly happy we must put our heart in God.

This putting our heart in God and striving to fulfil his will for us is what we call holiness, or sanctity. Holiness is making the effort to grow ever more in love for God, to respond to his invitation to love him with our whole heart and soul and mind and strength (cf. *Mk* 12:30), and to strive to do always what he is asking of us. When we consider that Jesus loves us to the point of suffering and dying for us, it is understandable that we should love him in return. And since God loves everyone, every single person he has created, it is clear that all are called to love him in return. In the words of the Second Vatican Council, "All Christians in any state or walk of life are called to the fullness of Christian life and to the perfection of charity" (*LG* 40 §2).

What must we do to grow in holiness? Again, the Second Vatican Council gives us the answer: "In order to reach this perfection the faithful should use the strength dealt out to them by Christ's gift, so that... doing the will of the Father in everything, they may wholeheartedly devote themselves to the glory of God and to the service of their neighbour.

Thus the holiness of the People of God will grow in fruitful abundance, as is clearly shown in the history of the Church through the lives of so many saints" (*LG* 40 §2; CCC 2013). As the passage makes clear, holiness consists essentially in doing the will of God, serving God and our neighbour out of love. In order to do this we must be very united with God through prayer, penance and the sacraments. This is within the reach of everyone.

2. FREEDOM AND RESPONSIBILITY

Because we were made in the image and likeness of God, with a spiritual soul, we are radically different from the highest animals. We have a rational intellect and a free will and we are capable of weighing up the various courses of action before us and then deciding freely what to do. Animals cannot do this. They only follow their instincts. As evidence of our rational intelligence, we humans are constantly making progress in so many fields – communication, transportation, medicine, etc. – whereas even the highest animals continue to live in the same way they always have.

What do we mean by freedom? The Catechism answers: "Freedom is the power, rooted in reason and will, to act or not to act, to do this or that, and so to perform deliberate actions on one's own responsibility" (*CCC* 1731). That is, free will involves the power to choose: to act or not to act, to follow one course of action or another. And because the person has deliberately chosen a course of action from among various possibilities, he or she is responsible for that choice. Responsibility necessarily goes with freedom. If we misuse our freedom in human affairs we have to answer to our family, to our employer or the government, and it is the same before God. If we choose rightly and do what God is asking of us, we find happiness and God will reward us both in this life and in the next. And if we go against God's will by committing sin, we will suffer the consequences. Our Lord himself speaks of the reward to be given to those who have been faithful: "Well done, good and faithful servant; you have been faithful over a little, I will set you over much; enter into the joy of your master" (*Mt* 25:23).

What is more, in a graphic expression the Catechism says that "by free will one shapes one's own life. Human freedom is a force for growth and maturity in truth and goodness; it attains its perfection when directed toward God, our beatitude" (CCC 1731). St Gregory of Nyssa expresses the same idea, saying that "we are in a certain way our own parents, creating ourselves as we will, by our decisions" (*De vita Moysis*, II, 2-3; in John Paul II, Enc. *Veritatis Splendor*, 71).

How true this is! The more we use our freedom wisely the more we shape our life for the better. Even more, as the Catechism puts it, "the more one does what is good, the freer one becomes. There is no true freedom except in the service of what is good and just. The choice to disobey and do evil is an abuse of freedom and leads to 'the slavery of sin'" (*CCC* 1733). So it is up to us how we want to live. We can live well and grow in virtue and freedom, or give ourselves over to sin and end up becoming slaves of sin. Anyone who has developed a habit of excessive alcohol consumption, of seeking sexual pleasure or of gambling will readily admit that they are no longer in control and that they have become in some sense a slave of sin. They have diminished their freedom.

Why did God make us free? So that we could do whatever we want? No, he made us free so that we could do whatever God wants and so find the fulfilment we seek both in this life and in the next. The Second Vatican Council sums it up, saying that God made man free "so that he might of his own accord seek his Creator and freely attain his full and blessed perfection by cleaving to him" (*GS* 17; CCC 1730). We want to do this, but how do we determine whether a particular act is the will of God or not? That is, whether it is good or bad, right or wrong? This is our third topic: the morality of human acts.

3. The morality of human acts

The Catechism explains the traditional three aspects of an act that determine its morality, aspects that are known as the sources of morality. Here we cannot go into the question in detail but it is very important to have clear ideas about the basic concepts because they will help us decide how to act in such a way as to find the fulfilment we seek. The three sources of morality of any freely chosen act are the object, the intention and the circumstances.

The first and primary aspect is the *moral object*, that is, the matter of the act. It answers the question, "What am I proposing to do?" For example, the object might be taking what belongs to another, telling a lie, praying or helping our neighbour. By its object an act will be either good or evil. That is, it will either be in conformity with God's law and with the true good of man, or it will be contrary to God's law and to our true good. Summing up – and this is of fundamental importance – there is an objective order of morality. As the Catechism puts it, "Objective norms of morality express the rational order of good and evil, attested to by conscience" (*CCC* 1751). In other words, morality is not something purely subjective or relative. There are some acts which, because they are contrary to the law of God and to the true good of man, are intrinsically evil and therefore always sinful. As the Catechism explains, "There are acts which, in and of themselves, independently of circumstances and intentions, are always gravely illicit by reason of their object; such as blasphemy and perjury, murder and adultery. One may not do evil so that good may result from it… It is therefore an error to judge the morality of human acts by considering only the intention that inspires them or the circumstances (environment, social pressure, duress or emergency, etc.) which supply their context" (*CCC* 1756). In other words, there are moral absolutes. And there are acts that are intrinsically evil.

The second source of morality is the *intention*. The intention is the reason why the act is done, the purpose, the goal sought. It answers the question, "Why am I doing this?" Every person acts for a reason and this reason is called the intention. Like the moral object, the intention is very important in determining the morality of our actions. There are two principles regarding the intention. First, a good intention – that is, one directed to the true good of man – is always necessary for the moral goodness of an act. If the intention is evil, like doing something in order to show off or to get revenge, the act will be sinful. Second, a good intention is not sufficient for the moral goodness of an act. The act itself must also have a good object. For example, one cannot steal or tell a lie in order to help someone in need. We all understand this. We express it in the two well-known phrases, "You cannot do evil that good may come from it" and "The end doesn't justify the means".

The third factor is the *circumstances*. They include such aspects as the time, the place, the possible influence of fear or anger, and so on. In the words of the Catechism, the circumstances are "secondary elements of a moral act. They contribute to increasing or diminishing the moral goodness or evil of human acts" (*CCC* 1754). The Catechism gives as an example the amount of a theft. It is not the same to steal $20 as to steal $20,000. Similarly, it is not the same to tell a joke at home or in a church; it is not the same to be rude to a stranger or to one's mother. Among the circumstances are the emotions, such as fear, anger, love, etc. While the circumstances can increase or diminish both the moral goodness or evil of an act and the person's responsibility, they can never make good or right an action that is in itself evil.

4. THE DIVINE MORAL LAW

We come now to our fourth topic, the divine moral law, which shows us God's plan for our happiness and for our flourishing as human beings. God wants us to be happy and he wants us to be with him forever in heaven, and so, like any good Father, he shows us the way. This is how we should always look on the moral law: as God's fatherly instruction to his children to show them the way to happiness and to warn them against taking the wrong way. In the words of the Catechism, the moral law is "fatherly instruction, God's pedagogy". It "prescribes for man the ways, the rule of conduct that lead to the promised beatitude; it proscribes the ways of evil which turn him away from God and his love" (*CCC* 1950). God's law is like the signposts along the road, pointing out the way to different destinations and warning against the dangers of sharp bends, steep inclines and so on.

God manifests his law to us in two ways: through the human nature he has given us and through revelation. The first way we call the natural law and the second divine positive law.

The natural law

Let us first consider the natural law. Can we come to know some basic principles of morality merely by reflecting on our human nature? Of course we can. We can know, for example, that human society is seriously disrupted if people do not respect one another's marriage, if people kill one another, steal their property, cheat on business deals, etc., and so these actions must be wrong. All civilisations have come to these conclusions and they all have laws regarding marriage, killing, stealing, fraud, etc. This law is called natural both because it is based on human nature and because we can know it by natural means without the need for God's revelation. In the words of St Thomas Aquinas, "The natural law is nothing other than the light of understanding placed in us by God; through it we know what we must do and what we must avoid. God has given this light or law at the creation" (*Dec. praec.* I; *CCC* 1955).

Long before the coming of Christ, civilisations recognised the existence of a natural law. The ancient Greeks and Romans wrote extensively on it. The Roman philosopher and jurist Cicero, for example, who lived in the first century BC, wrote: "For there is a true law: right reason. It is in conformity with nature, is diffused among all men, and is immutable and eternal; its orders summon to duty; its prohibitions turn away from offence ... To replace it with a contrary law is a sacrilege; failure to apply even one of its provisions is forbidden; no one can abrogate it entirely" (*Rep.* III, 22, 33; *CCC* 1956).

In this passage Cicero is pointing out three essential characteristics of the natural law. First, it is *universal*, applicable to all men of all times, because it is based on human nature, which all humans by definition have in common. It is just as wrong to kill an innocent human being in China or Africa as it is in Australia or the United States. Second, it is *eternal*, immutable, unchanging. Because human nature is unchanging it will always be wrong to kill an innocent human being. And third it *cannot be abolished*, any more than the law of gravity, which is based on the physical nature of things, can be abolished. Based on the natural law are human rights, which all humans have for the fact of being human, and the concept of natural justice, which protects these rights.

Divine positive law

In addition to knowing the moral law by reflecting on human nature, we can also know it through God's revelation to us. This second way we call divine positive law. Even though we could know the moral law by reason alone, God in his fatherly providence chose to reveal it to us in a formal, positive way so that all people could know it easily, with firm certainty and with no danger of error. Referring to the Ten Commandments given to Moses on two tablets of stone, St Augustine writes: "God wrote on the tables of the Law what men did not read in their hearts" (*En. in Ps.* 57, 1; *CCC* 1962). God revealed his law both in the Old Testament, especially through the Ten Commandments given to Moses, and in the New Testament through the teachings of Jesus Christ.

The Old Law was holy and spiritual but still imperfect, in that it showed the way to live rightly but it did not give the grace to follow that way. The grace would come with Jesus Christ in the New Law. Nonetheless the Ten Commandments, which reveal the natural law, remain forever valid. Christ himself said: "Do not think that I have come to abolish the law or the prophets; I have come not to abolish but to fulfil. For truly I tell you, until heaven and earth pass away, not one letter, not one stroke of a letter, will pass from the law until all is accomplished" (*Mt* 5:17-18).

The New Law taught by Jesus Christ is the perfection of the divine law. We find it especially in the Sermon on the Mount, where Christ refers back to the commandments of the Old Law and makes them more positive and demanding (cf. *Mt* 5:21-48). At the same time, he gives us the grace to fulfil them, so that through them we are helped to seek true holiness of life. The New Law is summed up in what has come to be called the golden rule: "Whatever you wish that men would do to you, do so to them; this is the law and the prophets" (*Mt* 7:12). Likewise we find it in Christ's "new commandment" to love one another as he has loved us (cf. *Jn* 15: 12; *CCC* 1970).

5. THE PRECEPTS OF THE CHURCH

Just as every country has laws that concretise the natural law for the right ordering of life in society, so the Church has laws that order the life of the Church. They refer to all aspects of the Church's life and activity: its government, worship, property, schools and universities, etc. Five of these laws, which relate to all the faithful, have come to be known as the precepts of the Church. As the Catechism puts it, these precepts are "meant to guarantee to the faithful the indispensable minimum in the spirit of prayer and moral effort, in the growth in love of God and neighbour" (*CCC* 2041).

The first precept is *"You shall attend Mass on Sundays and on holy days of obligation and rest from servile labour."* It requires all Catholics to sanctify Sundays and holy days of obligation by attending Mass and by resting from works and activities that could hinder this dedication to God. Holy days of obligation are special feast days on which we are obliged to attend Mass. In Australia these days are Christmas, celebrated on December 25, and the feast of the Assumption of Our Lady into heaven, celebrated on August 15.

The second precept, *"You shall confess your sins at least once a year"*, ensures preparation for the Eucharist by the reception of the sacrament of Penance. Strictly speaking, it only obliges us to confess any mortal sins we may have committed, but given the great benefits that come from this sacrament, it is good to go to confession frequently.

The third precept, *"You shall humbly receive your Creator in Holy Communion at least during the Easter season"*, guarantees as a minimum the reception of Communion during the long period between Ash Wednesday and Trinity Sunday (*CCC* 2042). But again, given the fruitfulness of the Eucharist, we will want to receive it as often as we can, even daily.

The fourth precept, *"You shall observe the days of fasting and abstinence established by the Church"*, safeguards the days of self-denial and penance which prepare us for the big feast days and help us acquire self mastery. The days of fast and abstinence in Australia are Ash Wednesday and Good Friday. On these days we may eat only one full meal and two smaller meals, and we must abstain from all meat and products made from meat. We should remember too that all Fridays are days of penance, on which we can choose from the areas of prayer, self-denial and works of charity.

The fifth precept, *"You shall help to provide for the needs of the Church"*, obliges us to contribute to the support of our pastors and to the material needs of the parish and the diocese, as well as of the universal Church (*CCC* 2043).

That brings us to the end of our first lesson on aspects of moral life in general. In the next lesson we will look at more such aspects, including the role of conscience, the virtues and emotions, sin and grace.

Until then, may you grow in love for the God who loves you so much he became man and died on the cross for you. God bless you.

QUESTIONS FOR DISCUSSION

1. How would you explain to a friend that human beings have a unique dignity which is altogether different from that of animals, a dignity that makes us a "someone", not a "something"?

2. What do we mean by holiness? If someone asked you why all are called to holiness, how would you answer?

3. What does St Gregory of Nyssa mean when he says that "we are, in a certain way, our parents, creating ourselves as we will, by our decisions"?

4. Many people think that a good intention is sufficient to make an act morally good. What examples could you give to show that this view is obviously wrong?

5. Some people look on the moral law given us by God as a restriction of our freedom. How would you show them that this is not the case?

POINTS TO REMEMBER

- The human person has a unique dignity that comes from being created in the image and likeness of God, with an intellect and free will that enable him to know and love his creator and to be with him forever in heaven.

- Because God has loved us first, all human beings are called to holiness, to love God with our whole heart and soul and to seek to do his will.

- Because we are free to choose how to act, we are also responsible for our acts.

- The three sources of morality of human acts are the moral object, the intention and the circumstances.

- God has made his law known to us through our reason, in what we call the natural law, and through revelation, in what we call divine-positive law.

17. CONSCIENCE, VIRTUES AND SIN

So faith, hope, love abide, these three; but the greatest of these is love
(1 Cor 13:13)

SUMMARY

In this lesson we continue our study of general aspects of moral life, looking at a number of very important topics.

The first is the role of conscience. Is conscience an inner voice that guides us independently of God's law, or does it look to God's law and apply it to the case at hand?

Next we study the virtues, those good habits that help us do what is right and avoid what is wrong. We look first at the four human or cardinal virtues and then at the three theological virtues. Then we study the gifts and fruits of the Holy Spirit, which also help us in our moral life.

Our fourth topic is the role of the emotions, or passions, which can be a big help in living a good life, but can sometimes make it more difficult.

Then we study the important topic of sin, looking at the definition of sin and the different types of sin, especially the distinction between venial, or lesser, sins and mortal, or serious, sins.

Finally, we study another very important help in our moral life, God's grace. We look at the definition of grace and then at three main types of grace.

Welcome back to our journey into truth. In the last lesson we looked at various aspects of moral life in general and today we will consider more such aspects before going on in the next lesson to begin our study of the Ten Commandments.

Let us begin with a prayer. Heavenly Father, in your goodness you made us in your image and likeness and you gave us free will, so that we could use our freedom to know, love and serve you on earth and be happy with you forever in heaven. Help us to understand your plan for us, so that we can live our lives as you want and come to eternal life with you. We make our prayer through Christ our Lord. Amen.

In this lesson we will study six very important topics, about which there is often considerable confusion. It is important to understand them well. The topics are conscience, the virtues, the gifts and fruits of the Holy Spirit, the passions, sin, and grace.

1. CONSCIENCE

If there is one topic about which there is a great deal of ignorance today it is the role of conscience. What is conscience? We all have a general notion of conscience as an inner voice that tells us what is right and wrong. The Catechism gives us the classical definition: "Conscience is a judgment of reason whereby the human person recognises the moral quality of a concrete act that he is going to perform, is in the process of performing, or has already completed" (*CCC* 1778). Looking closely at the definition, we see that conscience is first of all a judgment of reason, of our mind. It is not a feeling or an intuition. It is a judgment. Also, as the definition makes clear, conscience has a role to play in judging the morality of acts already completed, so that we may feel guilty or happy about acts done in the past, even days or years before.

On what basis does conscience make this judgment? It judges on the basis of what we have previously learned about the moral law, especially through the Ten Commandments. That is, conscience is not a law unto itself. Rather it looks to the law of God and applies that law to the particular act we are considering. In this sense it is like a sextant, which sailors use to know where they are by looking at the stars and other heavenly bodies. Without the stars, the sextant is useless. Without the law of God, conscience is blind.

This implies the important duty to form our conscience well: to learn God's law. We are doing this right now by studying moral life on our journey into truth. We have done it in the past too through what our parents taught us, what we learned in school, what we have heard from our pastors, what we have read and so on. Only when we have a well-formed conscience can we make judgements "in conformity with the true good willed by the wisdom of the Creator", as the Catechism puts it (*CCC* 1783). If we have doubts about the morality of an act, a good source is precisely the *Catechism of the Catholic Church*. It covers all the important moral issues and is an authoritative source of the Church's teaching. The Catechism makes the important point that "the education of conscience is indispensable for human beings who are subjected to negative influences and tempted by sin to prefer their own judgment and to reject authoritative teachings" (*CCC* 1783). When we are tempted to sin we will always find it easier to prefer our own judgment to that of God, but we should be honest enough to listen to what God is telling us and then follow it.

Are we obliged to follow our conscience? Yes we are, whenever our conscience is certain, not doubtful, and it is commanding or forbidding us to do something. To act against our conscience in that situation would be to commit sin, since we would be acting against what we understood to be the will of God. If on the other hand our conscience is doubtful, not certain, and we are unsure of whether the act is right or wrong, we should make every effort to resolve the doubt, consulting the Catechism or asking someone who we trust will give us the correct answer in keeping with the Church's teaching.

Is it possible to have an erroneous conscience? Yes it is, when for whatever reason we have not learned properly the teachings of the Church. If we are unaware that our conscience is in error we can still follow it, but if we become aware that we are mistaken we should make the effort to correct the error. As we have seen, God has given us his law to lead us to a happy and fruitful life, and we should therefore make the effort to find out what his law is. When we go against it we always suffer, both here and possibly hereafter.

2. THE VIRTUES

A big help in following our conscience and living the kind of life God wants for us is to grow in the virtues. What are virtues? The Catechism says: "A virtue is an habitual and firm disposition to do the good" (*CCC* 1803). More simply, virtues are good habits that facilitate doing what is good, just as vices are bad habits that facilitate doing what is wrong. The stronger the virtues, the easier it is to do what is right. The virtues can be divided broadly into human virtues, which we can acquire ourselves by the repetition of good acts, and infused virtues, which God infuses directly into the soul along with grace. We have already referred to them when we studied the sacraments, especially Baptism.

The human virtues

As regards the human virtues, the Catechism teaches: "Human virtues are firm attitudes, stable dispositions, habitual perfections of intellect and will that govern our actions, order our passions, and guide our conduct according to reason and faith. They make possible ease, self-mastery, and joy in leading a morally good life" (*CCC* 1804). There are four principal human virtues, sometimes called cardinal virtues, from the Latin word for hinge, since the other human virtues hinge on these four. They are mentioned in the book of Wisdom (cf. *Wis* 8:7) and ancient philosophers like Aristotle also wrote about them. These virtues are prudence, justice, fortitude and temperance. We acquire the human virtues by repeating good acts, so that each time we do the act it becomes easier and it forms a stronger habit. Just as the more someone practises the piano or a sport, the better they become at it and the easier it is for them, so the more we exercise the virtues, the easier it becomes for us to do what is right.

The Catechism defines *prudence* as "the virtue that disposes practical reason to discern our true good in every circumstance and to choose the right means of achieving it" (*CCC* 1806). That is, prudence helps us both to know what is our true good and to choose the best way of achieving it. It is prudence that guides the judgment of our conscience.

What is *justice*? In the words of the Catechism, "Justice is the moral virtue that consists in the constant and firm will to give their due to God and neighbour" (*CCC* 1807). In simple terms, justice commands us to give to each one what is owed to him. This includes God, to whom we owe our whole being, and so we worship God through the virtue of religion. We live justice with our neighbour by respecting his rights, being fair in all our dealings, observing the terms of contracts, paying lawful debts, etc. Justice is a fundamental virtue for harmony and stability in society. Without it there can be no peace. Indeed, the Second Vatican Council calls peace "the work of justice" (*GS* 78).

Fortitude is "the moral virtue that ensures firmness in difficulties and constancy in the pursuit of the good" (*CCC* 1808). Fortitude is sometimes called courage, and it is associated with will power. It helps us to resist temptations and to do what is right, even in the face of difficulties. For example, we need fortitude to overcome laziness and softness, to raise a family well, to succeed in our job, to grow in holiness, and so on. It can be likened to the spurs with which the rider urges the horse to continue running hard until the end of the race.

Temperance, in the words of the Catechism, is "the moral virtue that moderates the attraction of pleasures and provides balance in the use of created goods" (*CCC* 1809). Whereas fortitude is associated with a difficult good and it strengthens the will to pursue that good in spite of the difficulties, temperance is associated with a pleasurable good and its role is to moderate the unbridled search for that pleasure. It is associated with chastity in the pleasures of the flesh, sobriety in the pleasures of drink, and abstinence in the pleasures of food. It can be likened to the reins that hold the horse back.

It is important to know that, although the cardinal virtues are human virtues which anyone can acquire by the repetition of acts, they are also infused in the soul by God along with sanctifying grace. But unless the human virtues are firmly grounded in the soul, the infused virtues will have little effect in strengthening the person. For example, a man who is given over to drink will not change overnight simply because he becomes baptised and receives the infused virtue of temperance. In this sense the human virtues are fundamental in living a good life.

The theological virtues

In addition to the human virtues, which we can acquire on our own, God also gives us three infused virtues, known as the theological virtues, from the Greek word for God, *theos*. They are faith, hope and charity and they are essential if we are to grow in a true relationship of intimacy with God.

The Catechism defines *faith* as "the theological virtue by which we believe in God and believe all that he has said and revealed to us, and that Holy Church proposes for our belief, because he is truth itself" (*CCC* 1814). Faith gives us belief both in God himself and in what he has taught, based on his truthfulness. But since we may not be exactly sure what God has revealed, since the Scriptures can admit of different interpretations, we believe whatever "Holy Church proposes for our belief." Christ, after all, gave the Church the assistance of the Holy Spirit to guide her in the mission of teaching down the ages. Therefore, we can be sure that whatever the Church proposes for our belief is true. Faith also leads us to trust in God and surrender our whole lives to him.

What is *hope*? The Catechism answers: "Hope is the theological virtue by which we desire the kingdom of heaven and eternal life as our happiness, placing our trust in Christ's promises and relying not on our own strength, but on the help of the grace of the Holy Spirit" (*CCC* 1817). Thus hope is a longing for a good together with the trust that we will obtain it. It is sometimes defined as "the firm expectation of a difficult good not yet possessed". The object of hope is twofold: eternal life and the grace we need to attain it. We hope in God because he is faithful to his promises and he is all powerful and merciful.

"*Charity* is the theological virtue by which we love God above all things for his own sake, and our neighbour as ourselves for the love of God" (*CCC* 1822). In simple terms, charity is love for both God and neighbour. The reason why we love God is his goodness. We love God for his own sake and we love our neighbour for the sake of God.

Jesus calls charity the "new commandment" (cf. *Jn* 13:34). What is new is not the commandment to love but rather the way in which we are to love: "That you love one another as I have loved you" (*Jn* 15:12). Jesus loved us by sacrificing his life for us, and we should love others with generosity and a spirit of sacrifice. What is more, loving God is not just a matter of feelings; it is a matter of showing love by deeds, especially by keeping the commandments. After all, Jesus says: "Abide in my love. If you keep my commandments, you will abide in my love" (*Jn* 15:9-10; *CCC* 1824).

Charity is the most important of all the virtues since it unites us directly with God. In this sense St Paul writes: "So faith, hope, charity abide, these three. But the greatest of these is charity" (*1 Cor* 13:13).

3. THE GIFTS AND FRUITS OF THE HOLY SPIRIT

In addition to the virtues, we are helped to live a moral life and grow in holiness by the gifts of the Holy Spirit. What are these gifts? The Catechism defines them as "permanent dispositions which make man docile in following the promptings of the Holy Spirit" (*CCC* 1830). Their role, as the Catechism says, is to make us more docile to the promptings of the Holy Spirit in our soul. The Holy Spirit, for example, may give us the inspiration to pray, to show kindness to a stranger, to contact a friend or to do an act of penance, and the gifts help us to carry out these inspirations.

How do the gifts differ from the virtues? Whereas we exercise the virtues ourselves through freely chosen acts helped by grace, it is the Holy Spirit who moves us to make use of the gifts. Our role is to be docile to this action of the Holy Spirit. For example, a person wanting to convince a friend to go to confession may prepare the conversation very well, using the virtue of prudence. But in the actual conversation she may suddenly think of an argument she has never thought of before, inspired by the Holy Spirit through the gift of counsel. In this sense the gifts are likened by spiritual writers to the sails of a ship that catch the winds of the Holy Spirit, while the virtues are likened to the oars, which the crew must pull themselves.

How do we acquire the gifts? They are infused in the soul along with sanctifying grace, so that we will have them as long as we are in the state of grace. How many gifts are there? The tradition of the Church, following the prophecy of Isaiah, lists seven: wisdom, understanding, knowledge, counsel, fortitude, piety and fear of the Lord (cf. *Is* 11:1-2). The Catechism says that they "complete and perfect the virtues of those who receive them" (*CCC* 1831).

As a result of living close to God, helped by the virtues and the gifts of the Holy Spirit, we experience what have come to be called the "fruits of the Holy Spirit." They are like benefits or results of a life lived according to the law of God, according to the Spirit. The Catechism calls them "perfections that the Holy Spirit forms in us as the first fruits of eternal glory" (*CCC* 1832). St Paul lists them when contrasting the fruits of a life lived according to the spirit with those of a life following the flesh. Although St Paul lists nine, tradition has given us twelve: charity, joy, peace, patience, kindness, goodness, generosity, gentleness, faithfulness, modesty, self-control and chastity (cf. *Gal* 5:22-23).

4. THE PASSIONS

That brings us to the passions, which are perhaps better known as emotions. The Catechism defines passions as "emotions or movements of the sensitive appetite that incline us to act or not to act in regard to something felt or imagined to be good or evil" (*CCC* 1763). The Catechism summarises the basic passions: "The most fundamental passion is *love*, aroused by the attraction of the good. Love causes a *desire* for the absent good and the *hope* of obtaining it; this movement finds completion in the pleasure and *joy* of the good possessed. The apprehension of evil causes *hatred*, *aversion*, and *fear* of the impending evil; this movement ends in *sadness* at some present evil, or in the *anger* that resists it" (*CCC* 1765).

The passions are part of our makeup. Christ too experienced them. They are simply natural responses to something perceived to be good or evil, and God has given them to us for a good reason. We readily understand that emotions like love, joy, hope and desire help us to seek and enjoy the good things of life. But passions like fear, anger and hatred also help us – in this case to avoid what is evil or harmful. While it is good to hate sin, we should never hate the sinner who commits it.

How do the passions influence our acts? Firstly, given that they are simply feelings, not acts of the will, they are neither sinful nor meritorious in themselves. Just as it is not sinful to feel hungry or cold, it is not sinful to feel angry or sad. Only when the will enters and we freely choose to do something or not to do it do the passions influence the morality of our acts. The passions fall into the category of circumstances, which we considered in the last lesson. As we recall, the circumstances can make a good act more or less meritorious, or a sinful one more or less sinful, but they can never make an act good that is in itself evil. Thus, for example, if we feel angry towards someone who has hurt us and we give in to the anger, abusing the person by our speech, we will have sinned, even though the sin will be less culpable because we were moved by anger. But if we feel angry and make an effort to treat the person well, our kindness will be all the more meritorious because we had to go against the feeling of anger.

The passions can be very helpful in the moral life. For example, the deeply felt passion of love for God facilitates prayer, penance and works of charity. But when the love for God is not felt, when we experience rather spiritual dryness and a lack of desire, our prayer, penance and works of charity will be even more meritorious, because they require a greater act of the will, a greater love in the true sense of willing the good of another.

5. SIN

While we are called to a life of holiness, a true "life in Christ", and we are given the virtues and gifts of the Holy Spirit to help us grow in it, we don't always succeed in doing what we ought, and we sometimes offend God by sin. What do we mean by sin? A simple definition is "a wilful violation of God's law". For something to be sinful, it must be wilful, in the sense that we freely choose it, and it must be a violation of a law of God. The sin can be by thought, word, deed or omission of something we ought to have done. In addition to being an offence against God, who truly loves us and wants us to be happy, sin also hurts us, as we have seen.

What kinds of sins are there? The most important classification is the traditional one of venial and mortal sins; that is, the distinction between lesser sins and more serious ones. The word mortal comes from the Latin word for death, and mortal sin kills the life of grace and friendship with God in the soul. We find this distinction in the first letter of St John: "If any one sees his brother committing what is not a mortal sin, he will ask, and God will give him life for those whose sin is not mortal. There is sin which is mortal; I do not say that one is to pray for that. All wrongdoing is sin, but there is sin which is not mortal" (*1 Jn* 5:16-17). In simple terms, venial sins are lesser sins which do not destroy the state of friendship with God, although they do wound our relationship with him. Mortal sins destroy this relationship. In the words of the Catechism, "Mortal sin destroys charity in the heart of man by a grave violation of God's law; it turns man away from God, who is his ultimate end and his beatitude, by preferring an inferior good to him. Venial sin allows charity to subsist, even though it offends and wounds it" (*CCC* 1855). When the Catechism says that mortal sin destroys charity in the heart, it means that it takes away the state of sanctifying grace, of divine life in the soul, that we first received in Baptism. Through mortal sin we pass from the state of grace to the state of mortal sin.

For a sin to be *mortal* three conditions must be met. First, it must involve *grave matter*, like adultery, murder, stealing a large sum of money, etc. Second there must be *full knowledge* not only that the act is wrong but that it is seriously so: that it is a mortal sin. And third, there must be *deliberate consent*. If any of these conditions is lacking the sin may be venial or no sin at all. For example, if the person knew that something was wrong but not that it was a mortal sin, God would hold the person responsible for a venial sin but not for mortal sin. And if the person had no idea that it was wrong at all, due to an erroneous conscience, God would not hold them responsible for any sin, even venial. Similarly, strong passion could reduce the deliberateness of the consent, reducing the culpability of the sin.

As regards the effects of mortal sin, the principal one is the loss of the state of grace and with it, as we have seen, the eternal punishment of hell unless the person repents. Mortal sin, like venial sin, also involves temporal punishment, which must be made up either on earth through penance, good deeds and indulgences, or in Purgatory. The person cannot receive Communion until the sin has been absolved in the sacrament of Penance. Not only does the person lose all the merit they had acquired through their good acts, but they cannot gain any merit while in the state of mortal sin. Nonetheless, when they go to Confession they will regain all the merits they have lost. So it is clear that mortal sin is not just a broken rule but a serious disruption of our relationship with our loving Father God and it has serious consequences. But God is ever merciful and always ready to forgive us and restore us to friendship with him. We should seek his forgiveness regularly in the sacrament of Penance.

6. GRACE

We have been referring to grace throughout this course, especially when we studied original sin and the sacraments, so it will be sufficient here to recall briefly the main points.

First we should ask what we mean by the word grace. In general the word refers, as the Catechism says, to a "favour, the free and undeserved help that God gives us to respond to his call to become children of God, adoptive sons, partakers of the divine nature and of eternal life" (*CCC* 1996). That is, grace is a gift from God, a favour, something undeserved.

There are three main types of grace. The first is *sanctifying grace*. We spoke of it at length when we considered Baptism. There we saw that sanctifying grace is a sharing in the very life of God. We receive it for the first time in Baptism and it remains in the soul, as an habitual grace, as long as we do not lose it through mortal sin. This grace truly sanctifies – it makes us holy. As effects of sanctifying grace, we become children of God and heirs of heaven, the Blessed Trinity comes to dwell in our soul and, in the words of St Peter, we are made sharers in the divine nature (cf. *2 Pet* 1:4).

The second type of grace is what we call *actual grace*. Whereas sanctifying grace is an habitual grace which remains in the soul, actual grace is a passing help which God gives us to enable us to carry out good deeds. He gives actual grace to anyone who needs it: to non-believers to lead them to believe, to sinners to lead them to repent, to believers to lead them to pray or do penance, etc. We are constantly receiving actual graces from God and we should respond to them with docility so that God can lead us ever closer to him.

The third type of grace, as we have seen, is *sacramental grace*, a grace proper to each sacrament, which disposes us to live out the specific purpose of that sacrament.

That concludes our study of general aspects of moral life. In the next lesson we will begin our consideration of particular moral issues, following the Ten Commandments. Until then, may God draw you ever closer to him and fill you with his love. God bless you!

QUESTIONS FOR DISCUSSION

1. Many people think of conscience as an inner voice that automatically tells them what is right and wrong. What is conscience and why is it so important to form it well?

2. Why is it so important to grow in virtues, and how do we go about it?

3. We all have emotions, both positive ones like desire, hope and love and negative ones like fear, anger and hatred. How can we use the emotions to come closer to God and what must we do to avoid them leading us into sin?

4. While we want to do what is pleasing to God we all sin. What are some of the effects of mortal sin that make this type of sin so bad, and what can we do to commit it less often?

5. A big help in the spiritual life is God's grace. What can we do to receive more grace from God and how we can use these graces more effectively?

POINTS TO REMEMBER

- Conscience is a judgment of reason by which we recognise the morality of an act we are about to do, are doing or have done in the past.

- Virtues are good habits that make it easier to do good acts.

- The principal virtues are the theological virtues of faith, hope and charity and the cardinal virtues of prudence, justice, fortitude and temperance.

- The seven gifts of the Holy Spirit make us docile in following the promptings of the Holy Spirit.

- The passions are feelings or emotions that, while neither sinful nor meritorious in themselves, can help us do what is right and avoid doing what is wrong.

- Sin is a wilful violation of God's law.

- Venial sins are lesser sins which do not destroy our friendship with God, and mortal sins are serious sins which destroy the life of grace in the soul.

- Sanctifying grace is a sharing in the very life of God, and actual grace is a passing help from God.

18. THE FIRST THREE COMMANDMENTS

What great nation is there, that has statutes and ordinances so righteous as all this law which I set before you this day? (Deut 4:8)

SUMMARY

Having looked at general aspects of our moral life in the last two lessons, we come now to a detailed study of the Ten Commandments. In this lesson we study the first three commandments, all of which relate to the worship of God.

We begin by studying the reason why God gave us the commandments, which was to show us the way to happiness here on earth and to happiness hereafter in heaven, and also the importance of keeping the commandments.

Then we study the first commandment, which commands us to worship the one true God through the virtues of faith, hope, charity and religion, and to avoid sins against these virtues. We look especially at various present-day sins against this commandment.

Next we study the second commandment, which commands us to honour the name of God and to avoid such sins as blasphemy and taking false oaths.

Finally we study the third commandment of keeping the Lord's day holy. We look at the reasons why we should attend Mass every Sunday and why we should abstain from unnecessary work on that day.

Welcome once again to our journey into truth, our study of the marvellous truths of the Catholic faith. I hope you are enjoying the journey and that you are not only growing in knowledge of the faith but also coming to love it and to order your life in accordance with it. After all, we cannot be Catholics in name only. We must practise what we preach. Apart from bringing us closer to God and giving us the happiness we all seek, our example will also be a powerful force for evangelisation, for spreading the faith. As the Second Vatican Council says, "The witness of a Christian life and good works done in a supernatural spirit have great power to draw men to the faith and to God" (*AA* 6).

In this lesson we begin our study of the Ten Commandments and let us begin, as usual, with a prayer. Heavenly Father, in your goodness you revealed the moral law to us so that all could know it easily and without error. Help us to learn your law well, so that we can direct our lives in accordance with it and find the holiness and happiness you want for us. We make our prayer through Christ our Lord. Amen.

In this lesson we will study four topics. First, the reason for the commandments, and then the first three commandments, one by one.

1. THE REASON FOR THE COMMANDMENTS

We remember that God gave us the Ten Commandments through Moses to show us the way to happiness and to heaven. God is a loving father and he wanted to make easier our journey through life to our final destination of heaven, and so he revealed his law to us. He did it at the same time as he renewed his covenant with his people through Moses. He would be their God and they would be his people. The way they would honour the covenant and show their love for God was by keeping the commandments. This is the way we should always see the commandments. They are not merely laws to be fulfilled, but rather our loving response to the God who has loved us first and has called us to himself.

Keeping the commandments is important not only for our happiness here on earth but also for our eternal salvation. Our Lord himself said this to the young man who asked him, "Teacher, what good deed must I do, to have eternal life?" Jesus answered, "If you would enter life, keep the commandments" (*Mt* 19:16-19). So, a great deal is at stake. It is therefore very important that we learn God's law well so that we will know what is right and wrong and we can live our lives accordingly. To this end it is a very good idea to memorise the Ten Commandments, if you don't know them already.

The Ten Commandments are based on the natural law, which God has done us the favour of revealing to us. St Irenaeus puts it very succinctly: "From the beginning, God had implanted in the heart of man the precepts of the natural law. Then he was content to remind him of them. This was the Decalogue" (*Adv. haeres.* 4, 15, 1; *CCC* 2070). The word "Decalogue", by the way, comes from the Greek, meaning literally "ten words", and is another name for the Ten Commandments.

Since they are based on the natural law, the Ten Commandments oblige everyone. The Catechism is very clear: "Since they express man's fundamental duties towards God and towards his neighbour, the Ten Commandments reveal, in their primordial content, grave obligations. They are fundamentally immutable, and they oblige always and everywhere. No one can dispense from them" (*CCC* 2072).

As we will see, the Ten Commandments can be divided into two groups. The first three relate to love for God and the last seven to love for our neighbour. Jesus himself summarised them when he was asked which commandment was the greatest. He answered: "You shall love the Lord your God with all your heart, and with all your soul, and with all your mind. This is the greatest and first commandment. And a second is like it: You shall love your neighbour as yourself. On these two commandments hang all the Law and the prophets" (*Mt* 22:37-40).

In this lesson we will study the first three commandments. They relate to the worship of the one God, to honouring his name and to keeping the Lord's day holy.

2. THE FIRST COMMANDMENT – "I AM THE LORD YOUR GOD: YOU SHALL NOT HAVE STRANGE GODS BEFORE ME"

The first commandment is "I am the Lord your God: you shall not have strange gods before me" (*Ex* 20:2-3). The commandment in simple terms commands us to worship the one true God and to avoid sins against this worship. How do we worship God? The Catechism lists several ways.

First, we worship him by exercising the virtues of faith, hope and charity. By *faith* we believe in God and in everything he has revealed because God is Truth and everything he teaches us is true. At the same time we should avoid sins against faith. Among them is *voluntary doubt* of a truth revealed by God. While we can all have temptations to doubt, we should not give in to the temptation by accepting the doubt voluntarily. This sin can be serious, because it endangers the priceless and fundamental gift of faith. Even worse than voluntary doubt is the sin of *heresy*, where we obstinately deny a truth revealed by God. We say "obstinately", meaning that even after we have been warned that what we are saying is contrary to Catholic teaching, we persist in the denial. Other sins against faith are *apostasy*, which is the total rejection of the Catholic faith, and *schism*, the refusal to submit to the authority of the Pope.

We worship God too by the virtue of *hope*, trusting that the all powerful and all merciful God will give us all the means we need to reach heaven. There are two principal sins against hope: despair and presumption. By *despair* we cease to hope that God will save us or that he will forgive our sins. The sin is contrary to God's goodness and mercy. God will always forgive us, if we are truly sorry. By *presumption*, we presume either that we can save ourself without God's help, or that God will save us without any effort on our part.

By the virtue of *charity*, we worship God by showing him our love. Sins against charity include *lukewarmness*, or negligence in our spiritual struggle; *ingratitude*, or lack of appreciation for God's gifts to us; and *hatred of God*.

We also worship God through the acts of the *virtue of religion*, which include adoration, prayer and sacrifice. We worship him too by our *promises* and *vows*. We make *promises* to him in the sacraments of Baptism, Confirmation, Matrimony and Holy Orders, and we can also make personal promises to say a particular prayer, attend Mass more often, offer particular sacrifices, avoid a particular occasion of sin, and so on. Faithfulness to these promises is very pleasing to God. Some people may also make *vows* to God, by which they formally commit themselves to do some good act or live particular virtues. Most vocations in the Church require the person to make vows.

The first commandment not only commands us to worship the true God in the ways we have just considered, it also forbids worshipping false gods. The Catechism lists several such sins. The first is *superstition*. The classical definition of superstition, given by St Thomas Aquinas, is: "the vice inclining man to render divine worship either to a creature who does not deserve it or in a way contrary to its nature." The Catechism says of it: "Superstition is the deviation of religious feeling and of the practices this feeling imposes. It can even affect the worship we offer the true God, e.g., when one attributes an importance in some way magical to certain practices otherwise lawful or necessary. To attribute the efficacy of prayers or of sacramental signs to their mere external performance, apart from the interior dispositions that they demand, is to fall into superstition" (*CCC* 2111). For example, to think that our prayers will be heard only when we are kneeling in front of an image of Our Lady with candles lit on either side is a form of superstition. God will always hear and answer our prayers. As the Catechism says, what most matters is our interior dispositions, not the external performance of our acts.

Superstition can take many forms. The first is *idolatry*, which is the worship of idols or of any false god, such as the god of some other religion or even Satan. The Catechism points out that idolatry can be more wide ranging than we at first think. It says, "Man commits idolatry whenever he honours and reveres a creature in place of God, whether this be gods or demons (for example, satanism), power, pleasure, race, ancestors, the state, money, etc. Jesus says, 'You cannot serve God and mammon'" (*Mt* 6:24; *CCC* 2113). This point gives us much food for thought. While we can pursue goals such as professional success, fitness, success in sport, or even wealth, we should never turn them into a false god which takes precedence over our other duties.

Another form of superstition is *divination*, which seeks to predict or know by improper means what we cannot know naturally. The Catechism is very clear: "All forms of divination are to be rejected: recourse to Satan or demons, conjuring up the dead or other practices falsely supposed to 'unveil' the future. Consulting horoscopes, astrology, palm reading, interpretation of omens and lots, the phenomena of clairvoyance, and recourse to mediums all conceal a desire for power over time, history and, in the last analysis, other human beings, as well as a wish to conciliate hidden powers. They contradict the honour, respect and loving fear that we owe to God alone" (*CCC* 2116). One could add such practices as the use of ouija boards and tarot cards. A good Christian does not seek to know what he cannot know by natural means but rather puts himself trustingly in the hands of God and his providence, giving up unhealthy curiosity about these matters. What is more, one can sometimes be playing into the hands of Satan by seeking this knowledge. Other ways of sinning against God by superstition are *magic* and *sorcery*, "by which one attempts to tame occult powers, so as to place them at one's service and have a supernatural power over others" (*CCC* 2117).

The Catechism also mentions *irreligion* as a sin against the first commandment. If superstition is a perverse "excess" of religion, irreligion or irreverence is a lack of true religion. The Catechism mentions three forms of irreligion: tempting God, sacrilege and simony.

In the words of the Catechism, "*Tempting God* consists in putting his goodness and almighty power to test by word or deed" (*CCC* 2119). In a word it is to hope for an unusual manifestation of God's power, for example by expecting God to help us pass an exam when we haven't studied, or to reach our destination safely when we are driving recklessly. As regards *sacrilege*, the Catechism says that it "consists in profaning or treating unworthily the sacraments and other liturgical actions, as well as persons, things or places consecrated to God. Sacrilege is a grave sin especially when committed against the Eucharist, for in this sacrament the true Body of Christ is made substantially present for us" (*CCC* 2120). Examples of sacrilege include receiving Communion in the state of mortal sin, failing to confess knowingly a mortal sin in the sacrament of Penance, and using a chalice or other sacred vessel for a profane purpose. *Simony* is the buying or selling of spiritual things. It would be simony, for example, to sell a Rosary for more than the value of the Rosary itself simply because it has been blessed by the Pope.

Another important sin against the first commandment is *atheism*, which denies the existence of God. Atheism can be theoretical, in the case of a person who openly denies that God exists, or practical, in the case of a person who simply lives as if God did not exist. Atheism is often based on pride, on a false sense of human self-sufficiency, where the person rejects any dependence on a higher power, wanting to be their own God. We should pray very much for those in this situation, as well as for *agnostics*, who say it is impossible to know whether there is a God.

What does the Church teach regarding having statues and other images of Our Lord, Our Lady and the saints in our churches and homes? Is this not a form of idolatry? It would certainly be idolatry if we worshipped these statues, as the Israelites did when they made and worshipped the golden calf (cf. *Ex* 32:1-35), but we do not worship them. We use them to remind us of Our Lord, Our Lady and the saints, so that we can honour them and pray to them, just as we have photos of our loved ones in our homes to remind us of them. While the longer formulation of the first commandment forbids making images and worshipping them (cf. *Ex* 20:4), God himself in the Old Testament commanded the Israelites to make certain images: the bronze serpent, the ark of the covenant, the cherubim, etc. (cf. *CCC* 2130). The Catechism sums it up: "The honour paid to sacred images is a 'respectful veneration,' not the adoration due to God alone" (*CCC* 2132).

3. THE SECOND COMMANDMENT: "YOU SHALL NOT TAKE THE NAME OF THE LORD YOUR GOD IN VAIN"

The second commandment is "You shall not take the name of the Lord your God in vain." Even though in a sense the first commandment, which refers to the proper worship of God, includes honouring the name of God, God wanted to emphasise the importance of the divine name by giving us a separate commandment relating to it. We read in Scripture: "O LORD, our Lord, how majestic is your name in all the earth!" (*Ps* 8:1) In human affairs someone reveals his name to others only when there is a certain relationship of trust between them. God, entering into a close relationship with his people, revealed his name to Moses from the burning bush, calling himself Yahweh, "I am who I am" (*Ex* 3:14). As the Catechism says in an earlier point: "A name expresses a person's essence and identity and the meaning of this person's life. God has a name; he is not an anonymous force. To disclose one's name is to make oneself known to others; in a way it is to hand oneself over by becoming accessible, capable of being known more intimately and addressed personally" (*CCC* 203).

Therefore, the second commandment commands us to use God's name with great respect, to witness to it by professing our faith before others without fear, and to keep any promises made to others in God's name. It forbids *blasphemy*, which "consists in uttering against God – inwardly or outwardly – words of hatred, reproach, or defiance, in speaking ill of God, in failing in respect toward him in one's speech, in misusing God's name" (*CCC* 2148). This includes any abuse of the names of Jesus Christ, Our Lady, the saints and the Church, which are all closely related to God. The Catechism says that while blasphemy is in itself a grave sin, because it offends God himself (cf. *CCC* 2148) , it can be a venial sin due to lack of deliberation, ignorance or the force of habit which one is trying to overcome. It is good to know that to say "O my God!", for example when witnessing an accident, is not blasphemy, but to say "Jesus Christ" in anger certainly would be.

The second commandment also forbids *taking a false oath*. As the Catechism explains, "Taking an oath or swearing is to take God as witness to what one affirms. It is to invoke the divine truthfulness as a pledge of one's own truthfulness" (*CCC* 2150). Therefore it is a serious matter to take a false oath. This includes lying under oath in court, which is the sin of perjury, and swearing under oath to do something when one has no intention of doing it. In general, except when demanded by the situation, as in court, we should avoid taking unnecessary oaths. As Jesus said, "You have heard that it was said to the men of old, 'You shall not swear falsely, but shall perform to the Lord what you have sworn.' But I say to you, do not swear at all... Let what you say be simply 'Yes' or 'No'; anything more than this comes from the evil one" (*Mt* 5:33-34).

4. THE THIRD COMMANDMENT: "REMEMBER TO KEEP HOLY THE LORD'S DAY"

This brings us to the third commandment, "Remember to keep holy the Lord's Day". God commanded the Israelites to rest on the seventh day of the week, the Sabbath, just as he himself had rested on the seventh day after working for six days in the creation of the world. He told them, "The seventh day is a sabbath of solemn rest, holy to the LORD" (*Ex* 31:15). The word *sabbath*, by the way, means precisely *rest*.

For the Jews, the sabbath was the seventh day of the week, Saturday, and it is on that day that they still celebrate the Lord's day. But the first Christians began to worship God on the first day of the week, Sunday. In the *Acts of the Apostles* St Luke tells us: "On the first day of the week, when we were gathered together to break bread..." (*Acts* 20:7). The breaking of the bread was of course the celebration of the Eucharist.

The first Christians celebrated on Sunday for several reasons: it was on Sunday that Jesus rose from the dead, Sunday was the first day of creation, and being also the eighth day, it symbolises the new creation ushered in by Christ's Resurrection. St Justin, in the middle of the second century, explains this practice: "We all gather on the day of the sun, for it is the first day [after the Jewish sabbath, but also the first day] when God, separating matter from darkness, made the world; and on this same day Jesus Christ our Saviour rose from the dead" (*1 Apol.* 67; *CCC* 2174).

The Catechism calls Sunday "the foremost holy day of obligation in the universal Church" (*CIC*, can. 1246 §1; *CCC* 2177) and therefore it is a day on which we attend Mass. When we consider how good God has been to us in becoming man and in dying on the cross for us, and how much he has blessed us throughout the week, the least we can do on Sunday is make the sacrifice to attend Mass to worship him and thank him for all his blessings. When we do this, he gives himself to us through his Word in the readings, through the prayers and especially through holy Communion. In view of this we can apply to our attendance at Mass Christ's question to the apostles in the Garden of Gethsemane, "Could you not watch with me one hour"? (*Mt* 26:40)

In this we are edified by the example of so many Catholics who go to great lengths to attend Mass each Sunday and even during the week, and so many Christian martyrs down the ages who risked their very lives to attend Mass. In one incident early in the fourth century, forty-nine Christians were arrested and put to death in Abitene in North Africa while attending Mass in a home. When the Roman official asked them why they had defied the edict of the emperor which forbade attending Mass they answered, "We cannot live without Sunday".

Although we should want to attend Mass anyway for the reasons we have given, the Church has always taught that attendance is a serious obligation. In the words of the Catechism, "The Sunday Eucharist is the foundation and confirmation of all Christian practice. For this reason the faithful are obliged to participate in the Eucharist on days of obligation, unless excused for a serious reason (for example, illness, the care of infants) or dispensed by their own pastor. Those who deliberately fail in this obligation commit a grave sin" (*CCC* 2181). Apart from the examples of illness and the care of infants given in the Catechism, other serious reasons that would excuse someone from attending Mass would be the need to work or the great distance one would have to travel. If there is no Mass in the place, or for any other reason it is simply impossible to attend, there is of course no obligation. Days of obligation on which we must attend Mass are all Sundays and those days which the bishops' conference in each country has declared to be such. In Australia the holy days of obligation are Christmas day and the feast of the Assumption of Our Lady into heaven, August 15.

Apart from attending Mass we should also rest from unnecessary work on Sundays in order to regain our strength and spend time with God and our family. What types of activities should we avoid on Sundays? The Catechism answers: "On Sundays and other holy days of obligation, the faithful are to refrain from engaging in work or activities that hinder the worship owed to God, the joy proper to the Lord's Day, the performance of the works of mercy, and the appropriate relaxation of mind and body" (*CCC* 2185). Naturally, family needs – for example the need to prepare meals – or other important services can excuse us from the obligation of Sunday rest. But we should be careful not to let legitimate excuses on a given occasion become habitual. For example, as a general rule we should avoid doing the laundry, shopping, painting the house, etc., if these activities can be done on other days. Sunday is the Lord's day and we should try to keep it holy.

This concludes our study of the first three commandments, all of which refer to the worship of God. In the next lesson we will study the fourth commandment, which refers to relations between parents and children and to the respect owed to all those in authority. Until then, may God bless you and keep you in his love.

QUESTIONS FOR DISCUSSION

1. Many people look on the Ten Commandments as a series of prohibitions that restrict their freedom. How can we explain the commandments to them in a very positive way?

2. Why is it so important to keep the commandments?

3. Which sins against the first commandment do you think are most common today, especially sins against faith and sins of idolatry and divination?

4. Disrespectful use of God's name is quite common, both in films and in workplaces. What can we do when we hear God's name abused?

5. What are some arguments we can use to help children and adults see the importance of attending Mass every Sunday?

POINTS TO REMEMBER

- The Ten Commandments are God's fatherly instruction to show his children the way to happiness here on earth and in heaven.

- The first commandment commands us to love and worship the true God and to avoid worshipping false gods.

- The second commandment commands us to use God's name always with respect and to avoid misusing it.

- The third commandment commands us to keep Sundays holy by attending Mass and avoiding unnecessary work.

- It is a grave sin to miss Mass on Sundays unless we are excused for a serious reason such as illness, the need to travel a great distance or the need to work.

19. THE FOURTH COMMANDMENT: HONOUR YOUR FATHER AND MOTHER

"Honour your father and your mother, that your days may be long in the land which the LORD gives you" (*Ex* 20:12).

SUMMARY

Continuing our study of the Ten Commandments, in this lesson we look at the fourth commandment, which refers to relations between parents and their children as well as to relations between others in authority and those under them.

We begin by considering the vital importance of the family in God's plan, both for society and for the Church.

Then we look at the duties of children towards their parents, both when the children are young and in the care of their parents, and when they are older and need to look after their ageing parents.

After this we study the duties of parents towards their children, including the important duty of educating them in the faith.

Our fourth topic is the rights and duties that stem from participation in civil society, whether as citizens or as leaders.

Finally, we study the relations between the Church and the political community, including the right of the Church to pass judgment on matters of politics in certain circumstances.

Welcome once again to our journey into the truths of the Catholic faith. As you will recall, in the last lesson we studied the first three commandments given by God to Moses, all of which relate directly to our worship of God, to our love for him. In this lesson we begin our study of the last seven commandments, which relate to love for our neighbour. Our topic today is the fourth commandment: honour your father and mother.

Let us begin, as usual, with a prayer. Heavenly Father, you allow human beings to share in your creative power by bringing forth children as the fruit of married love. Just as we love and honour you, our Father, so you teach us to love and honour our parents. And just as you provide for all our needs, so parents are called to provide for their children. Help us to see our duties towards our parents and those in our care as a reflection of your loving kindness towards us. We make our prayer through Christ our Lord. Amen.

The Catechism explains that the fourth commandment of honouring our father and mother shows us the order of charity, since after love for God the first ones we should love are our parents. While the commandment seems to refer only to the love and honour owed by children to their parents, in reality it is much broader, covering all relationships between those in authority and those under them.

In this lesson we will study five topics: the family in God's plan, the duties of children towards their parents, the duties of parents towards their children, rights and duties in civil society, and finally the Church and the political community.

1. THE FAMILY IN GOD'S PLAN

Our first topic is the family in God's plan. What exactly is a family? The Catechism gives a very succinct definition: "A man and a woman united in marriage, together with their children, form a family" (*CCC* 2202). This is the traditional understanding and it is God's plan for human beings. It is understandable that the family should be constituted in this way since it is within a family formed by a man and a woman united in marriage that children can best be raised. Naturally if one spouse has died or left, the remaining spouse with the children can still be considered a family.

What is more, the Christian family is a reflection of the Blessed Trinity. In the words of the Catechism, the family is a "communion of persons, a sign and image of the communion of the Father and the Son in the Holy Spirit. In the procreation and education of children it reflects the Father's work of creation. It is called to partake of the prayer and sacrifice of Christ. Daily prayer and the reading of the Word of God strengthen it in charity. The Christian family has an evangelising and missionary task" (*CCC* 2205). As is clear from this, the Christian family has a great dignity and mission.

The family has fundamental importance too for human society since it is what the Catechism calls "the original cell of social life" (*CCC* 2207). Just as the human body is composed at its most basic level of individual cells, so society is composed of the cells of families. If the cells are healthy, so will the whole body be. It is in the family that children learn moral values, that they begin to relate to others and learn to care for the young and the old, the sick and the handicapped, and to exercise freedom and responsibility. As such, family life is a school of social virtues and it contributes greatly to the well being of society. For this reason, the state should do all in its power to assist families in carrying out their mission, while always recognising and safeguarding the rights of parents to make their own decisions.

2. The duties of children towards their parents

We look now at the duties of children toward their parents. The foundation of the honour owed by children to their parents is the very fatherhood of God, which parents make present to their children. This honour and respect stem from the gratitude which children naturally feel towards their parents, who gave them the gift of life and who love and sacrifice themselves for them. The *Book of Sirach* expresses this duty powerfully: "With all your heart honour your father, and do not forget the birth pangs of your mother. Remember that through your parents you were born; what can you give back to them that equals their gift to you?" (*Sir*

7:27-28) Children can never give back to their parents what their parents gave them, but they can show them all their love and respect. They do this, among other ways, by being docile and obedient to them.

As long as the children live at home, they should obey their parents in all that they ask when it is for their own good or for that of the family. Similarly, children should obey the reasonable directives of their teachers and all those to whom their parents have entrusted them. Obedience, however has three limits:

1. If a child is convinced in conscience that it would be morally wrong to obey a particular command, he or she must disobey it. For example, if a mother urged her daughter to have an abortion, the daughter could not obey.

2. Strictly speaking, obedience towards parents ceases when the child reaches the majority of age, now 18, or leaves home (cf. *CCC* 2217). Nonetheless, while they are still at home, children should always show great respect to their parents and carry out their wishes.

3. Children are not obliged to obey their parents in the choice of a profession or state in life, whether this be marriage, a vocation to celibacy, or whatever. Nonetheless, they should always listen to their parents' advice in these matters before choosing the course to follow. Parents, at the same time, should be careful not to exert undue pressure on their children in the choice of a profession or of a spouse or a vocation (cf. *CCC* 2230).

What responsibilities do children have when they become adults? Naturally, as they grow older, children should always continue to love and respect their parents. They should stay in contact with them, show them their concern, seek their advice and give them material and moral support in their old age and in times of illness, loneliness or other difficulties. The *Book of Sirach* says: "Whoever honours his father will be gladdened by his own children, and when he prays he will be heard... O son, help your father in his old age, and do not grieve him as long as he lives; even if he is lacking in understanding, show forbearance; in all your strength do not despise him..." (*Sir* 3:5, 12-13). This assistance to parents in their old age is a good way of repaying the sacrifice the parents made for their children when they were infants and in constant need of care. Moreover, if children see their parents putting themselves out to care for their grandparents in their old age, they in turn will be led to show greater respect to their parents when they are in the same position.

In addition to what they owe their parents, Christians owe special gratitude to those from whom they have received the grace of Baptism, the gift of faith and life in the Church. These include parents, grandparents, other members of the family, godparents, pastors, catechists, and other teachers and friends (cf. *CCC* 2220).

3. THE DUTIES OF PARENTS TOWARDS THEIR CHILDREN

We come now to the duties of parents towards their children. The first and most obvious duty of parents is to love and respect their children, seeing them as truly a gift from God. Also, they should provide for the physical and spiritual needs of their children, including food, shelter, clothing, health care, education, and so on. In general, parents should educate their children in the right use of their reason and freedom.

The education of children in all aspects is a paramount duty of parents. As the Catechism says, quoting the Second Vatican Council, "'The role of parents in education is of such importance that it is almost impossible to provide an adequate substitute.' The right and the duty of parents to educate their children are primordial and inalienable" (*GE* 3; *CCC* 2221). This duty begins with the parents regarding their children as children of God and respecting them as human persons. In a real sense, parents educate their children on behalf of God, who is the first educator (cf. *CCC* 2222).

Parents live out this responsibility by creating a home where tenderness, forgiveness, respect, fidelity and service are the rule. They should teach their children the virtues, including self-denial, sound judgment and self-discipline, which are necessary for true freedom. In the words of the *Book of Sirach*: "He who loves his son will not spare the rod... He who disciplines his son will profit by him" (*Sir* 30:1-2). Naturally, parents teach their children best by giving them good example (cf. *CCC* 2223).

As those first responsible for the education of their children, parents have the right to choose a school for them which corresponds to their own convictions and which will best help them in their task as Christian educators. This right is fundamental. Public authorities have the duty of respecting this right of parents and of ensuring that they can exercise it properly (cf. *CCC* 2229).

Parents also have the privilege and responsibility of evangelising their children, of educating them in the faith. They should initiate their children at an early age into the mysteries of the faith, of which they are the "first heralds" for their children, and they should introduce them from their earliest years into the life of the Church. This education begins with the family members helping one another to grow in faith by the witness of their own Christian life. Parents have the great mission of teaching their children to pray and to discover their vocation to holiness as children of God (cf. *CCC* 2225-26).

One of the most important duties of parents is to respect and encourage the vocation of their children, whether it be in the single state or in marriage. They must be convinced that the first vocation of the Christian is to seek holiness by following and loving Christ. As Jesus himself said, "He who loves father or mother more than me is not worthy of me; and he who loves son or daughter more than me is not worthy of me" (*Mt* 10:37). Therefore, parents should welcome God's call to one of their children to follow him, whether in the religious life, in priestly ministry or in the lay state (cf. *CCC* 2233). The vocation of one of their children is truly one of the greatest blessings God can bestow on a couple.

4. Rights and duties in civil society

We come now to our fourth topic, rights and duties in civil society. As we said earlier, the fourth commandment refers not only to the relations between parents and children but more generally to all relations between those in authority and those under them. It commands us to honour those who have received authority in society from God, and it clarifies the duties of those who exercise this authority.

What are some of the duties of civil authorities? First, they should exercise their authority in a spirit of service towards those in their care. Also, they should govern according to the principles of justice, not commanding anything that is contrary to the dignity of persons and the natural law. They should facilitate the exercise of freedom and responsibility of all. In apportioning burdens and favours, they should take into account the needs and possibilities of each person in order to foster justice, harmony and peace. They should respect the fundamental rights of the human person, especially those of families and the disadvantaged. They should respect the political rights attached to citizenship, for example the right to vote, to run for public office, and so on. These rights, which are for the common good, cannot be suspended by public authorities without legitimate and proportionate reasons (cf. *CCC* 2235-37).

If civil authorities have duties towards those under them, so too citizens have duties towards those in authority. First, they should regard those in authority as representatives of God, for St Peter writes: "Be subject for the Lord's sake to every human institution" (*1 Pet* 2:13). Citizens have the right, and at times the duty, to voice their just criticism of whatever seems harmful to the dignity of persons and to the good of the community. They should contribute to the good of society in a spirit of truth, justice, solidarity and freedom. They should fulfil their roles in the life of the political community by obeying the laws, paying taxes, exercising the right to vote, and defending their country if the need arises (cf. *CCC* 2238-40).

The ancient *Letter to Diognetus* expresses how Christians are to live in society: they "reside in their own nations, but as resident aliens. They participate in all things as citizens and endure all things as foreigners... They obey the established laws and their way of life surpasses the laws... So noble is the position to which God has assigned them that they are not allowed to desert it" (*Ad Diognetum* 5, 5 and 10; 6, 10).

The more prosperous nations are obliged, to the extent that they are able, to welcome people from other countries who come in search of the security and means of livelihood they cannot find in their country of origin. Naturally, political authorities may make the exercise of the right to immigrate subject to various conditions, especially with regard to the immigrants' duties towards their new country. Immigrants, in turn, are obliged to respect with gratitude the material and spiritual heritage of the country that receives them and to obey its laws (cf. *CCC* 2241).

How should a citizen react with respect to an unjust law? The Catechism answers: "The citizen is obliged in conscience not to follow the directives of civil authorities when they are contrary to the demands of the moral order, to the fundamental rights of persons or the teachings of the Gospel" (*CCC* 2242). The justification is found in the distinction between serving God and serving the political community: "We must obey God rather than men" (*Acts* 5:29). But even in this case, as the Second Vatican Council teaches, citizens "should still not refuse to give or to do what is objectively demanded of them by the common good; but it is legitimate for them to defend their own rights and those of their fellow citizens against the abuse of this authority within the limits of the natural law and the Law of the Gospel" (*GS* 74 §5; *CCC* 2242). For example, in all ages Christians have refused to do what was against the law of God and many have become martyrs in doing so.

5. THE CHURCH AND THE POLITICAL COMMUNITY

We come now to our final topic, the political community and the Church. Here we look at how the Church relates to the political community.

Every society's laws and institutions reflect a vision of man and his destiny, and most societies have formed their institutions in the recognition of a certain pre-eminence of man over things. This is how it should be. But at a higher level, only the divinely revealed religion has clearly recognised that man in turn has his origin and destiny in God, the Creator and Redeemer. For this reason the Church invites political authorities to measure their judgments and decisions against this inspired truth about God and man. Societies that do not recognise this higher vision of man or reject it in the name of independence from God, often take upon themselves a totalitarian power over man and his destiny, as history shows (cf. *CA* 45, 46; cf. *CCC* 2244, 2257). Think, for example, of the twentieth-century communist regimes, of Nazi Germany, and so on.

How does the Church relate to the political community in general? The Church, because of her divine commission of leading souls to God, is not to be confused in any way with the political community, which seeks the common good of man on earth. The Church is both the sign and the safeguard of the transcendent character of the human person and she respects and encourages the political freedom and responsibility of the citizen (cf. *GS* 76 §3; *CCC* 2245).

But doesn't the Church sometimes pass judgment on matters of politics? Quoting the Second Vatican Council, the Catechism says that it is a part of the Church's mission "to pass moral judgments even in matters related to politics, whenever the fundamental rights of man or the salvation of souls requires it" (*GS* 76; *CCC* 2246). Thus, for example, bishops or the Pope himself may occasionally comment on such matters as proposed new legislation, the running of a country, a war, and so on, whenever these bear on fundamental human rights, the salvation of souls, the common good, etc.

That concludes our study of the fourth commandment, where we have seen not only the duties of children towards their parents and of parents towards their children, but also some principles that govern the relations between those in authority and those under them. In the next lesson we will consider the fifth commandment: You shall not kill. Until then, may God watch over you and keep you in his love.

QUESTIONS FOR DISCUSSION

1. Why is the family so important for the well-being of society and what can Catholic families do to make their contribution more effective?

2. How should parents react if one of their children announces that he or she feels called to serve God in a vocation in the Church?

3. Ageing parents can sometimes be seen as a burden by their grown-up children. How should their children see them and look after them in their old age?

4. What are some ways citizens can contribute to a more just and flourishing society?

5. While Church and state are distinct from one another, what are some ways the Church can contribute to a better society?

POINTS TO REMEMBER

- The fourth commandment commands us to show honour and respect to all those with authority over us and to be diligent in looking after those entrusted to our care.

- The family has great importance for society since it is the original cell of social life.

- Children should always love and honour their parents, even though their obedience to them has certain limits.

- Parents should love and respect their children, seeing them as a gift from God.

- Parents have a duty to educate their children in the faith, so that they can one day be with them in heaven.

- Citizens are obliged to contribute to the good of their country by obeying just laws, paying taxes and participating in the choice of their leaders.

20. THE FIFTH COMMANDMENT: YOU SHALL NOT KILL

I have set before you life and death, blessing and curse; therefore choose life, that you and your descendants may live (Deut 30:19)

SUMMARY

In this lesson we study the fifth commandment, which forbids killing the innocent and commands us to respect human life at all stages. The commandment is very broad, forbidding not only killing but also harming both the spiritual and the physical life of oneself or another.

We look first at five forms of wrongful killing: murder, abortion, embryo destruction, euthanasia and suicide. There is much confusion about some of these at the present time and so it is important to study why they are so wrong.

Next we look at three exceptions to the wrongfulness of killing: self-defence, war and capital punishment. In all of these the person killed is not innocent but is rather an unjust aggressor.

Finally, we consider respect for the dignity of persons, studying in particular the sin of scandal, which endangers the spiritual life of another, and care for one's health and bodily integrity.

Welcome back to our journey into the truths of the Catholic faith. I hope you are enjoying the trip. Really, the more we come to know about our faith, the more we appreciate and love it. In the last lesson we studied the fourth commandment: Honour your father and mother. There we saw not only the duties of children towards their parents and of parents towards their children, but also the relations between those in authority and those under them in the Church and in civil society. In this lesson we will study the fifth commandment: You shall not kill.

Let us begin as usual with a prayer. Heavenly Father, you gave us the gift of life so that we can know, love and serve you on this earth, and be happy with you forever in heaven. Help us to give thanks every day for this great gift and to use it wisely. Help us to respect the life of others from conception until natural death, and to do all we can to bring them to eternal life with you. We make our prayer through Christ, our Lord. Amen.

We tend to think that the fifth commandment forbids only killing another person, but it is much broader than that. In simple terms, it forbids both killing and harming the life of our neighbour and of ourselves, our spiritual life as well as our physical life. And of course it commands us to love and respect everyone and to do all we can to bring them to heaven.

The general principle that governs how life is to be treated is the sacredness of human life. As the Catechism puts it, "Human life is sacred because from its beginning it involves the creative action of God and it remains for ever in a special relationship with the Creator, who is its sole end. God alone is the Lord of life from its beginning until its end: no one can under any circumstance claim for himself the right directly to destroy an innocent human being" (CDF, Instr. *Donum Vitae*, intro. 5; *CCC* 2258). In the words of Scripture: "In [God's] hand is the life of every living thing and the breath of all mankind" (*Job* 12:10; *CCC* 2318).

In this lesson we will study three main topics: wrongful killing, which includes murder, abortion and euthanasia; exceptions to the prohibition of killing, including self-defence, capital punishment and war; and finally respect for the dignity of persons, which includes avoiding scandal and caring for one's health.

1. WRONGFUL KILLING

First then, wrongful killing. When we use a title like "wrongful killing" we are implying that there are forms of killing which are not wrongful and, strange as it may sound, this is indeed the case. While the fifth commandment states "You shall not kill", it admits of exceptions like killing in self-defence, capital punishment and war. What is absolute and does not admit of any exceptions is the prohibition of killing the innocent. The book of Exodus makes this very clear: "Do not slay the innocent and the righteous" (Ex 23:7). The Catechism comments: "The deliberate murder of an innocent person is gravely contrary to the dignity of the human being, to the golden rule and to the holiness of the Creator. The law forbidding it is universally valid: it obliges each and everyone, always and everywhere" (CCC 2261). We will now look at five forms of wrongful killing: murder, abortion, embryo destruction, euthanasia and suicide.

Murder

The first and most obvious violation of the fifth commandment is murder or homicide, which is the intentional killing of an innocent human being. The Old Testament says that this sin, which is always grave, cries out to heaven for vengeance (cf. Gen 4:10). The Catechism says that, of the various categories of murder, "infanticide, fratricide, parricide [the killing of one's parents] and the murder of a spouse are especially grave crimes by reason of the natural bonds which they break" (CCC 2268). Infanticide is one of the most grave forms of killing, since the infant is the most innocent and defenceless of human beings. This includes of course deformed and handicapped babies. We can never kill an innocent human being.

In addition to forbidding direct intentional killing, the fifth commandment also forbids doing anything which could indirectly bring about another's death (cf. CCC 2269). Examples given by the Catechism are exposing someone to mortal danger without grave reason, and refusing assistance to a person in danger, with the intention that they will die. It would also include reckless driving of a motor vehicle and driving under the influence of alcohol, which results in the death of another.

Abortion

The second form of killing the innocent is abortion, which is the destruction of the unborn child in the womb. When we consider the sacredness of human life from the moment of conception it is easy to understand why abortion is so wrong. In the prophecy of Jeremiah God speaks of his care for the unborn child: "Before I formed you in the womb I knew you, and before you were born I consecrated you" (*Jer* 1:5). God loves every human being from the moment it is conceived and for all eternity. In view of this, it is understandable that the Church has always forbidden abortion. Already in the first century, a document known as the *Didache* says: "You shall not kill the embryo by abortion and shall not cause the newborn to perish" (*Didache*, 2, 2; *CCC* 2271).

Not only does abortion end the life of the unborn child, it often does serious harm to the mother and father, who can suffer from post-abortion grief, manifesting itself as depression, emotional instability and so on. But God still loves those who have done wrong and he is always ready to forgive them if they come back to him sorry for what they have done. Others too should never condemn those who have had abortions but should rather show them every kindness and help them to return to God.

Embryo destruction

A third form of wrongful killing is the destruction of human embryos. This has the same moral consideration as abortion, since the embryo is simply a human being at an earlier stage of development. In the words of the Catechism, "Since it must be treated from conception as a person, the embryo must be defended in its integrity, cared for, and healed, as far as possible, like any other human being" (*CCC* 2274). Thus it is not morally acceptable to conduct procedures that harm or kill the embryo or to discard unwanted embryos. A Church document says that "it is immoral to produce human embryos intended for exploitation as disposable biological material" (CDF, *Donum Vitae*, I, 5; *CCC* 2275). This would include using embryos for stem cell research or for tissues for the treatment of various conditions. The embryo, after all, is a human being. If it were allowed to develop in the womb, it would one day be born like any other human being. All of us were one day an embryo.

Nonetheless it is lawful to conduct tests and procedures on human embryos that can improve their life, just as it is with adults. The Catechism teaches: "One must hold as licit procedures carried out on the human embryo which respect the life and integrity of the embryo and do not involve disproportionate risks for it, but are directed toward its healing, the improvement of its condition of health, or its individual survival" (CDF, *Donum Vitae*, I, 3; *CCC* 2275).

Euthanasia

A fourth type of wrongful killing is euthanasia. What is euthanasia? The Catechism defines it as "an act or omission which, of itself or by intention, causes death in order to eliminate suffering." That is, euthanasia is the killing of an innocent human being, as is murder, but with the particular aim of eliminating the person's suffering.

The Church is very clear about the moral evil of euthanasia. In the words of the Catechism, it "constitutes a murder gravely contrary to the dignity of the human person and to the respect due to the living God, his Creator. The error of judgment into which one can fall in good faith does not change the nature of this murderous act, which must always be forbidden and excluded" (*CCC* 2277). While it is always acceptable and indeed advisable to do everything possible to reduce a person's suffering, it is not lawful to end the person's life in order to achieve this. God, after all, is the master of life and it is up to him to decide when the person is ready to die.

This does not rule out discontinuing certain procedures that prolong the life of the person when it is clear that these procedures are not achieving their aim or that they are burdensome to the person, dangerous or disproportionate to the expected outcome. As the Catechism explains, "Here one does not will to cause death; one's inability to impede it is merely accepted. The decisions should be made by the patient if he is competent and able or, if not, by those legally entitled to act for the patient, whose reasonable will and legitimate interests must always be respected" (CCC 2278). For example, it is acceptable to disconnect life support when it is clear that without it the person would die anyway of their underlying condition.

But even if death is thought imminent, the ordinary care owed to a sick person must always be continued, including the provision of food and water. The use of painkillers – for example, morphine – to alleviate the suffering of the dying, even at the risk of shortening their life, is morally acceptable. This is the role of palliative care, which aims to help the patient to be as comfortable as possible in the last phase of an illness. It is a special form of charity (cf. CCC 2279).

Suicide

We come finally to a fifth form of wrongful killing: the killing of oneself or suicide. What is wrong with suicide? Can't we do with our life whatever we want? No, our life is not something we possess, to be used however we want. Life is always a gift from God, to be administered wisely until we are called to give an account of it in the judgment. The Catechism expresses it beautifully: "It is God who remains the sovereign Master of life. We are obliged to accept life gratefully and preserve it for his honour and the salvation of our souls. We are stewards, not owners, of the life

God has entrusted to us. It is not ours to dispose of" (*CCC* 2280). It is God who has given us the gift of life and he will decide when it is time for it to end.

Apart from being an offence against God, who is the Master of life, suicide goes against the natural inclination to preserve our life, an inclination written into our nature by God. It is one of our strongest inclinations. In this way suicide is gravely contrary to the just love of self which everyone should have. After all, Our Lord tells us to love your neighbour "as yourself" (*Mk* 12:31). And it is a grave lack of love for our neighbour, because it affects many people deeply, especially our family and friends.

Although, objectively speaking, suicide is a grave sin, one can never make judgments about the subjective guilt of persons who commit suicide. Grave psychological disturbances, depression, anguish or grave fear of hardship, suffering or torture can diminish the responsibility of someone who ends their own life (cf. *CCC* 2282). We should always pray very much for those who have committed suicide, begging God to forgive them and take them to himself.

2. EXCEPTIONS TO THE WRONGFULNESS OF KILLING

We come now to our second topic: exceptions to the wrongfulness of killing. As we said before, while it is always wrong to kill an innocent person, it is sometimes permissible to kill someone who is not innocent but is threatening to harm, is harming or has harmed others. There are three such situations: self-defence, war and capital punishment.

Self-defence

Love for our neighbour should lead us to do everything possible to help him and defend his life, but if someone is attacking us and is threatening our life, we can use whatever means are necessary to protect ourselves, even to the point of killing the attacker. It is important that one not use more force than necessary, but if killing is the only way to defend ourselves, we may go to this length. The reason why one can kill in self-defence is that love for oneself is a fundamental duty and it takes precedence even over love for our neighbour. The Catechism explains this, quoting St Thomas Aquinas:

> If a man in self-defence uses more than necessary violence, it will be unlawful: whereas if he repels force with moderation, his defence will be lawful... Nor is it necessary for salvation that a man omit the act of moderate self-defence to avoid killing the other man, since one is bound to take more care of one's own life than of another's (*STh* II-II, 64, 7; cf. *CCC* 2264).

Capital punishment

The second situation in which it is permissible to kill another is capital punishment, the putting to death of a convicted criminal by the state. It is called "capital" punishment, by the way, from the Latin word for "head", *caput*, since the more common way of putting criminals to death in ancient times was beheading.

The Catechism explains that it is a requirement of the common good that the state curb the spread of behaviour harmful to society, and that it therefore "has the right and the duty to inflict punishment proportionate to the gravity of the offence" (*CCC* 2266). It goes on to explain that in addition to defending public order and protecting people's safety, punishment should also contribute to the correction of the guilty person. As regards the death penalty, the Catechism teaches:

> Assuming that the guilty party's identity and responsibility have been fully determined, the traditional teaching of the Church does not exclude recourse to the death penalty, if this is the only possible way of effectively defending human lives against the unjust aggressor. If, however, non-lethal means are sufficient to defend and protect people's safety from the aggressor, authority

will limit itself to such means, as these are more in keeping with the concrete conditions of the common good and more in conformity with the dignity of the human person. Today, in fact, as a consequence of the possibilities which the state has for effectively preventing crime, by rendering one who has committed an offence incapable of doing harm – without definitively taking away from the possibility of redeeming himself – the cases in which the execution of the offender is an absolute necessity 'are very rare, if not practically non-existent'" (Pope John Paul II, Enc. *Evangelium Vitae* 56; *CCC* 2267).

As is clear, the mind of the Church is clearly to discourage the use of the death penalty, so that only in very rare cases would it be necessary and therefore permissible.

War

The third case in which killing another human being is permissible is war. The Catechism deals with it in the context of stressing the duty of doing everything possible to foster peace on earth. Indeed, as Our Lord says in the Sermon on the Mount, "Blessed are the peacemakers, for they shall be called sons of God" (*Mt* 5:9). What is peace? In the words of the Catechism, "Peace is not merely the absence of war, and it is not limited to maintaining a balance of powers between adversaries. Peace cannot be attained on earth without safeguarding the goods of persons, free communication among men, respect for the dignity of persons and peoples, and the assiduous practice of fraternity. Peace is 'the tranquillity of order.' Peace is the work of justice and the effect of charity" (St Augustine, *De Civ. Dei*, 19, 13, 1; *CCC* 2304).

There will be peace if we strive to love our neighbour as our self, to help our neighbour in whatever way we can and to avoid anger, hatred and quarrelling, not only war. Our Lord himself said, "Everyone who is angry with his brother shall be liable to judgment" (*Mt* 5:21; *CCC* 2302). He went even further to say, "Love your enemies and pray for those who

persecute you, so that you may be sons of your Father who is in heaven"
(*Mt* 5:44-45).

If everyone lived out these exhortations, there would be no war, but
we know that war has been with us practically from the beginning. The
Catechism teaches: "Because of the evils and injustices that accompany
all war, the Church insistently urges everyone to prayer and to action so
that the divine Goodness may free us from the ancient bondage of war"
(*CCC* 2307). Nonetheless, in the words of the Second Vatican Council,
"as long as the danger of war persists and there is no international
authority with the necessary competence and power, governments
cannot be denied the right of lawful self-defence, once all peace efforts
have failed" (*GS* 79 §4; *CCC* 2308).

When the leaders of a country have decided that there is a legitimate
reason to go to war, the members of the armed forces can feel justified
in fighting for their country and of course killing enemy soldiers. In the
words of the Catechism, "Those who are sworn to serve their country
in the armed forces are servants of the security and freedom of nations.
If they carry out their duty honourably, they truly contribute to the
common good of the nation and the maintenance of peace" (*CCC*
2310). As regards those with a conscientious objection to fighting in the
war, the authorities should allow them to serve in some other way so that
they are not required to bear arms.

3. RESPECT FOR THE DIGNITY OF PERSONS

This brings us to our third and final topic, respect for the dignity of
persons. Here we will look at the sin of scandal and at care for one's
health and bodily integrity.

Scandal

As we saw earlier, the fifth commandment forbids not only taking or
harming the physical life of a person, but also harming the spiritual

life of another by leading them into sin. This is what is called scandal, which is an attitude or behaviour which leads another to commit sin. For example, it would be scandal for someone to lead another person into a sin against chastity, or to encourage another to read a book contrary to faith or to attend an immoral film. In the words of the Catechism, "The person who gives scandal becomes his neighbour's tempter. He damages virtue and integrity; he may even draw his brother into spiritual death" (*CCC* 2284). Clearly, one of the worst things one can do to another is lead that person into sin, and even more into mortal sin, or spiritual death, which can lead to eternal damnation.

Scandal is especially serious when it is done by those in authority, such as teachers, priests or parents, and when those who are led into sin are especially vulnerable, such as children or the handicapped. This prompted our Lord to utter the curse: "Whoever causes one of these little ones who believe in me to sin, it would be better for him to have a great millstone fastened round his neck and to be drowned in the depth of the sea" (*Mt* 18:6). We should not forget that scandal can also be committed on a broader scale when, for example, parliamentarians pass laws that legalise immoral conduct, film makers produce films that display human sexuality in an immoral way, or business leaders encourage fraud or corruption.

Respect for health and bodily integrity

As regards care for our health and bodily integrity we should look on health, like life itself, as a gift entrusted to us by God and so we should take reasonable care of it. This includes eating a balanced diet, avoiding excesses, taking any prescribed medicines, and getting sufficient rest and exercise. A notable failure in any of these areas would be a sin against the fifth commandment. This could include excessive eating or drinking of alcohol, smoking tobacco excessively and using prohibited drugs. Drunkenness, where the person has lost control of his rationality, is generally a grave sin. At the same time we should not make the body an absolute value by promoting a cult of the body or idolising physical perfection or success at sports.

Naturally surgery, including the removal of organs or the amputation of limbs, is permissible when it is necessary for the health or life of the person. As regards organ transplants, which have saved the life and well-being of many people, the Church teaches that it is essential that the donor or those who speak for him or her have given informed consent for the donation of organs. Naturally when the donor has died, it is essential to be certain that death has in fact occurred before the organs are removed. When organs are donated by a living person, the good sought for the recipient must be proportionate to the dangers incurred by the donor.

Respect for the body extends to its handling after death. The body must always be treated with respect and charity since, along with the soul, it forms an integral part of the human person and it will rise again on the last day. While the Church prefers burial, it allows cremation as long as this does not demonstrate a denial of faith in the resurrection of the body (cf. *CCC* 2300-2301).

That concludes our study of the fifth commandment. In the next lesson we will study the sixth commandment – You shall not commit adultery – which protects marriage and the virtue of chastity. Until then, may God bless you and guide you gently through the week.

QUESTIONS FOR DISCUSSION

1. What are some good arguments to show that abortion is a most serious evil?

2. Why is the Church so opposed to the use of human embryos for experiments and other purposes that result in their death?

3. Today there is much confusion about the immorality of euthanasia. How would you convince a friend that it is always wrong and should not be legalised?

4. Over the years the Church has toughened its stand against the death penalty. Why should capital punishment be used only in very limited circumstances?

5. Scandal is a serious sin in that it leads another into sin and possibly jeopardises his eternal salvation. What are some common ways in which people commit scandal these days?

POINTS TO REMEMBER

- Because human life is sacred, the fifth commandment commands us to foster the spiritual and physical life of ourselves and our neighbour.

- It is always a grave sin to kill an innocent person.

- Among the forms of wrongful killing are murder, abortion, embryo destruction, euthanasia and suicide.

- An unjust aggressor may be killed in self-defence, war and capital punishment.

- We must always avoid giving scandal, which consists in leading another into sin.

- We should always take reasonable care of our health, regarding it as a gift from God.

21. THE SIXTH COMMANDMENT: YOU SHALL NOT COMMIT ADULTERY

What therefore God has joined together, let no man put asunder (Mt 19:6)

SUMMARY

In this lesson we study the sixth commandment, which not only forbids adultery but protects marriage and the virtue of chastity.

Our first topic is human sexuality in the plan of God. Here we consider how human sexuality is ordered to forming bonds of communion with others, especially in marriage, and how it relates to the vocation to love.

Next we study the virtue of chastity, which is fundamental in human relationships and which requires a lifelong struggle. Then we look at offences against chastity, in particular lust, masturbation, fornication, pornography, prostitution, rape and homosexual acts, all of which are in themselves serious sins.

Our fourth topic is the morality of the sexual act in marriage and the importance of being open to life. We study why the use of contraception is contrary to love as well as to life and why artificial means of bringing about the conception of a child are also unacceptable.

Lastly we look at offences against the dignity of marriage, including adultery, divorce and polygamy.

Welcome back to our journey into the truths of the Catholic faith. In the last lesson we studied the fifth commandment – You shall not kill –

which, as you will recall, refers not only to killing someone, but in general to taking or harming the life, whether physical or spiritual, of oneself or another. In this lesson we look at the sixth commandment – You shall not commit adultery – which refers to the virtue of chastity and the sins opposed to it, both in marriage and in the single life.

But let us begin, as usual, with a prayer. Heavenly Father, you made us in your image and likeness, male and female you created us. You gave us a vocation to love, as a reflection of your eternal love and communion in the Blessed Trinity. Help us to live our vocation to the full and so to show the world your infinite love for each and every one of us. We make our prayer through Christ our Lord. Amen.

In this lesson we will study five main topics: human sexuality in the plan of God, the virtue of chastity, sins opposed to chastity, marriage in God's plan, and sins opposed to marriage.

1. HUMAN SEXUALITY IN THE PLAN OF GOD

We begin in the Blessed Trinity where we find the foundation for our call to love and communion. The Blessed Trinity, as we recall, is an eternal and infinite communion of love among the three divine persons. In making mankind in his image and likeness God was calling us too to a vocation of love and communion. Pope John Paul II writes: "God is love and in himself he lives a mystery of personal loving communion. Creating the human race in his own image ... God inscribed in the humanity of man and woman the vocation, and thus the capacity and responsibility, of love and communion... Love is the fundamental and innate vocation of every human being" (*FC* 11; *CCC* 2392).

All human beings, then, are called to love. In his first encyclical, Pope John Paul elaborated on this point: "Man cannot live without love. He remains a being that is incomprehensible for himself, his life is senseless, if love is not revealed to him, if he does not encounter love, if he does not experience it and make it his own, if he does not participate intimately in it" (*RH* 10). Most people will live out their vocation to love in marriage, while others will do so in the single state. But all are called to love – to be loved and to give love.

We know that God created us male and female and our sexuality is intimately related to our vocation to love. The Catechism explains: "Sexuality affects all aspects of the human person in the unity of his body and soul. It especially concerns affectivity, the capacity to love and to procreate, and in a more general way the aptitude for forming bonds of communion with others" (*CCC* 2332). Thus, while especially ordered to the ability to love and bring forth children, sexuality has a more general ordering to forming bonds of communion with others.

Sexuality, as is obvious, is especially ordered to marriage. In the words of the Catechism, "Everyone, man and woman, should acknowledge and accept his sexual identity. Physical, moral and spiritual difference and complementarity are oriented toward the goods of marriage and the flourishing of family life. The harmony of the couple and of society depends in part on the way in which the complementarity, needs and mutual support between the sexes are lived out" (*CCC* 2333). A very important aspect of the Church's teaching on sexuality is the equal dignity of man and woman. In the words of Pope John Paul II, "In creating men 'male and female,' God gives man and woman an equal personal dignity" (*FC* 22).

2. THE VIRTUE OF CHASTITY

We know that as a consequence of original sin, we all experience a certain disorder in our nature, and this affects our ability to control our sexuality and use it for the purpose for which God intended it. We see the effects of this lack of self control in such aspects as widespread sexual promiscuity among young people, marital infidelity, the growing use of pornography and so on.

For this reason we need the virtue of chastity, which helps us to integrate sexuality within the unity of our nature, bringing about the harmony we all seek. Chastity is traditionally defined as "the virtue which moderates the desire for sexual pleasure according to right reason." That is, God intended – and right reason confirms – that sexual pleasure should be sought only in acts of love open to life between a man and a woman united in marriage.

We need the virtue of chastity to help us live in this way, with our sexual desires under control. When we have the virtue we experience the harmony, balance and self-control which we all seek. Thus chastity brings self-mastery and freedom. As the Catechism puts it, "Chastity includes an apprenticeship in self-mastery which is a training in human freedom. The alternative is clear: either man governs his passions and finds peace, or he lets himself be dominated by them and becomes unhappy" (*CCC* 2339). People who were formerly dominated by their passions and are now able to control them speak precisely of being liberated, of being free again. They regain their integrity, their wholeness.

How do we grow in chastity? We grow in it through being sincere with ourselves and acknowledging our weakness, through prayer in which we ask God to help us, through penance and self-denial to strengthen our will and gain more grace, through frequent reception of the sacraments of Penance and the Eucharist, and especially through controlling our desire for sexual pleasure when it is not appropriate.

3. OFFENCES AGAINST CHASTITY

It is important to know that as a general rule, external sins against chastity – that is, sins of action as distinct from internal sins of thought or desire – are of themselves grave, or mortal, sins. However, if they are done in ignorance of their seriously disordered nature or without full consent in the will, they may be venial sins or no sin at all. Following the Catechism, we will consider seven sins.

The first one is *lust*, defined by the Catechism as "disordered desire for or inordinate enjoyment of sexual pleasure. Sexual pleasure is morally disordered when sought for itself, isolated from its procreative and unitive purposes" (*CCC* 2351). Our Lord spoke of lust when he said, "You have heard that it was said, 'You shall not commit adultery.' But I say to you that every one who looks at a woman lustfully has already committed adultery with her in his heart" (*Mt* 5:27-28). We can all be tempted to lust and we must be on guard to reject the temptations immediately.

The second sin is *masturbation,* understood as "the deliberate stimulation of the genital organs in order to derive sexual pleasure." As regards the morality of this practice, the Catechism teaches: "Both the Magisterium of the Church, in the course of a constant tradition, and the moral sense of the faithful have been in no doubt and have firmly maintained that masturbation is an intrinsically and gravely disordered action" (*CCC* 2352; CDF, Decl. *Persona humana* 9). It is gravely disordered in that, instead of being directed towards another person in an act of love, it is turned inward towards oneself, in the search of selfish pleasure. While in itself masturbation is a mortal sin, the Catechism points out that the serious nature of the sin may be lessened by such factors as "affective immaturity, force of acquired habit, conditions of anxiety or other psychological or social factors" (*CCC* 2352).

The third sin against chastity is *fornication,* commonly referred to as sex before marriage. The Catechism says of it: "Fornication is carnal union between an unmarried man and an unmarried woman. It is gravely contrary to the dignity of persons and of human sexuality which is naturally ordered to the good of spouses and the generation and education of children" (*CCC* 2353).

The fourth sin is the use of *pornography.* The Catechism teaches: "*Pornography* consists in removing real or simulated sexual acts from the intimacy of the partners, in order to display them deliberately to third parties. It offends against chastity because it perverts the conjugal act, the intimate giving of spouses to each other. It does grave injury to the dignity of its participants (actors, vendors, the public), since each one becomes an object of base pleasure and illicit profit for others. It immerses all who are involved in the illusion of a fantasy world. It is a *grave offence*. Civil authorities should prevent the production and distribution of pornographic materials" (*CCC* 2354). One of the worst aspects of pornography is that it divorces the use of sexuality from love, making it merely an object of pleasure for the viewer. It thus portrays men, women, or even children, as mere objects of sexual gratification, as mere bodies, rather than as persons. The ready availability of pornography on the internet is causing grave harm to many persons.

The fifth sin against chastity is *prostitution*. As the Catechism says, like pornography it reduces the person "to an instrument of sexual pleasure. The one who pays sins gravely against himself: he violates the chastity to which his Baptism pledged him and defiles his body, the temple of the Holy Spirit... While it is always gravely sinful to engage in prostitution, the imputability of the offence can be attenuated by destitution, blackmail or social pressure" (*CCC* 2355).

The sixth sin is *rape*, which everyone finds particularly abhorrent. In the words of the Catechism, rape is "the forcible violation of the sexual intimacy of another person. It does injury to justice and charity. Rape deeply wounds the respect, freedom and physical and moral integrity to which every person has a right. It causes grave damage that can mark the victim for life. It is always an intrinsically evil act. Graver still is the rape of children committed by parents (incest) or those responsible for the education of the children entrusted to them" (*CCC* 2356). The effects of the sexual abuse of young people are often life-long, causing serious emotional and mental problems.

Finally, the seventh sin against chastity mentioned by the Catechism is *homosexual acts*. As the Catechism explains, "Homosexuality refers to relations between men or between women who experience an exclusive or predominant sexual attraction toward persons of the same sex... Basing itself on Sacred Scripture, which presents homosexual acts as acts of grave depravity, tradition has always declared that 'homosexual acts are intrinsically disordered' (CDF, Decl. *Persona humana*, 8). They are contrary to the natural law. They close the sexual act to the gift of life. They do not proceed from a genuine affective and sexual complementarity. Under no circumstances can they be approved" (*CCC* 2357).

While homosexual acts are sinful, the homosexual condition itself, commonly known as same-sex attraction, is not sinful. Persons with same-sex attraction have the same dignity as everyone else and they too were redeemed by the precious blood of Christ, who desires their eternal salvation. As the Catechism explains, "They must be accepted with respect, compassion and sensitivity. Every sign of unjust discrimination in their regard should be avoided. These persons are called to fulfil God's will in their lives and, if they are Christians, to unite to the sacrifice of the Lord's Cross the difficulties they may encounter from their condition" (*CCC* 2358).

4. THE MARRIAGE ACT AND OPENNESS TO LIFE

As you will recall, we studied God's plan for marriage when we considered the sacrament of Matrimony in Lesson 15. There we considered that God made man male and female and he gave them a mutual attraction for each other which leads them into a life-long commitment of love in marriage, through which they bring children into the world. Marriage is a covenant, a commitment between a man and a woman to give themselves to each other as spouses for the whole of their life, and it is based on God's covenant with his people, especially Christ's covenant with his Church. In this covenant we see the essential characteristics of Christian marriage: unity, indissolubility and openness to life. Now we look at some moral aspects of the marriage act and its openness to life, and then at sins against the dignity of marriage.

Morality of the marriage act
First, what is the morality of the sexual act in marriage? Quoting the Second Vatican Council the Catechism answers: "The acts in marriage by

which the intimate and chaste union of the spouses takes place are noble and honourable; the truly human performance of these acts fosters the self-giving they signify, and enriches the spouses in joy and gratitude" (*GS* 49 §2; *CCC* 2362).

Moreover, the joy and pleasure experienced in these acts is willed by God and is a foretaste of the eternal joy of heaven. The Catechism quotes some beautiful words of Pope Pius XII in this regard: "The Creator himself... established that in the [generative] function, spouses should experience pleasure and enjoyment of body and spirit. Therefore, the spouses do nothing evil in seeking this pleasure and enjoyment. They accept what the Creator has intended for them. At the same time, spouses should know how to keep themselves within the limits of just moderation" (Pius XII, Discourse, 29 October 1951; *CCC* 2362).

Openness to life and contraception

As regards openness to life, the marriage act as intended by God has both a *unitive* aspect, the one-flesh union which is an expression of the spouses' love for each other, and a *procreative* aspect, the openness to life of the act through which children come into the world. The Church has always taught that these two aspects may never be separated, so that the marriage act is both love-giving and life-giving. Quoting Pope Paul VI's encyclical *Humanae Vitae* (1968), the Catechism teaches that "it is necessary that each and every marriage act remain ordered per se to the procreation of human life. This particular doctrine, expounded on numerous occasions by the Magisterium, is based on the inseparable connection, established by God, which man on his own initiative may not break, between the unitive significance and the procreative significance which are both inherent to the marriage act" (*HV* 11, 12; *CCC* 2366).

Through their love open to life spouses have the awesome capacity to bring a new human being into existence, thus sharing in the very creative power and fatherhood of God. Not for nothing is this gift called procreation. One of the greatest joys of spouses is indeed the birth of a child, who enriches their marriage immeasurably. Pope John Paul II writes:

> In its most profound reality, love is essentially a gift; and conjugal love, while leading the spouses to the reciprocal "knowledge" which makes them "one flesh," does not end with the couple, because it makes them capable of the greatest possible gift, the gift by which they become cooperators with God for giving life to a new human person. Thus the couple, while giving themselves to one another, give not just themselves but also the reality of children, who are a living reflection of their love, a permanent sign of conjugal unity and a living and inseparable synthesis of their being a father and a mother (FC 14).

In view of this teaching, it is understandable that the use of contraception in any form, including sterilisation, is not permitted. Indeed, a marriage act using contraception would not be an act of true love, which is a total giving of the spouses to each other. Through contraception the spouses do not give themselves totally but withhold something, putting a barrier between them. In the words of Pope John Paul II: "Thus the innate language that expresses the total reciprocal self-giving of husband and wife is overlaid, through contraception, by an objectively contradictory language, namely, that of not giving oneself totally to the other. This leads not only to a positive refusal to be open to life but also to a falsification of the inner truth of conjugal love, which is called upon to give itself in personal totality (FC 32; CCC 2370).

Naturally, if there are serious reasons why the couple should not have another child for the time being or even indefinitely, the couple may make use of their marriage only during the infertile periods of the wife through what is called natural family planning. Here the marriage act is of itself open to life even though the couple know that it is highly unlikely that it will result in the conception of a baby. And always the couple are open to receive a new child, should God send them one. This is very different from the "contraceptive mentality" which is closed off to life and would take measures to prevent the birth of the child.

Artificial means of conception

Since the unitive and procreative aspects of the marriage act can never be separated, it is understandable too that artificial means of bringing about the conception of a child are not permitted. Among such means are artificial insemination and in-vitro fertilisation. The Church has always taught that a child should be conceived through a loving act of a husband and a wife, not through the act of scientists in a laboratory. To be sure, such a way of bringing about conception would convert the child into a product and would not be in keeping with the dignity of the human person. The Catechism teaches that these artificial techniques

> dissociate the sexual act from the procreative act. The act which brings the child into existence is no longer an act by which two persons give themselves to one another, but one that 'entrusts the life and identity of the embryo into the power of doctors and biologists and establishes the domination of technology over the origin and destiny of the human person. Such a relationship of domination is in itself contrary to the dignity and equality that must be common to parents and children' (CDF, *Donum Vitae* II, 5; *CCC* 2377).

In response to the claim of childless couples that they have a "right to a child" and therefore can resort to artificial means to have one, the Church teaches:

> A child is not something owed to one, but is a gift. The "supreme gift of marriage" is a human person. A child may not be considered a piece of property, an idea to which an alleged "right to a child" would lead. In this area, only the child possesses genuine rights: the right "to be the fruit of the specific act of the conjugal love of his parents", and "the right to be respected as a person from the moment of his conception" (CDF, *Donum Vitae* II, 81; *CCC* 2378).

5. Offences against the dignity of marriage

This brings us to our final topic: offences against the dignity of marriage itself. We will consider three offences: adultery, divorce and remarriage, and polygamy.

Adultery

The sixth commandment states "You shall not commit adultery". By adultery we understand, of course, sexual relations between two persons of whom at least one is married to someone else. In marrying, the spouses committed themselves to remain faithful to each other all their lives and adultery is a violation of that promise. It is not only a sin against chastity, but also against justice and charity. The Catechism explains: "Adultery is an injustice. He who commits adultery fails in his commitment. He does injury to the sign of the covenant which the marriage bond is, transgresses the rights of the other spouse and undermines the institution of marriage by breaking the contract on which it is based. He compromises the good of human generation and the welfare of children who need their parents' stable union" (CCC 2381).

Divorce and remarriage

The second sin against marriage is divorce and remarriage. Our Lord was very clear on this: "Every one who divorces his wife and marries another commits adultery, and he who marries a woman divorced from her husband commits adultery" (Lk 16:18). The spouses promised to remain with each other for the whole of their life and divorce is the breaking of that bond. Since marriage is a sign of the covenant between Christ and his Church, divorce also does harm to that covenant (cf. CCC 2384). Naturally, if there are serious reasons why the couple should not remain together they are always free to separate, but they should not presume to break the marriage bond through civil divorce. If obtaining a civil divorce is necessary to secure the protection of the law as regards property, maintenance or the custody of children, this is not a sin.

Persons who have divorced and been remarried civilly can only be admitted to the sacraments of the Church if they obtain an annulment of the first marriage from a Church tribunal and then remarry validly, or the first spouse dies, or they agree to live together in the second union as brother and sister, without having sexual relations. If none of these is possible and there are good reasons why they should not separate, for example the need to care for children, they are always most welcome to attend Mass and to take part in parish activities, but they cannot receive the sacraments.

Polygamy

The final sin against marriage that we consider is polygamy, where a man has more than one wife. Given that marriage is a reflection of Christ's covenant with his one Church, from this viewpoint alone it is clear that marriage should be a covenant between one man and one woman. Added to this is the fact that God has disposed through the laws of nature that there are approximately equal numbers of men and women in the world so that widespread polygamy would leave many men without wives. The Catechism explains that another very important reason why polygamy is not acceptable is that "it is contrary to the equal personal dignity of men and women who in matrimony give themselves with a love that is total and therefore unique and exclusive" (*FC* 19; *CCC* 2387). In polygamy men and women are not equal in dignity. The husband has several wives but the wives have to share one husband.

That concludes our study of the sixth commandment which, as you can see, includes a multitude of issues relating to human sexuality and God's plan for marriage. In the next lesson we will study the seventh commandment – You shall not steal – which involves issues of justice. Until then, may God bless you and fill you with his love.

QUESTIONS FOR DISCUSSION

1. We have seen how all people are called to love and to be
    loved. Why is love so important?

2. The virtue of chastity, with self-control over the sexual
    appetite, is difficult for everyone. What are some ways of
    growing in this important virtue?

3. The use of pornography is becoming a particularly serious
    problem, not only for single people but also for those who
    are married. Why is pornography so bad and what can we
    do to avoid it ourselves and help others to avoid it?

4. Many people do not make a distinction between
    homosexual acts, which are intrinsically disordered, and
    the homosexual condition or same-sex attraction, which is
    not sinful. How should we look on and treat people with
    same-sex attraction?

5. How would you explain to a friend why the use of
    contraception is wrong?

POINTS TO REMEMBER

- Everyone has a vocation to love and to be loved.

- Chastity is the virtue which moderates the desire for sexual
  pleasure according to right reason.

- As a general rule, sins of action against chastity are grave
  sins. They include masturbation, fornication, use of
  pornography, prostitution, rape and homosexual acts.

- Because the marriage act is an act of true love open to life,
  the use of contraception and direct sterilisation are never
  permitted.

- Among the sins against the dignity of marriage are adultery,
  divorce and remarriage, and polygamy

22. THE SEVENTH COMMANDMENT: YOU SHALL NOT STEAL

Behold, the wages of the labourers who mowed your fields, which you kept back by fraud, cry out; and the cries of the harvesters have reached the ears of the Lord of hosts (Jas 5:4)

SUMMARY

In this lesson we study the seventh commandment, which relates not only to stealing but to a broad range of issues in the area of justice and the use of material goods.

First we study the right to private property and how it relates to the right of all to what they need for a decent life, otherwise known as the universal destination of the world's goods.

Then we consider respect for the property of others. Here we study the sin of stealing, which can take many forms, and the need to make restitution if we have taken or damaged the property of another.

Our third topic is respect for creation, where we study how we are stewards of the creation which God has entrusted to us.

We go on to study various topics related to work, including the meaning of work, the role of the state in regulating it, the role of management and that of workers.

Lastly, we consider the love we should have for the poor, and the works of mercy.

Welcome once again to our journey into truth. In the last lesson we

271

studied the sixth commandment – You shall not commit adultery – which relates to issues of human sexuality and marriage. In this lesson we will study the seventh – You shall not steal – which covers issues in the area of justice.

Let us begin as usual with a prayer. Heavenly Father, you reveal yourself as a God of mercy and at the same time a God of justice. In your goodness you give us, along with grace, the infused virtue of justice, which moves us to give to each one his due. Help us to live justice first of all with you, to whom we owe all that we are, by worshipping you and striving always to do your will. And help us to give their due to all those around us so that we can contribute to building a more just society. We make our prayer through Christ our Lord. Amen.

As we recall, the first three commandments relate to our love for God, and the last seven to love for our neighbour. Each of the last seven has as its object a particular good of our neighbour. The fourth refers to our love for our family and all those in authority over us, the fifth to our neighbour's life, the sixth to our neighbour's chastity and marriage, the seventh to our neighbour's goods, the eighth to our neighbour's good name, and the ninth and tenth to internal sins against the sixth and seventh.

The seventh, like the others we have studied, has a wide scope, in this case relating to earthly goods. The Catechism summarises it, saying that the commandment "forbids unjustly taking or keeping the goods of one's neighbour and wronging him in any way with respect to his goods. It commands justice and charity in the care of earthly goods and the fruits of men's labour. For the sake of the common good, it requires respect for the universal destination of goods and respect for the right to private property. Christian life strives to order this world's goods to God and to fraternal charity" (*CCC* 2401).

In this lesson we will study five main topics: the right to private property, respect for the property of others, respect for creation, the world of work and love for the poor.

1. The right to private property

Two great principles of Catholic social teaching govern the use and ownership of the world's goods. The first is that God intended the world's goods – that is the air, the water, the resources, the food and so on – to be available for all human beings. This principle is known as the universal destination of the world's goods. As the Catechism puts it, "The goods of creation are destined for the whole human race" (*CCC* 2402). The second principle follows from the first. In order to ensure that each person has access to what he needs for himself and for those in his care, it is fitting that people be able to own property. This principle is the right to private property. The ownership of property not only gives security and the ability to provide for the future, it also enhances the sense of freedom and responsibility, and indeed the dignity, of persons.

But the universal destination of goods always takes precedence over private property if there are people who are going without the basic necessities of life. If this happens, those with private property must come to their assistance so that everyone has what he needs. In the words of the Second Vatican Council, "In his use of things man should regard the external goods he legitimately owns not merely as exclusive to himself but common to others also, in the sense that they can benefit others as well as himself" (*GS* 69 §1). In this way the owner of property is "a steward of providence, with the task of making it fruitful and communicating its benefits to others, first of all his family" (*CCC* 2404).

2. Respect for the property of others

That brings us to our second topic, respect for the property of others. Here we consider the principal sin against the seventh commandment: stealing or theft. Theft is defined as taking another's property against the reasonable will of the owner. We can understand what is wrong with theft by applying the golden rule. Just as we would not want anyone to steal our goods, it is a matter of justice that we should not steal the goods of our neighbour. Moreover, in every country stealing is a crime punishable by law.

However, as the Catechism explains, there are two situations in which taking the property of another is not stealing: "if consent can be presumed or if refusal is contrary to reason and the universal destination of goods" (CCC 2408). As regards the first, since stealing is taking goods "against the reasonable will of the owner", there are circumstances in which we can presume that the owner would be happy for us to take his property. For example, if the owner of an apple tree gives us some apples each year and in a given year he is away when the apples are ripe, we can presume that he would be happy for us to take some of his apples as usual. This would not be stealing since the consent of the owner is presumed.

The second situation is the case of "obvious and urgent necessity, when the only way to provide for immediate, essential needs (food, shelter, clothing...) is to put at one's disposal and use the property of others" (CCC 2408; cf. GS 69 §1). Since God intended the world's goods for the use of all, if someone is going hungry and no one will give him anything, he can take from another what he needs to relieve his immediate needs – eggs, a chicken, some bread or fruit – without being guilty of the sin of stealing.

The Catechism goes on to give examples of sins against the seventh commandment that involve the unjust taking and keeping of the property of another. They include deliberate keeping of goods lent or of objects lost without a reasonable effort to find the owner, business fraud and paying unjust wages. Other sins mentioned include corruption, taking for private purposes the common goods of an enterprise, work poorly done, tax evasion, forgery of cheques and invoices, excessive expenses and waste, and wilfully damaging the property of another (cf. CCC 2409). This is just a sample of the many possible sins against the seventh commandment.

An important principle in this area is that when someone has stolen or damaged another's property, the offender is morally obliged to make reparation, or restitution, for the harm caused. This would involve returning the stolen goods to the owner or paying for them, as well as paying for any losses the owner suffered as a result of not having the goods in his possession. For example, if someone broke the windscreen of a taxi, he would be liable to pay not only for the cost of the windscreen but also for the amount of money the driver would have earned while the car was off the road being repaired (cf. *CCC* 2412). If many years have passed and the person cannot remember from whom items were stolen, it is sufficient to make reparation by giving extra donations to charitable causes.

Reparation is so important that the priest cannot forgive the sin in confession unless the offender is willing to do all in his or her power to make good the harm caused. It is not sufficient simply to be sorry. One must be determined to make reparation insofar as possible.

As regards whether stealing is a venial or a mortal sin, this will depend on the amount of harm caused to the owner. Some thefts will be only a venial sin and some clearly mortal. A traditional "rule of thumb" is that the theft of the equivalent of a day's wages of a person would constitute a mortal sin. But it is not a matter of drawing lines between venial and mortal sins. We should resolve not to steal at all.

Is gambling a sin? The Catechism teaches: "Games of chance (card games, etc.) or wagers are not in themselves contrary to justice. They become morally unacceptable when they deprive someone of what is necessary to provide for his needs and those of others. The passion for gambling risks becoming an enslavement" (*CCC* 2413). As we all know, the habit of gambling can become an addiction, an enslavement, causing serious harm to the person and often to their family and friends. It is therefore important to know when to stop gambling so that it does not become an entrenched habit, and to encourage others to seek professional help if they have this problem.

3. RESPECT FOR CREATION

We come now to our third topic: respect for creation. The whole matter of care for the environment and creation is a justice issue governed by the seventh commandment, which commands respect for the integrity of creation. Creation, with its resources, plants and animals, is destined by God for the common good of all generations, past, present and future. It is a matter of justice, not only with respect to God but also with respect to our fellow human beings of the present and future generations, to care for what God has given us. The Catechism teaches: "Use of the mineral, vegetable and animal resources of the universe cannot be divorced from respect for moral imperatives. Man's dominion over inanimate and other living beings granted by the Creator is not absolute; it is limited by concern for the quality of life of his neighbour, including generations to come; it requires a religious respect for the integrity of creation" (*CCC* 2415). In a word, man is a steward of creation on behalf of the Creator, not the master of it.

In his encyclical *Caritas in Veritate* (2009), Pope Benedict XVI wrote: "In nature, the believer recognises the wonderful result of God's creative activity, which we may use responsibly to satisfy our legitimate needs, material or otherwise, while respecting the intrinsic balance of creation. If this vision is lost, we end up either considering nature an untouchable taboo or, on the contrary, abusing it. Neither attitude is consonant with the Christian vision of nature as the fruit of God's creation" (*CV* 48).

As regards our attitude to animals, while we should always treat them well and not cause them to suffer or die unnecessarily, they are there for the service of man, who has stewardship over them. "Hence", the Catechism says, "it is legitimate to use animals for food and clothing. They may be domesticated to help man in his work and leisure. Medical and scientific experimentation on animals, if it remains within reasonable limits, is a morally acceptable practice since it contributes to caring for or saving human lives" (*CCC* 2417).

4. THE WORLD OF WORK

That brings us to our fourth topic, the world of work. The Catechism stresses that economic activity in general must always have the good of man as its goal. It says that "the development of economic activity and growth in production are meant to provide for the needs of human beings. Economic life is not meant solely to multiply goods produced and increase profit or power; it is ordered first of all to the service of persons, of the whole man, and of the entire human community" (*CCC* 2426). Or, more briefly, "Man is himself the author, centre and goal of all economic and social life" (*CCC* 2459).

The Catechism goes on to consider the rich variety of meanings that work has. Human work proceeds from persons created in the image of God and called to prolong the work of creation by subduing the earth, both with and for others. Hence work is a duty, as St Paul writes to the Thessalonians: "If any one will not work, let him not eat" (*2 Thes* 3:10). Moreover, work honours and develops the gifts and talents the worker has received from God, thus improving the worker himself. What is more, work can be redemptive. By enduring the toil and hardships of work in union with Jesus Christ, who worked as a carpenter and redeemed us by his death on the Cross, man collaborates in some way with Christ in his work of redemption. In so doing, he also

shows himself to be a disciple of Jesus by taking up his cross daily in his work. In all of this it is clear that work can be a means of sanctification, of growth in holiness. By offering his work to God, doing it well and with love, in a spirit of prayerfulness, the worker is truly sanctified and united with God. Finally, by bringing Christian values into work, values like honesty, charity and justice, work becomes a means for the Christianisation of society itself (cf. *CCC* 2427). Truly work has momentous value when we look at like this. This is in addition to the value of work as a means of providing a livelihood for the worker and his or her family and as a service to society.

What is the role of the state in economic activity? In a long quote from

Pope John Paul II's encyclical *Centesimus Annus* (1991), the Catechism says: "Economic activity, especially the activity of a market economy, cannot be conducted in an institutional, juridical or political vacuum. On the contrary, it presupposes sure guarantees of individual freedom and private property, as well as a stable currency and efficient public services. Hence the principal task of the state is to guarantee this security, so that those who work and produce can enjoy the fruits of their labours and thus feel encouraged to work efficiently and honestly... Another task of the state is that of overseeing and directing the exercise of human rights in the economic sector. However, primary responsibility in this area belongs not to the state but to individuals and to the various groups and associations which make up society" (*CA* 48; *CCC* 2431).

As regards the role of management and the importance of profits, the Catechism says that business leaders "are responsible to society for the economic and ecological effects of their operations. They have an obligation to consider the good of persons and not only the increase of profits. Profits are necessary, however. They make possible the investments that ensure the future of a business and they guarantee employment" (*CCC* 2432). Once again we see how the good of persons takes precedence over the increase of profits, even though profits are of course necessary to ensure the viability of the business.

The Catechism stresses the importance of avoiding discrimination in the area of employment: "Access to employment and to professions must be open to all without unjust discrimination: men and women, healthy and disabled, natives and immigrants. For its part society should, according to circumstances, help citizens find work and employment" (cf. *LE* 19; *CA* 48; *CCC* 2433).

As regards payment for work, the Catechism gives some criteria. A just wage is the legitimate fruit of work and therefore to refuse or withhold it can be a grave injustice. In determining fair pay both the needs and the contributions of each person must be taken into account. As the Second Vatican Council says, "Remuneration for work should guarantee man the opportunity to provide a dignified livelihood for himself and his family on the material, social, cultural and spiritual level, taking into account the role and the productivity of each, the state of the business, and the common good" (GS 67 §2). That is, there can be circumstances in which the state of the business does not allow the payment of high wages, but in general firms should pay their workers what is traditionally called a *family wage*, a wage sufficient to support an average family.

What is more, agreement between the parties is not sufficient to justify morally the amount to be paid in wages (cf. CCC 2434). For example, it can happen in a place of widespread unemployment that workers are so desperate to find work that they will freely agree to work for a wage which is insufficient to feed their family. While they have agreed to work for this wage, this does not mean that the wage is just.

Is it legitimate for workers to go on strike? The Catechism answers: "Recourse to a strike is morally legitimate when it cannot be avoided, or at least when it is necessary to obtain a proportionate benefit. It becomes morally unacceptable when accompanied by violence, or when objectives are included that are not directly linked to working conditions or are contrary to the common good" (CCC 2435). For example, strikes for political or ideological reasons are unacceptable, as are strikes which would cripple the economy and thus harm a large number of innocent people, or strikes which leave people without essential services such as food supply, health care, or police protection.

Related to the question of work is that of unemployment, which has many serious consequences. As the Catechism says, it "almost always wounds its victim's dignity and threatens the equilibrium of his life. Besides the harm done to him personally, it entails many risks for his family" (CCC 2436). Therefore business leaders, workers and government officials should do everything possible to maximise employment opportunities.

5. LOVE FOR THE POOR

This brings us to our fifth and final topic, love for the poor. It is very much related to the seventh commandment, which teaches us how to use material goods, not only for ourselves but also for the good of others.

To begin with, God blesses those who come to the aid of the poor and he rebukes those who turn away from them. Jesus says in the Sermon on the Mount: "Give to him who begs from you, do not refuse him who would borrow from you" (*Mt* 5:42). And he promises eternal life to those who serve him through the poor: "Come, O blessed of my Father, inherit the kingdom prepared for you from the foundation of the world; for I was hungry and you gave me food, I was thirsty and you gave me drink, I was a stranger and you welcomed me..." (*Mt* 25:34-35).

As we all know, the Church's love for the poor is a part of her constant tradition. This love is inspired by the Gospel of the Beatitudes, of the poverty of Jesus and of his concern for the poor. It is seen today in all the charitable and welfare works carried out by Church agencies all over the world and by the great work of the St Vincent de Paul Society. Love for the poor is even one of the reasons for the duty of working, so as to be able to give to those in need (cf. *CCC* 2444).

Love for the poor is incompatible with immoderate love of riches or their selfish use. St James is particularly scathing in condemning those who are attached to their wealth. He writes:

> Come now, you rich, weep and howl for the miseries that are coming upon you. Your riches have rotted and your garments are moth-eaten. Your gold and silver have rusted, and their rust will be evidence against you and will eat your flesh like fire. You have laid up treasure for the last days. Behold, the wages of the labourers who mowed your fields, which you kept back by fraud, cry out; and the cries of the harvesters have reached the ears of the Lord of hosts. You have lived on the earth in luxury and in pleasure; you have fattened your hearts in a day of slaughter. You have condemned, you have killed the righteous man; he does not resist you (*Jas* 5:1-6; *CCC* 2445).

St John Chrysostom says that failure to give to the poor is equivalent to stealing from them. He writes: "Not to enable the poor to share in our goods is to steal from them and deprive them of life. The goods we possess are not ours, but theirs" (*Hom. in Lazaro* 2, 5; *CCC* 2446). And St Gregory the Great writes in a similar vein: "When we attend to the needs of those in want, we give them what is theirs, not ours. More than performing works of mercy, we are paying a debt of justice" (*Regula Pastoralis* 3, 21; *CCC* 2446). This can be understood in terms of the principle of the universal destination of the world's goods. God intended that all would have access at least to what was necessary for their survival, so that the poor have a right in justice to this minimum. In this sense the goods we possess belong to the poor.

The various deeds by which we help our neighbour in need are summed up in what are traditionally called the works of mercy. They are divided into seven corporal works of mercy, which refer to our neighbour's bodily needs, and seven spiritual works, which refer to his spiritual needs. The corporal works are to feed the hungry, give drink to the thirsty, clothe the naked, shelter the homeless, visit the sick, visit the imprisoned and bury the dead. The spiritual works of mercy are to counsel the doubtful, instruct the ignorant, admonish sinners, comfort the afflicted, forgive offences, bear wrongs patiently and pray for the living and the dead (cf. *Mt* 25:31-46; *CCC* 2447).

St Rose of Lima gives us a beautiful example of love for the poor. When her mother scolded her for caring for the poor and the sick at home, St Rose answered: "When we serve the poor and the sick, we serve Jesus. We must not fail to help our neighbours, because in them we serve Jesus" (P. Hansen, *Vita mirabilis*; *CCC* 2449).

That concludes our study of the seventh commandment which, as we have seen, covers a wide range of matters all related to the virtue of justice and the use of material goods. In the next lesson we will study the last three commandments. Until then, may God bless you and guide you gently through the week.

QUESTIONS FOR DISCUSSION

1. God intended the world's goods to be available for all.
   What are some ways we can use our own goods to benefit
   those in need?
2. There are many ways we can in effect steal almost without
   realising it. What are some of these ways?
3. Why is making restitution for what we have stolen so
   important that the priest cannot forgive the sin of stealing
   if we are unwilling to make it?
4. What are some ways we can exercise care for creation as
   stewards of God?
5. Which of the various meanings of work do you find most
   helpful in carrying out your own work with more sense of
   purpose?

POINTS TO REMEMBER

- The seventh commandment requires us to respect the
  property of others and forbids us to damage or steal it.
- The Church upholds the right to private property but this
  right must always give way to the prior right of all to a
  share of the world's goods.
- Theft is taking another's property against the reasonable
  will of the owner.
- If we have stolen or damaged another's property, before we
  can be forgiven we must be prepared to make restitution
  for the harm caused.
- We should respect God's creation, regarding ourselves as
  stewards of it.
- Human work perfects not only God's creation but the
  worker as well and can be a true means of sanctificati

23. THE LAST THREE COMMANDMENTS

If you love me, you will keep my commandments (Jn 14:15)

SUMMARY

In this lesson we study the last three commandments. The eighth commandment relates to the virtue of truthfulness and respect for our neighbour's good name, the ninth to internal sins against chastity and the tenth to internal sins against our neighbour's goods.

We begin with the eighth commandment, studying the important virtue of truthfulness, which is vital for the flourishing of any society. We must be able to trust that others are telling us the truth if we are to live in peace and harmony with them. Next we look at sins against the truth, the most obvious one being lying. We study the seriousness of lying, the reason why it is wrong and the special sin of lying under oath, which is perjury.

Our third topic is sins against the good name of another. Here we study the three principal sins of rash judgment, detraction and slander, plus that of revealing secrets without good reason.

Then we study the ninth commandment, which forbids coveting or desiring our neighbour's wife and commands us to live purity of heart, which is very much associated with the virtue of modesty.

Finally, we study the tenth commandment, which forbids coveting our neighbour's goods through greed and envy, and commands us to live detachment from material things.

Welcome once again to "Journey into Truth", our excursion into the marvellous truths of the Catholic faith. In this lesson we will study the last three of the Ten Commandments and in the final lesson we will study prayer, the Our Father and Hail Mary in particular.

In the last lesson, as you recall, we studied the seventh commandment – You shall not steal – which deals with a variety of issues related to the virtue of justice and the use of material goods. In this lesson we will begin with the eighth commandment – You shall not bear false witness against your neighbour – which refers to the virtue of truthfulness and the good name of our neighbour. Then we will consider the last two commandments, which forbid internal sins against the sixth and seventh commandments.

But let us begin with a prayer. Heavenly Father, you communicated your divine truth by sending us your eternal Word, Jesus Christ, who revealed himself as the Way, the Truth and the Life. Jesus is the fulness of truth and he taught us to live always in the truth. Help us to use the gift of speech to communicate only the truth and to respect the good name of our neighbour. We make our prayer through Christ our Lord. Amen.

In this lesson we will study five main topics: the eighth commandment and the virtue of truthfulness, sins against the truth, sins against the good name of our neighbour, the ninth commandment and the tenth commandment.

1. THE EIGHTH COMMANDMENT AND THE VIRTUE OF TRUTHFULNESS

The eighth commandment, as we have said, is You shall not bear false witness against your neighbour. The Catechism sums up the commandment, saying:

"The eighth commandment forbids misrepresenting the truth in our relations with others. This moral prescription flows from the vocation of the holy people to bear witness to their God who is the truth and wills the truth. Offences against the truth express by word or deed a refusal to commit oneself to moral uprightness: they are fundamental infidelities to God and, in this sense, they undermine the foundations of the covenant" (*CCC* 2464).

As this point says, God is the truth and so to live in God is to live in the truth, to be truthful in everything we say and do. To be sure, our very nature seeks truth. We see this in children, who are always asking questions: Why is the sky blue? Where do babies come from? and so on. The Second Vatican Council teaches: "It is in accordance with their dignity that all men, because they are persons ... are both impelled by their nature and bound by a moral obligation to seek the truth, especially religious truth. They are also bound to adhere to the truth once they come to know it and direct their whole lives in accordance with the demands of truth" (*DH* 2 §2; *CCC* 2467).

To seek the truth, to hold to the truth and to communicate the truth are all aspects of the virtue of truthfulness, which the Catechism defines as "the virtue which consists in showing oneself true in deeds and truthful in words, and in guarding against duplicity, dissimulation and hypocrisy" (*CCC* 2468). The virtue is also called sincerity or candour. This virtue is absolutely fundamental for our dealings with others and for the wellbeing of society. St Thomas Aquinas puts it bluntly: "Men could not live with one another if there were not mutual confidence that they were being truthful to one another" (*STh* II-II, 109, 3 *ad* 1).

The virtue of truthfulness is related to justice in that it gives to another what is his due. That is, people have a right to know that what is communicated to them is true. This does not mean, naturally, that we are obliged to tell everyone the whole truth. In the words of the Catechism, "Truthfulness keeps to the just mean between what ought to be expressed and what ought to be kept secret: it entails honesty and discretion" (*CCC* 2469). We are all aware of situations in which it is not opportune to tell someone the whole truth about a particular matter. For example, parents need not reveal to their children certain aspects of their own relationship or their financial situation. The solution in these cases is not to tell lies, but simply to remain silent about certain matters.

Among the truths we are obliged to communicate are the truths of our faith. Christ himself, before Pontius Pilate, says that he "has come into the world, to bear witness to the truth" (*Jn* 18:37). And John the Baptist bore witness to the truth before King Herod, who had John put to death for telling him he should not have married his brother Philip's wife (cf. *Mk* 6:14-29). So too the Christian, as a follower of Jesus Christ, should not be afraid to share the faith with others. Christ says to all: "So every one who acknowledges me before men, I also will acknowledge before my Father who is in heaven" (*Mt* 10:32).

2. SINS AGAINST THE TRUTH

Our second topic is sins against the truth. The most obvious sin against the truth is the lie, which St Augustine defines as "speaking a falsehood with the intention of deceiving" (*De mendacio* 4, 5). Of great importance in the definition is the phrase "with the intention of deceiving." Thus if someone says sincerely that today is Tuesday when in fact it is Wednesday, he is telling an untruth but not a lie. Only when a person knowingly tells an untruth with the intention of deceiving is it a lie. In view of this, when another says something which is clearly untrue, we must be careful not to accuse him of lying, for he may sincerely believe he is telling the truth. Jesus denounces lying as the work of the devil: "You are of your father the devil... there is no truth in him. When he lies, he speaks according to his own nature, for he is a liar and the father of lies" (*Jn* 8:44; *CCC* 2482).

How serious is the sin of lying? In the words of the Catechism, "The gravity of a lie is measured against the nature of the truth it deforms, the circumstances, the intentions of the one who lies, and the harm suffered by its victims. In general a lie in itself, insofar as it is contrary to truthfulness, is a venial sin, but it becomes mortal when it does grave injury to the virtues of justice and charity" (*CCC* 2484). Only when it causes grave harm to another would a lie be a mortal sin.

Especially serious is telling a lie under oath in court, which is the original meaning of bearing false witness against our neighbour. As the Catechism says, "When it is made publicly, a statement contrary to the truth takes on a particular gravity. In court it becomes false witness. When it is under oath, it is perjury" (*CCC* 2476). Perjury is especially serious because it calls upon God to bear witness to a lie, and also because it can contribute to the conviction of someone who is innocent, or the acquittal of someone who is guilty.

The Catechism goes on to describe why lying is wrong: "It is a profanation of speech, whereas the purpose of speech is to communicate known truth to others. The deliberate intention of leading a neighbour into error by saying things contrary to the truth constitutes a failure in justice and charity. The culpability is greater when the intention of deceiving entails the risk of deadly consequences for those who are led astray" (*CCC* 2485).

In a very strong statement, the Catechism goes on to say that "since it violates the virtue of truthfulness, a lie does real violence to another. It affects his ability to know, which is a condition of every judgment and decision. It contains the seed of discord and all consequent evils. Lying is destructive of society; it undermines trust among men and tears apart the fabric of social relationships" (*CCC* 2486).

3. SINS AGAINST THE GOOD NAME OF ANOTHER

That brings us to our third topic, sins against the good name of another. Bearing false witness against our neighbour also includes sins which harm his good name. We are all aware that our good name, our good reputation in the eyes of others, is very important to us. It affects our dealings with others and our ability to function well in society. Without a good reputation people will not trust us and we will find it difficult to get a job or to enter into meaningful relationships. Therefore it is very important to respect our neighbour's reputation, just as we expect others to respect ours. St Thomas Aquinas is very clear on this: "It is a serious matter to take away the good esteem of another, because among man's temporal possessions nothing is more precious than his good name; if he lacks this he is prevented from doing many good things. Therefore it is said: 'Take care of your good name; for this will be a more lasting possession of yours than a thousand valuable and precious treasures'" (*STh* II, II, q. 73, a. 2).

There are three principal sins against the good name of our neighbour: rash judgment, detraction and slander.

Rash judgment

The first sin, rash judgment, remains in our mind and consists in assuming as true, without sufficient reason, the moral fault of our neighbour (cf. *CCC* 2477). For example, we may judge that some member of our family has taken our wallet when in fact we have simply left it in the car. Or we may judge that because someone is late for an appointment he or she is at home watching the end of a television program, when it fact they have been held up in a traffic jam.

While we can judge another's external behaviour – for example, that someone arrived late for work three days in a row – we can never presume to judge why they did it. It would be a rash judgment to conclude that they were lazy and trying to cheat the employer, where in fact their wife may have been in hospital and they had to drive their children to school. Rash judgment consists precisely in making a judgment of the intentions or motives of others without sufficient foundation. Therefore, when we do not know the motives, in order to avoid sinning by rash judgment we should endeavour as a general rule to interpret the other's conduct in a favourable way, giving them the benefit of the doubt. After all, that is how we would like others to treat us.

Our Lord himself was very clear: "Judge not, that you be not judged. For with the judgement you pronounce you will be judged, and the measure you give will be the measure you get" (*Mt* 7-1-2).The Second

Vatican Council sums it up: "God alone is the judge and searcher of hearts; for that reason he forbids us to make judgments about the internal guilt of anyone" (*GS* 28).

Detraction

The second sin, detraction, consists in disclosing, without good reason, another's faults and failings to persons who did not know them (cf. *CCC* 2477). Here the other person has in fact done something wrong but we reveal this fault to others without a sufficient reason. For example, we may be aware that someone is addicted to gambling or to alcohol but we have no right to reveal this to others, for that would be to blacken the person's good name. Just as we would not want others to blacken our reputation in this way, so we must avoid doing so to them. The most common form of detraction is what is known as gossip, where people pass on to others negative aspects of someone's life. When others want to pass on gossip, we should show no interest and, if possible, say something good about the person.

In what circumstances would it be permissible to pass on this information? Only when it is necessary for the good of the person with the fault, for the common good or for the good of some other innocent person would we be justified in disclosing negative information. For example, if we knew that a young person had a habit of using drugs or was contemplating suicide, we could disclose this to their parents. Or if we knew that someone running for public office had a history of dishonesty, we could make this fact known. In general, there will be few cases in which we can reveal the hidden faults of others.

Slander

The third sin against the good name of our neighbour is slander, sometimes called calumny. It consists in telling lies that damage another's reputation (cf. *CCC* 2477). It is obvious that slander is even worse than detraction since it involves a lie that damages our neighbour's reputation. We all know how we would feel if someone told lies about us and so we should be careful to avoid doing so to others.

What is so harmful about detraction and slander is that it is practically impossible to restore a person's good name once it has been damaged. Even though the person who began the gossip or lie apologises publicly and defends the good name of the other, people will always harbour suspicions that the person may actually be guilty of the fault.

Because everyone has a right to a good name, sins against the good name of another are a violation of justice as well as of charity. As with other sins against justice, there is an obligation to make restitution for the harm caused by detraction and slander, but it is usually almost impossible to restore the person's good reputation. "The mud sticks", as they say.

To avoid falling into these sins, it is important to avoid curiosity about others' lives, to show a dislike for gossip, to be very careful in talking about others, saying only positive things about them, and to listen to both sides before making a judgment about others.

Revealing secrets

Another way of sinning against the good name of others is the revelation of secrets without good reason. We may come to know certain sensitive things through observing them ourselves, through friends who reveal them to us or through our professional work, for example in the case of doctors, counsellors, lawyers, accountants and politicians. In all these cases we are obliged not to reveal confidential information if revealing it could harm another in any way. Nonetheless, there can be circumstances in which secrets may be revealed for a proportionate reason. The Catechism says that this may be done only "in exceptional cases where keeping the secret is bound to cause very grave harm to the one who confided it, to the one who received it or to a third party, and where the very grave harm can be avoided only by divulging the truth" (*CCC* 2491). In general, then, any private information we may have which is prejudicial to another is not to be divulged without a proportionate reason.

4. THE NINTH COMMANDMENT: YOU SHALL NOT COVET YOUR NEIGHBOUR'S WIFE

This brings us to the ninth commandment, You shall not covet your neighbour's wife. The word covet, by the way, means to desire in a disordered way and so the commandment forbids internal sins against the sixth commandment, in the area of chastity. As we saw when we studied the sixth commandment, Our Lord himself spoke of these disordered lustful desires: "You have heard that it was said, 'You shall not commit adultery.' But I say to you that every one who looks at a woman lustfully has already committed adultery with her in his heart" (*Mt* 5:27-28).

The ninth commandment calls us to live purity of heart, so that our affections and desires are always properly ordered. What do we mean by the heart, in this sense? The Catechism explains that in common language we refer to the heart as the seat of moral personality. For example, Scripture says: "Out of the heart come evil thoughts, murder, adultery, fornication ..." (*Mt* 15:19). The struggle against the wayward desires of the flesh, therefore, entails purifying the heart and practising temperance.

Jesus calls us to purity of heart in the Sermon on the Mount, when he gives us the beatitudes: "Blessed are the pure in heart, for they shall see God" (*Mt* 5:8). What do we mean by "pure in heart?" As the Catechism explains, "'Pure in heart' refers to those who have attuned their intellects and wills to the demands of God's holiness" (*CCC* 2518). That is, they have their thoughts and desires ordered to their true good, to God, not to what is sinful and offensive to God. Purity of heart is very important in moral life. In the words of the Catechism, "The 'pure in heart' are promised that they will see God face to face and be like him. Purity of heart is the precondition of the vision of God." What is more, the

Catechism goes on to say, "even now it enables us to see according to God, to accept others as 'neighbours'; it lets us perceive the human body – ours and our neighbour's – as a temple of the Holy Spirit, a manifestation of divine beauty" (CCC 2519). What a great difference there is between someone with purity of heart who looks on his neighbour's body as a manifestation of divine beauty, and someone who looks on the body with lust, as an object of pleasure.

Purity of heart is very much associated with the virtue of modesty. As the Catechism says, "modesty protects the intimate centre of the person. It means refusing to unveil what should remain hidden ... It guides how one looks at others and behaves toward them in conformity with the dignity of persons and their solidarity" (CCC 2521). The Catechism goes on to give a beautiful explanation of the role of modesty: "Modesty protects the mystery of persons and their love. It encourages patience and moderation in loving relationships; it requires that the conditions for the definitive giving and commitment of man and woman to one another be fulfilled. Modesty is decency. It inspires one's choice of clothing. It keeps silence or reserve where there is evident risk of unhealthy curiosity. It is discreet" (CCC 2522). We all understand the difference between a modest person and a lewd or sensuous one.

What does the ninth commandment forbid? It is traditionally taught that there are three types of internal sins against chastity: taking pleasure in past sins, desire of future impure acts, and taking pleasure in imaginary impure acts. With all of them it is important to remember that impure thoughts, memories or imaginations on their own are not sinful; it is only the consent of the will, the deliberate taking pleasure in them, that makes them sinful.

5. THE TENTH COMMANDMENT: YOU SHALL NOT COVET YOUR NEIGHBOUR'S GOODS

This brings us to the tenth and final commandment: You shall not covet your neighbour's goods. Just as the ninth commandment forbids internal sins against the sixth commandment, so the tenth forbids internal sins against the seventh: You shall not steal. It forbids greed, or avarice, a disordered desire for material things, which can lead to such sins as stealing and fraud. Greed is a sort of idolatry, a worshipping of material goods rather than worshipping their creator. The *Roman Catechism* explains it graphically:

> When the Law says, "You shall not covet," these words mean that we should banish our desires for whatever does not belong to us. Our thirst for another's goods is immense, infinite, never quenched. Thus it is written: "He who loves money never has money enough" (*Roman Catechism*, III, 37; cf. *Sir* 5:8; *CCC* 2536).

We know the truth of the statement that whoever loves money never has money enough. We see how some very wealthy people are never satisfied and their greed leads them to invent dishonest schemes to make even more money, until they are finally caught and sent to jail.

The tenth commandment forbids envy of others' goods, which is "sadness at the sight of another's goods and the immoderate desire to acquire them for oneself, even unjustly" (*CCC* 2539). It can lead to the worst forms of injustice, including killing another to obtain his property. We read in the book of Wisdom: "Through the devil's envy death entered the world" (*Wis* 2:24). And St John Chrysostom writes:

> We fight one another, and envy arms us against one another... If everyone strives to unsettle the Body of Christ, where shall we end up? We are engaged in making Christ's Body a corpse ... We declare ourselves members of one and the same organism, yet we devour one another like beasts (*Hom. in 2 Cor.* 27, 3-4).

Envy, like greed, is one of the seven deadly or capital sins and the Fathers of the Church wrote powerfully about it. For example, St Augustine saw envy as "the diabolical sin" (*De catechizandis rudibus* 4, 8), and St Gregory the Great wrote: "From envy are born hatred, detraction, calumny, joy caused by the misfortune of a neighbour, and displeasure caused by his prosperity" (*Moralia in Job* 31, 45; *CCC* 2539).

What can we do to overcome the tendency to envy and greed? In the first place we should make a constant effort to grow in our love for God, who is the infinite good and who alone can satisfy the longings of our heart. We recall the words of St Augustine: "You have made us for yourself, and our heart is restless until it rests in you" (*Conf.* 1, 1, 1). The more we love God the less we will be concerned about the things of this world. At the same time we should make an effort to be more detached from material things, following Our Lord's advice: "Therefore do not be anxious, saying, 'What shall we eat?' or 'What shall we drink?' or 'What shall we wear?' For the Gentiles seek all these things; and your heavenly Father knows that you need them all. But seek first his kingdom and his righteousness, and all these things shall be yours as well" (*Mt* 6:31-33). Jesus sums it up in the Beatitudes: "Blessed are the poor in spirit, for theirs is the Kingdom of Heaven" (*Mt* 5:3).

Just as we were made by God, in his image and likeness, so we are called to be with God forever in heaven. If we are detached from the things of this world we will have a greater desire to see God and be with him for all eternity.

This concludes our study of the commandments and of the third part of the Catechism, our moral life in Christ. In the next lesson we will end our journey into truth by considering our life of prayer, especially prayer to our Father God and to Our Lady. Until then, may God bless you and keep you in his love.

QUESTIONS FOR DISCUSSION

1. What is so bad about telling lies?

2. We often make rash judgments about someone only to discover that we were very wrong. How can we avoid making these judgments?

3. What is so bad about gossip?

4. The virtue of modesty is often sadly lacking. What are some common examples of immodesty and what can we do to help restore the practice of this important virtue?

5. Greed has been an important cause of economic hardship for many. What can we do to avoid falling into this vice ourselves?

POINTS TO REMEMBER

- The eighth commandment requires us to live in the truth and to respect our neighbour's good name.

- The principal sin against truthfulness is the lie, which is saying something false with the intention of deceiving.

- The three principal sins against the good name of another are rash judgment, detraction and slander.

- Secrets must always be kept unless keeping them could cause grave harm to the one who confided them, to the one who received them or to another person.

- The ninth commandment forbids sins of thought against chastity and commands us to live purity of heart and modesty.

- The tenth commandment forbids greed and envy and it commands us to live detachment from material things.

24. Prayer to the Father through Mary

But when you pray, go into your room and shut the door and pray to your Father who is in secret; and your Father who sees in secret will reward you (Mt 6:6)

Summary

We come now to the end of our journey into the truths of the Catholic faith. We turn to Part Four of the Catechism, which deals with Christian prayer, to study our relationship with God our Father, the Our Father itself and prayer to Mary, our mother.

First we study what it means to call God our Father and how we should live if we want to be good daughters and sons of his.

Then we study the prayer Our Saviour taught us and which is said by Christians everywhere: the Our Father. We look at each phrase of the prayer and what it means for us.

Thirdly, following a traditional custom, we call upon the intercession of Mary, our mother, who leads us to Christ and who in turn leads us to the Father. Here we consider the beautiful words of the Hail Mary and what they mean for us.

We end our journey into truth considering how we can put our faith into practice so as to grow in a personal, loving relationship with Christ, who will lead us to the Father's house in heaven.

Welcome to the final lesson of our journey into truth. I hope you have enjoyed the trip and that you are truly growing in the faith.

You will recall that in the fifth lesson we studied various aspects of the personal relationship with God which is prayer. There we considered, among other things, the nature and importance of prayer, the different types of prayer, and the times and places for prayer. In this lesson we conclude our journey of faith by considering what is truly the goal of our life: union with God our Father through his Son Jesus Christ by the hand of Our Lady. We will study in particular the Our Father and the Hail Mary.

But first let us pray. Heavenly Father, you are the beginning and the end of our whole existence. You are not only our creator but our loving Father, who knew us from all eternity, who have a personal plan for each one of us, who watch over us in your loving providence, and who want us to be with you forever in heaven. Help us to grow in love for you and to relate to you as your children, so that we may find the happiness you want for us in this life and in the next. Our Father who art in heaven, hallowed be thy name. Thy kingdom come. Thy will be done on earth, as it is in heaven. Give us this day our daily bread, and forgive us our trespasses, as we forgive those who trespass against us, and lead us not into temptation, but deliver us from evil. Amen (*Mt* 6:9-13).

All Christians are familiar with this beautiful prayer, the Our Father, and we all love it. Others too, when they come to learn it, take it to heart and find it a joy to say. After all, God is truly a father and it is good to pray to him as his children. In this lesson we will study four topics: God as father, the Our Father, prayer to Mary and putting our faith into practice.

1. GOD AS FATHER

As Christians we have the joy of knowing that the God who created the universe out of nothing is not just a creator, an all-powerful supreme being, who could in the end be very distant from his creatures. Rather he reveals himself as a God who is very close to us, who is our Father. It is Jesus himself who teaches us to call God our Father: "Our Father who art in heaven". St Cyprian, a third-century Father of the Church from North Africa, explains what this means for us:

> How merciful the Lord Jesus is towards us, how abundantly kind and good! He permits us, when praying in the sight of God, to call God our Father and to be called sons of God even as Christ is Son of God. Not one of us would dare to use that name in prayer, had not he himself allowed us to pray in that way. We must remember, then, dearest brothers, we must realise that when we call God 'Father', we ought to act like sons of God, so that as we are pleased to have God as our Father, so he will be pleased with us (*De Dom. orat.*, 11-12).

This relationship with God as our Father is truly an awesome gift. It is not only that we can *call* God our Father; we truly *are* his sons and daughters by Baptism. As we have seen, when we are baptised we are reborn as sons and daughters of God, we become members of Christ, the eternal Son of God, and so become children of God the Father by adoption (cf. *CCC* 1213, 2782). St Cyprian explains: "The new man, reborn and restored to his God by grace, says first of all, 'Father!' because he has now begun to be a son" (*De Dom. orat.* 9).

The Lord's Prayer, where we call God Father, not only reveals the Father to us, it also reveals our own dignity as children of God. In the often-quoted words of the Second Vatican Council, "Christ ... in the very revelation of the mystery of the Father and of his love, fully reveals man to himself and brings to light his most high calling" (*GS* 22 § 1; cf. *CCC* 2783). St Ambrose explains it like this:

> O man, you did not dare to raise your face to heaven, you lowered your eyes to the earth, and suddenly you have received the grace of Christ: all your sins have been forgiven. From being a wicked servant you have become a good son ... Then raise your eyes to the Father who has begotten you through Baptism, to the Father who has redeemed you through his Son, and say: "Our Father..." But do not claim any privilege. He is the Father in a special way only

of Christ, but he is the common Father of us all, because while he has begotten only Christ, he has created us. Then also say by his grace, "Our Father," so that you may merit being his son (*De Sacr.* 5, 4, 19).

If through Baptism we receive the gift of divine filiation, of being adopted as children of God our Father, what should this mean for us? The Catechism answers: "The free gift of adoption requires on our part continual conversion and new life. Praying to our Father should develop in us two fundamental dispositions:

1. "First, *the desire to become like him*: though created in his image, we are restored to his likeness by grace; and we must respond to this grace" (*CCC* 2784). That is, as children of God by Baptism, we should strive to become more Christlike, and thus to resemble our Father God more and more, as Christ does. "Like father, like son", goes the popular saying. St John Chrysostom explains: "You cannot call the God of all kindness your Father if you preserve a cruel and inhuman heart; for in this case you no longer have in you the marks of the heavenly Father's kindness" (*De orat. Dom.* 3). It is a reminder always to live as good children of God, striving to be more like him in kindness, patience, forgiveness, generosity and so on.

2. The second fundamental disposition required of us as children of our Father God is "a *humble and trusting heart* that enables us 'to turn and become like children': for it is to 'little children' that the Father is revealed" (*Mt* 18:3; *Mt* 11:25; *CCC* 2785). That is, if we really believe that God is our Father, we will approach him with humility and trust, like little children before their father. When things are going wrong in our life or we are anxious about the future, we can place absolute trust in God our Father, who loves us and will always give us what is best. St Augustine comments: "Our Father: at this name love is aroused in us ... and the confidence of obtaining what we are about to ask... What would he not give to his children who ask, since he has already granted them the gift of being his children?" (*De serm. Dom. in monte* 2, 4, 16).

2. THE OUR FATHER

That brings us to our second topic, a consideration of the prayer Christ gave us, the Our Father, also known as the Lord's Prayer. This is the essentially Christian prayer, taught by Jesus himself and recorded in the Gospel of Matthew. It is said by all Christians. Tertullian called the Lord's Prayer "the summary of the whole gospel" (*De orat.* 1; *CCC* 2761). St Augustine too comments on how complete the Our Father is: "Run through all the words of the holy prayers [in Scripture], and I do not think that you will find anything in them that is not contained and included in the Lord's Prayer" (*Ep.* 130, 12, 22). And St Thomas Aquinas writes: "The Lord's Prayer is the most perfect of prayers ... In it we ask, not only for all the things we can rightly desire, but also in the sequence that they should be desired. This prayer not only teaches us to ask for things, but also in what order we should desire them" (*STh* II-II, 83, 9).

As we begin the Our Father the first thing we notice is that we say "our Father", not "my Father". This means that we are praying not as individuals asking only for our personal needs, but as members of the Church, in union with all Christians. We are praying for the needs of all, not just for our own.

When we say "who art in heaven" we do not mean that God is in some far off place, very distant from us, but rather that he is in a way of being which is exceedingly holy, yet very close to us. St Augustine goes so far as to say: "'Our Father who art in heaven' is rightly understood to mean that God is in the hearts of the just, as in his holy temple" (*De serm. Dom. in monte* 2, 5, 18). So our Father God is in our soul in the state of grace as well as in the heaven that awaits us at the end of our life, where we will be in the company of the Father, Son and Holy Spirit, as well as of Our Lady and all the angels and saints.

After saying "Our Father who art in heaven" we go on to make seven petitions. The first three are centred on God himself: "hallowed be thy name, thy kingdom come, thy will be done". The last four are centred on our own needs, asking for our daily bread, forgiveness of our sins, strength to overcome temptation and deliverance from evil.

When we say "hallowed be thy name" we are asking that God's name be held holy by ourselves and by all. We know that many people misuse the name of God and so we ask that we may always honour that name and use it in a holy way, with reverence and love. In so doing we ourselves become more holy and so we glorify God by our very lives.

The second petition is "thy kingdom come". In a very real sense the kingdom of God has already come in the person of Jesus Christ and in his Church, which is the beginning of the kingdom on earth. But not all acknowledge Christ's reign over them, and so we pray that, beginning with ourselves, Christ may reign in the hearts of all, that all may accept him into their lives and honour him as their God and king, living lives of true holiness. This petition can also refer to Christ's second coming at the end of time, when his kingdom will be brought to fulfilment.

The third petition is "thy will be done on earth as it is in heaven". What is God's will? The Catechism answers: "Our Father 'desires all men to be saved and to come to the knowledge of the truth'" (*1 Tim* 2:3-4; *CCC* 2822). To pray that God's will be done is therefore to pray that all may believe in God and find eternal salvation. But it is also to pray that each one of us may do what God is asking of us personally. God has a particular will for each one of us in every moment, and it is up to us to discover it and carry it out. So when we pray "thy will be done" we are not saying empty words. We must be ready to do God's will in every moment. In this Christ is the model. As he said to his Father in the garden, "not my will, but yours, be done" (*Lk* 22:42; *CCC* 2824). By imitating Christ, we will do God's will on earth as it is done in heaven and we will grow in the holiness to which we are all called.

In the fourth petition, the first of those referring to our own needs, we say "give us this day our daily bread". We say "give us" with the confidence that God, our loving Father, will hear and answer our prayer. And we say "us", not "me", to make clear that we are praying not only for our own personal needs but for those of all mankind. When we say "bread" we are referring not just to bread itself but to all our needs. As the Catechism says, it refers to all "the nourishment life requires: all appropriate goods and blessings, both material and spiritual" (*CCC* 2829?). This includes the Bread of Life, which is the Eucharist, and also the Word of God contained in the Scriptures, for which so many are hungering.

In the fifth petition we ask God to "forgive us our trespasses, as we forgive those who trespass against us". Asking God to forgive us our sins is only natural, since we all sin and our sins offend God, our loving Father, who is the only one who can forgive us. God is always ready to forgive us when we come before him in humility and sorrow, and he does it especially through the sacraments of Baptism and Penance. But we must also be ready to forgive those who have trespassed, or sinned, against us, and so we say "as we forgive those who trespass against us". Immediately after giving the apostles the Our Father, Jesus himself explains how important it is to forgive others if we want to be forgiven ourselves. He says, "For if you forgive others their trespasses, your heavenly Father will also forgive you; but if you do not forgive others, neither will your Father forgive your trespasses (*Mt* 6:14-15). This is strong, and it exhorts us to forgive from the heart all those who have offended us in any way. Then we can be assured that God will forgive us our sins.

The sixth petition is "and lead us not into temptation". What do we mean by this? Are we asking God not to allow us to be tempted at all, or rather to be strong enough not to fall in the temptations we all experience? The Catechism says that the Greek word used actually means both (cf. *CCC* 2846). Since we know by experience that there will always be temptations, it would be unrealistic to ask God to free us from them altogether. What we are really asking, then, is to be strong enough to resist temptations and not fall into sin. In this we can take heart from Jesus Christ himself who, after fasting and praying for forty days, was tempted three times in the desert and overcame the temptations, giving us hope (cf *Mt* 4:1-11). And we know from St Paul that God always gives us the grace to overcome temptations. He writes: "God is faithful, and he will not let you be tempted beyond your strength, but with the temptation will also provide the way of escape, so that you may be able to endure it" (1 *Cor* 10:13). It is good to know too that when we resist temptations we actually grow in holiness through them, since our virtue is being tested and we show God that we truly love him.

The seventh and last petition of the Our Father asks God to "deliver us from evil". What do we mean by "evil" in this sense? Is it the bad things and misfortunes that can happen to us or rather the evil one himself, Satan? The Catechism answers: "In this petition, evil is not an abstraction, but refers to a person, Satan, the Evil One, the angel who opposes God" (*CCC* 2851). How will we resist his attacks? The answer is of course prayer and union with God. The more we love Christ, the stronger we will be in resisting temptations. St Ambrose reassures us: "The Lord who has taken away your sin and pardoned your faults also protects you and keeps you from the wiles of your adversary the devil, so that the enemy, who is accustomed to leading into sin, may not surprise you. One who entrusts himself to God does not dread the devil. 'If God is for us, who is against us?'" (*De Sacr.* 5,4,30; cf. *Rom* 8:31)

At the end of the Lord's Prayer, as with all prayers, we answer "Amen". St Cyril of Jerusalem explains: "Then, after the prayer is over you say 'Amen', which means 'So be it', thus ratifying with our 'Amen' what is contained in the prayer that God has taught us" (*Cat. myst.* 5, 18; *CCC* 2856). The Hebrew word "amen" comes from the same root as the word "believe". So not only at the end of the Lord's Prayer, but now at the end of our journey into truth, we repeat and confirm the words with which we began: "I believe; Amen". We assent to everything we have studied in these lessons with the conviction that it comes from God himself through the Church he founded.

Indeed, in the words of a previous point in the Catechism, "Jesus Christ himself is the 'Amen.' He is the definitive 'Amen' of the Father's love for us. He takes up and completes our 'Amen' to the Father: 'For all the promises of God find their Yes in him. That is why we utter the Amen through him, to the glory of God' (2 *Cor* 1:20; *CCC* 1065).

3. PRAYER TO MARY

That brings us to our third topic, prayer to Mary. As we come to the end of our journey of faith, we follow a traditional custom of seeking the intercession of Our Lady, who is our mother and who leads us to Jesus and the Father. If Jesus is the only way to the Father, Mary is the shortest way to Jesus and so the Church gives us the celebrated phrase, "To Jesus through Mary".

One of the most ancient and powerful prayers to Mary is the one that is repeated fifty times in the Rosary: the Hail Mary. Its first part comes from the Scriptures and it expresses some of our most heartfelt sentiments towards our spiritual mother. The Hail Mary begins with the words of the angel Gabriel in the Annunciation: "Hail Mary". The word "hail", in addition to being a greeting, can also mean "rejoice". As the Catechism says, "It is God himself who, through his angel as intermediary, greets Mary" (*CCC* 2676). We join God in greeting this most blessed of all women.

Next we say, also with the angel, "full of grace, the Lord is with thee." In these words we see a suggestion of Mary's Immaculate Conception, that she was already full of grace in anticipation of Jesus' death on the cross, by which he would redeem all mankind. As the Catechism puts it, "Mary is full of grace because the Lord is with her" (*CCC* 2676). She has the Blessed Trinity dwelling in her soul and so she is truly full of grace. The words of the angel echo those of the prophet Zephaniah: "Rejoice ... O Daughter of Jerusalem ... the LORD your God is in your midst" (*Zeph* 3:14, 17a).

After this we say, "Blessed art thou among women and blessed is the fruit of thy womb, Jesus." These words, with the exception of the name

Jesus, were pronounced by Mary's kinswoman Elizabeth when Mary went to visit her and help her until the birth of John the Baptist (cf. *Lk* 1:42). The Catechism comments: "'Filled with the Holy Spirit,' Elizabeth is the first in the long succession of generations who have called Mary 'blessed'" (*Lk* 1:41, 48; *CCC* 2676). If the Holy Spirit himself, through Elizabeth, calls Mary "blessed among women", and Mary herself says that "all generations will call me blessed" (*Lk* 1:48), all Christians of whatever denomination should pay her the honour due to her. She is truly the most blessed woman in history, the one chosen to be the very Mother of God on earth. The name "Jesus" was added to the Hail Mary by Pope Urban IV in the thirteenth century.

The second part of the Hail Mary, which was added by Pope St Pius V in the year 1568, begins with the words "Holy Mary, Mother of God". The Catechism comments: "Because she gives us Jesus, her son, Mary is Mother of God and our mother; we can entrust all our cares and petitions to her: she prays for us as she prayed for herself: 'Let it be to me according to your word.' (*Lk* 1:38) By entrusting ourselves to her prayer, we abandon ourselves to the will of God together with her: 'Thy will be done'" (*CCC* 2677). Thus we can pray with total confidence to Mary, who is the Mother of God and our mother.

We go on to say, "Pray for us sinners, now and at the hour of our death". Here we beg Our Lady to pray for us, who are poor sinners, now in our present needs and also at the hour of our death, when she will intercede for all her children. The Catechism expresses it beautifully: "By asking Mary to pray for us, we acknowledge ourselves to be poor sinners and we address ourselves to the 'Mother of Mercy,' the All-Holy One. We give ourselves over to her now, in the Today of our lives. And our trust broadens further, already at the present moment, to surrender 'the hour of our death' wholly to her care. May she be there as she was at her son's death on the cross. May she welcome us as our mother at the hour of our passing to lead us to her son, Jesus, in paradise" (*CCC* 2677). We

can be confident that if we say the Hail Mary frequently during our life,
Our Lady will be there at the hour of our death to intercede for us before
the Father.

4. PUTTING OUR FAITH INTO PRACTICE

And so, by the hand of Our Lady, we come to the conclusion of our
long journey into truth, our excursion into the marvellous truths of the
Catholic faith. I hope you have enjoyed the trip and that you have learned
much about the riches of the Catholic faith. We are privileged to have the
gift of faith, which enables us to believe that Jesus Christ is truly the Son
of God and that the Catholic Church he founded has the fulness of the
means God has given us for our salvation.

What matters now is not only to believe what we have learned but to
put that belief into practice. This is not difficult. We practise our faith
first of all through prayer, in its different forms and moments: morning
prayers, meditation, the Rosary, the Angelus, grace before meals, night
prayers... We practise it especially through that most powerful of prayers,
the Mass, where we unite our prayer with the sacrifice of Christ on
Calvary for the salvation of all souls, and where we hear God's word in
the readings and receive Jesus Christ himself in Holy Communion. And
we practise it through regular celebration of the sacrament of Penance,
where we confess our sins and receive forgiveness of them along with
many graces to help us grow in holiness. All of this helps us to grow in
a very personal and loving relationship with Jesus Christ and to live our
daily lives in a way consistent with our faith. Then the light of Christ
will shine more brightly in the world through us and many others will
be drawn to Christ and through him to the Father. We can be sure that
we will be firmly on the road to heaven as well as to happiness here on
earth. We ask Our Lady, Help of Christians and Queen of All Saints, to
intercede for us so that we may be the saints God wants us to be and so
that we will come to the glory of eternal life in heaven. God bless you.

QUESTIONS FOR DISCUSSION

1. The foundation of our whole spiritual life is the awareness that God is not just a creator but a loving Father. What should this mean for us in our daily life, especially when we face difficulties?

2. Why does Jesus teach us to say "our Father" and not "my Father"?

3. Which phrase of the Our Father strikes you particularly and gives you more food for thought and action?

4. Recourse to Mary is traditional at the end of spiritual activities. What can we do to grow in devotion to Mary ourselves and abandon ourselves trustingly into her motherly care?

5. What are some practical ways we can not only hold on to our faith but grow in it throughout our lives so as to find the joy we seek both in this life and in the next?

POINTS TO REMEMBER

• The knowledge that God is our Father should fill us with trust that he will always give us what is best.

• The Our Father is the essentially Christian prayer, given to us by Jesus himself, and so we should say it often and well, aware of its deep meaning.

• Since God is always ready to forgive us our sins, we should be ready to forgive those who have sinned against us.

• Jesus is the only way to the Father and Mary is the shortest way to Jesus.

• We should say the Hail Mary often, in union with the whole Church, confident that Our Lady will be there to intercede for us always.

Common Prayers

Sign of the Cross

In the name of the Father and of the Son and of the Holy Spirit. Amen.

Our Father

Our Father, who art in heaven, hallowed be thy name. Thy kingdom come, thy will be done, on earth as it is in heaven. Give us this day our daily bread, and forgive us our trespasses, as we forgive those who trespass against us. And lead us not into temptation, but deliver us from evil. Amen.

Hail Mary

Hail, Mary, full of grace, the Lord is with thee. Blessed art thou among women and blessed is the fruit of thy womb, Jesus. Holy Mary, Mother of God, pray for us sinners, now and at the hour of our death. Amen.

Glory be to the Father

Glory be to the Father and to the Son and to the Holy Spirit, as it was in the beginning, is now, and ever shall be, world without end. Amen.

Apostles' Creed

I believe in God, the Father almighty, Creator of heaven and earth, and in Jesus Christ, his only Son, our Lord, who was conceived by the Holy Spirit, born of the Virgin Mary, suffered under Pontius Pilate, was crucified, died and was buried; he descended into hell; on the third day he rose again from the dead; he ascended into heaven, and is seated at the right hand of God the Father almighty; from there he will come to judge the living and the dead. I believe in the Holy Spirit, the holy catholic Church, the communion of saints, the forgiveness of sins, the resurrection of the body, and life everlasting. Amen.

Hail, Holy Queen

Hail, holy Queen, mother of mercy, hail our life, our sweetness and our hope. To thee do we cry, poor banished children of Eve, to thee do we send up our sighs, mourning and weeping in this valley of tears. Turn then, most gracious advocate, thine eyes of mercy toward us, and after this, our exile, show unto us the blessed fruit of thy womb, Jesus. O clement, O loving, O sweet Virgin Mary.

V. Pray for us, O Holy Mother of God.

R. That we may be made worthy of the promises of Christ. Amen.

Act of Contrition

O my God, I am heartily sorry for all my sins, because they have offended thee, my God, who art all good and worthy of all my love. I love thee with my whole heart and with the help of thy grace I will not sin again. Amen.

Spiritual Communion

I wish, my Lord, to receive you with the purity, humility, and devotion with which your Holy Mother received you, with the spirit and fervour of the saints. Amen.

The Angelus

V. The angel of the Lord declared unto Mary;

R. And she conceived of the Holy Spirit.

 Hail Mary...

V. Behold the handmaid of the Lord;

R. Be it done unto me according to thy word.

 Hail Mary...

V. And the Word was made flesh;

R. And dwelt among us.

 Hail Mary...

V. Pray for us, O holy Mother of God;

R. That we may be made worthy of the promises of Christ.

Let us pray. Pour forth, we beseech thee, O Lord, thy grace into our hearts, that we, to whom the incarnation of Christ, thy Son, was made known by the message of an angel, may by his passion and cross be brought to the glory of his resurrection, through the same Christ our Lord.

R. Amen.

The Regina Coeli (during the Easter season)

V. Queen of heaven, rejoice! Alleluia.

R. For he whom you did merit to bear. Alleluia.

V. Has risen, as he said. Alleluia.

R. Pray for us to God. Alleluia.

V. Rejoice and be glad, O Virgin Mary. Alleluia.

R. For the Lord is truly risen. Alleluia.

Let us pray. O God, who gave joy to the world through the resurrection of your Son, Our Lord Jesus Christ, grant, we beseech you, that through the intercession of the Virgin Mary, his Mother, we may obtain the joys of everlasting life, through the same Christ our Lord.

R. Amen.

Prayer to the Guardian Angel

Angel of God, my guardian dear, to whom God's love entrusts me here, ever this day be at my side, to light and guard, to rule and guide. Amen.

Morning offering

O my Jesus, through the Immaculate Heart of Mary, I offer you my prayers, works, joys and sufferings of this day for all the intentions of your Sacred Heart. Amen.

Memorare

Remember, O most gracious Virgin Mary, that never was it known that anyone who fled to thy protection, implored thy help, or sought they intercession, was left unaided. Inspired by this confidence I fly to thee, O Virgin of virgins, my Mother. To thee do I come, before thee I stand, sinful and sorrowful. O Mother of the Word Incarnate, despise not my petitions, but in thy mercy hear and answer me. Amen.

Grace before meals

Bless us, O Lord, and these your gifts which we are about to receive from your bounty, through Christ our Lord. Amen.

Grace after meals

We give you thanks, Almighty God, for all your benefits, who live and reign forever and ever. Amen.

FORMULAS OF CATHOLIC DOCTRINE

The seven Sacraments

1. Baptism
2. Confirmation
3. Eucharist
4. Penance (Reconciliation)
5. Anointing of the Sick
6. Holy Orders
7. Matrimony

The Ten Commandments

1. I am the Lord your God. You shall not have strange gods before me.
2. You shall not take the name of the Lord your God in vain.
3. Remember to keep holy the Sabbath day.
4. Honour your father and your mother.
5. You shall not kill.
6. You shall not commit adultery.
7. You shall not steal.
8. You shall not bear false witness against your neighbour.
9. You shall not covet your neighbour's wife.
10. You shall not covet your neighbour's goods.

The five precepts of the Church

1. You shall attend Mass on Sundays and on holy days of obligation.
2. You shall confess your sins at least once a year.
3. You shall receive Holy Communion at least during the Easter season.
4. You shall observe the days of fasting and abstinence established by the Church.
5. You shall help to provide for the needs of the Church.

The three theological virtues
1. Faith
2. Hope
3. Charity

The four cardinal virtues
1. Prudence
2. Justice
3. Fortitude
4. Temperance

The Golden Rule (cf. Mt 7:12)
Do to others as you would have them do to you.

The seven gifts of the Holy Spirit
1. Wisdom
2. Understanding
3. Knowledge
4. Counsel
5. Fortitude
6. Piety
7. Fear of the Lord

The twelve fruits of the Holy Spirit
1. Charity
2. Joy
3. Peace
4. Patience
5. Kindness
6. Goodness
7. Generosity
8. Gentleness

9. Faithfulness

10. Modesty

11. Self-control

12. Chastity

The seven corporal works of mercy

1. Feed the hungry.

2. Give drink to the thirsty.

3. Clothe the naked.

4. Shelter the homeless.

5. Visit the sick.

6. Visit the imprisoned.

7. Bury the dead

The seven spiritual works of mercy

1. Counsel the doubtful.

2. Instruct the ignorant.

3. Admonish sinners.

4. Comfort the afflicted.

5. Forgive offences.

6. Bear wrongs patiently.

7. Pray for the living and the dead.

The seven capital sins

1. Pride

2. Covetousness

3. Lust

4. Anger

5. Gluttony

6. Envy

7. Sloth

INDEX

abortion 237, 245-8. 257

adultery 173, 190, 201, 218, 256, 258ff, 272, 291

agnostics 228

alcohol 200, 248, 255, 289

Alphonsus Liguori, St 63

Ambrose, St 28, 298, 303

Amen 297, 304

angels 37, 39, 43, 45, 51, 59, 70, 124, 126, 128, 133, 300

Anointing of the Sick 167-8, 176ff, 182

Anselm, St 24, 107

anthropic principle 6, 42

apostasy 225

Aquinas, St Thomas 9, 23, 41, 107, 121, 203, 226, 252, 285

artificial insemination 267

astrology 227

Athanasius, St 119

atheism 228

Augustine, St 4, 7, 10, 21, 24, 42, 88, 95, 110-11, 124, 127, 193, 204, 253, 286, 294, 299-300

Baptism 27, 36, 48, 81-2, 85, 92, 96-7, 100, 113, 132, 134-41, 156, 165, 179, 185, 191, 211, 218-9, 226, 238, 263, 298-9, 302

    effects of 146-8

meaning of 143-5

    minister and ceremonies 149-50

Basil, St 43, 50. 111

Benedict XVI, Pope 10, 121, 123-4, 276

Bernadette Soubirous, St 108

Bernard, St 107

bishops 9, 18. 27, 90, 95, 97-9, 101-3, 149, 158, 178, 181-7, 194, 232, 242

blasphemy 201, 222, 229-30

Bonaventure, St 41, 107

burial 17, 144, 156

Caesarius of Arles, St 31

capital punishment 245-7, 251-2, 157

Caritas in Veritate 276

catechumen 149

Catherine Labouré 108

celibacy 99, 186, 237

Centesimus Annus 276

character 139, 147, 152, 242

charity 82, 114, 147, 174-6, 185, 198, 206, 213-7, 231-2, 235-6, 250, 253, 256, 263, 268, 271, 277, 286-7, 290

chastity 62, 99, 173, 212, 215, 255-6, 258-63, 268, 270, 272, 283, 291-2, 295

childless couples 267

chrism 135, 139, 150-2

Christmas 72, 136, 197, 205, 232